The Classic Guide to ATHLETICS

The Classic Guide to ATHLETICS

Montague Shearman

AMBERLEY

First edition published 1887

This edition first published 2015

Amberley Publishing
The Hill, Stroud
Gloucestershire, GL5 4EP

www.amberley-books.com

Copyright © Amberley Publishing, 2015

All rights reserved. No part of this book may be reprinted
or reproduced or utilised in any form or by any electronic,
mechanical or other means, now known or hereafter invented,
including photocopying and recording, or in any information
storage or retrieval system, without the permission in writing
from the Publishers.

British Library Cataloguing in Publication Data.
A catalogue record for this book is available from the British Library.

ISBN 978 1 4456 4483 7 (print)
ISBN 978 1 4456 4503 2 (ebook)

Typesetting and Origination by Amberley Publishing.
Printed in the UK.

Contents

	Editor's Note	6
	Introduction	8
1	The History of Athletic Sports in England	16
2	A Modern Championship Meeting	64
3	Running and Runners	78
4	Jumping, Weight-Putting, etc.	128
5	Training	150
6	Athletic Meetings	164
7	Athletic Government	198

Editor's Note

The history of athletics dates back to the era of blood and sand in Ancient Greece, where the grand Olympian Games paid tribute to the mighty god, Zeus. Over time, the honoured games have cemented themselves within our culture, venturing outside of Greece and spreading across the world as a global sporting phenomenon. Now, the infamous collection of sporting events focuses less on Greek mythology and more on the fierce competition, determination and dedication to sport.

From road running, race walking, cross-country running, mountain running and track and field, athletics has proven to be one of the most regularly competed sports to exist. The fact that it does not require the use of expensive equipment makes athletics even more available to potential athletes, giving them the opportunity to showcase their individual sporting talent.

Beyond the Greek games, athletic contests have existed in various countries: in Ancient Egypt there are illustrations of high-jumping on tombs; there was the Celtic festival of the 'Tailteann Games' in Ireland in 1800, and in seventeenth-century England, the introduction of the Cotswold Olympick Games. It was the Royal Military College in Sandhurst, England, that claimed to be the first to use the metric system for athletics in 1812 and 1825, but there was no evidence to support this. However, there is evidence of recorded athletics meetings in the UK, with one in 1840 organised by the Royal Shrewsbury School Hunt. This was followed by an organised competition by the Royal Military Academy at Woolich in 1849, and a series of meetings available only to undergraduates at Exeter College, Oxford, in 1850.

Editor's Note

With so vast a history to cover, when it came to the studious task of compiling a guidebook for the progression of athletics, it needed to come from someone well-equipped with the foundations of the games. Thus, it was in 1887 that Sir Montague Shearman did just that. More than qualified for the role, Shearman had enough knowledge and experience with athletics to pen *Athletics and Football*. Starting off as a founding member of the Amateur Athletics Association – commonly known as the A.A.A., which was established in England in 1880 – Shearman later became the first honorary secretary from 1880 to 1883, vice-president until 1910, and eventually, president.

As well as a judge and art collector, Shearman remained the ever resilient sportsman, continuing to work despite suffering a speech impairment from an operation triggered by an old football injury. He passed away, aged seventy-two, in 1930, at his London home, just one year after his retirement.

Laura Nicklin
Editor
2015

Introduction

It may seem strange that I should be asked to turn aside from the studies and occupations which have so closely engaged my time during the last twenty years, to write a few lines upon a subject in which during that period, and for years before, I have taken the greatest interest, namely, athletics; and yet it is not altogether unfitting, inasmuch as I am probably as well qualified as any to speak from personal experience of the advantages which are gained in a sedentary life from the power of practising active exercises. Except cycling and lawn-tennis, both of which have been practically invented

A steeplechase.

during the last fifteen years, no pursuit has seen so great an advance or revival as athletic sports. It may be, and it probably is, the case (as those who read the pages of this book will learn), that for a great many years prior to the year 1850 athletic sports had been from time to time pursued by both amateurs and professionals, who had with more or less assiduity, according to the particular ability or powers of the competitor, performed before the public; there had been, no doubt, remarkable instances of individual men who possibly had been as great at running, walking, jumping, and swimming as those who have excelled in modern times; but it is perfectly certain that prior to the date last mentioned – I mean the year 1850 – athletics were not practised as a recognised system of muscular education, nor was there any authentic record of individual performances. I doubt, moreover, whether either times or distances were taken and measured with sufficient accuracy to make the earlier records in any way trustworthy.

Speaking of our Universities, I have seen the foundation of the present prosperous clubs at both Cambridge and Oxford, and, with the exception of the crick-run at Rugby and the steeplechase at Eton, prior to 1850 no public school had any established athletic contest. I do not, however, propose in the few lines which I intend to pen to attempt any history of athletic sports; the following pages will, I am sure, contain records attractive both to the athlete and the public, of those who, in years gone by and down to the present time, have excelled on the road, the turf, and the running-path. I wish for a few moments to regard the subject from the point of view of the consideration of the advantages to be gained in the practice of athletics, and, secondly, to make a few suggestions as to the best mode in which these advantages may be increased so as to be of still greater utility and benefit.

We are brought face to face in England, and other populous countries, with the difficult problem which is called into existence by over-population, and the utter absence of space and opportunity for the youth of the present day to find sufficient scope for his energies. The tendency to crowd into the curriculum of both school and college a large and ever-increasing number of subjects has rendered the strain of education far heavier than in times gone by, and this tension will certainly increase.

In old days, when a fair grounding in Greek and Latin, or a moderate knowledge in mathematics, was a sufficient preparation for almost any profession (the brilliant few being left to excel in those subjects by the sheer force of their natural abilities), the culture of the body and the simultaneous development of physical and mental strength were of less importance, or at any rate their value was less recognised. I need scarcely remind those who read these pages that, thirty years ago, it was the exception for a senior wrangler or a senior classic to figure in the University boat or the eleven. The names of those few who did excel stand out among their contemporaries, and it was by no means an uncommon experience to find that those who had surpassed in intellectual contests in school and college utterly broke down in their professions in after life. I attribute this in no small degree to the fact that for many boys and men there was scarcely any inducement to develop or use their physical strength, nothing which led them to those pursuits which, without engrossing the mind too much, develop the body gradually and contemporaneously with mental growth. How many a first class man at Oxford, or wrangler or first class classic at Cambridge, could only find exercise in the daily and monotonous grind of an hour or an hour and a half's walk; cricket and boating both taking up too much time, and not unfrequently leading many to expenses which they could ill afford?

I maintain that one great good which has arisen from the stimulus given from the years 1860 to 1870 to athletic sports is the facility which those pursuits afford for the development of physical strength, and the inducement to active exercise offered to men who, either from want of inclination or want of means, would otherwise never have taken any. I have known intimately a great many reading men, who have told me how deeply they regretted that there was nothing of the kind in their time, and many others have assured me of the advantages which they have derived from the interest which these pursuits have given to them, and the inducement to take exercises which otherwise they would have wholly neglected. It must not be forgotten that more genuine exercise can be got in a shorter space of time from running than probably from any other pursuit, except boxing and gymnastics, with the great advantage of the former over the two latter that the exercise is taken in the open air.

There is, moreover, the great interest which attaches to the contests in other colleges, universities, and clubs, affording an object of attraction at times when it is not necessary for men themselves to compete, and bringing together men who otherwise would remain unknown to one another, whereby acquaintanceships and friendships are formed which are of the greatest value. A very distinguished judge who joined the Inns of Court rifle corps in the earliest days of its existence told me that he much regretted that there was no rifle corps when he was called to the bar, as he was satisfied that many young men reading for the bar were by such means brought into contact with older members of the profession, whom under ordinary circumstances they would have had no opportunity of meeting.

It is unnecessary here for me to enlarge upon the immense advantage to be gained from the simultaneous development of physical and mental power; that subject has been so fully treated, and the beneficial results so conclusively demonstrated, by those who have studied the matter from a scientific and medical point of view, particularly in connection with the Swedish system, that any argument of mine would be out of place. I can only say that I am firmly convinced that the brain is better developed, and is more capable of sustained effort, if its growth be accompanied by a proportionate physical development than in the case of the brain over-developed without any corresponding bodily improvement.

I desire here to say a few words upon the subject of the best method of athletic training in schools. I am of course aware that superlative excellence and cases of remarkable prowess are to a great extent inborn – or to put the converse, that some boys and men, however much they practise, will never succeed in reaching the standard readily attained by born athletes. But superlative excellence in special cases is by no means that which is most to be aimed at. Innate talent for any pursuit will as a rule develop itself whatever be its surroundings, but I think at all public schools boys should be taught to run properly. There is as much difference between good running and bad running as there is between good rowing and bad rowing, and the standard of excellence will be certainly increased by a high normal standard among the average boys.

To mention one other point, it will be admitted that no boy is more likely to do harm in a school than the loafer. Ask the masters of any public school what class of boys cause them the most anxiety, or bring the least credit on a school; they will tell you the boys who loaf, and have no zest for play or work.

Numbers of boys are not strong enough to play football, or are not successful at cricket, and cannot afford the expense of racquets. To many of these the incentive to exercise by the prospect of being able to compete in races and other athletic tests is an incalculable benefit, particularly if one or more of the masters, who have often themselves been distinguished in muscular pursuits, superintend and take an interest in their training and practice.

All boys should, in my opinion, be made to take some regular exercise of the kind best suited to them, and in the first instance under regular and careful supervision.

Attention to such a matter as this will prevent boys from being made to play games for which they are not adapted; for instance, very little practice or tuition in running would find out the boys who are unfitted for football or incapable of extreme exertion; and, again, the boys who show a turn of speed in advance of their age will develop more rapidly into high-class performers. I am, however, altogether opposed to any boys being made to race too long distances, particularly game and plucky boys who do not know when they are beaten. I think no boy under fourteen should run a race of greater length than half a mile; he may trot longer distances so as to strengthen the muscles of the feet, legs, and back, care being taken that he runs throughout as much as possible in good form.

Only those who have had personal experience of results have the slightest idea of the improvement made by a few lessons in the proper style of running, getting well on to the toes with a springy tread, the hips working freely, the chest out and arms well carried. I am satisfied that the growth of boys is improved, and that their lungs are strengthened, by moderate and judicious coaching.

In strong corroboration of this I would call attention to the extraordinary improvement in times and performances which has taken place during the last twenty years. This has, no doubt, been to a certain extent due to a circumstance to which I have already referred – namely, the inaccuracy of the old records both as to distances and times; but, allowing for unwarranted conclusions based on comparison, there can be little doubt that five-and-twenty years ago the number of men who in ordinary condition could run a mile in five minutes was exceedingly few, so much so that anything under five minutes was supposed to be good time for amateurs, whereas at the present time 4 min 30 sec may be taken to be below the standard of first-class performances, and, as the following pages will show, the mile has been run by undoubted amateurs under 4 min 25 sec. The improvement in the quarter-mile is quite as remarkable, although it was more speedily attained, being due to improvement in style. Between 1865 and 1872 the standard time was reduced from 55 seconds to 50 and 51; the time of the other distances – as, for instance, half-mile and three miles – has correspondingly improved. In the hurdles it is exceedingly difficult to make out any comparison; nor do I think there has been the same improvement in pace, although the number of first-class performers has increased enormously.

Probably the most remarkable instance is the improvement in jumping, both in height and length. It is not many years ago that to clear six feet was considered beyond human powers, and to cover 22 ft 6 in. and 23 ft little short of an impossibility, and yet both these feats have been performed by more than one athlete. I do not wish to close these observations without some reference to such contests as throwing the hammer and putting the weight: in my opinion they are contests which should be encouraged, as they afford scope to those who are unable to compete in running and jumping, and are very valuable for the development of the chest and arms.

The same arguments may also with justice be employed in favour of walking; and while on the subject of walking, I wish to call particular attention to the extraordinary feats of long-distance walking which have been performed in late years, by which I mean distances of 40 and 50 miles and upwards, which are, in my opinion, of far greater value than the so-called performances of walking eight or more miles in the hour by a mode of progression so nearly resembling a shamble or trot as to defy the most watchful of judges. I have known many instances of development of chest, lungs, and great improvement of general stamina, resulting in a vastly improved constitution, from steady walking of long distances.

I gladly take this opportunity of paying a tribute to the great services rendered to athletic pursuits by the late J. G. Chambers, Esq., of Eton and Cambridge, who for years devoted himself to initiating and maintaining contests of all kinds, and by his untiring energy and foresight did probably more than any one in modern times to maintain and improve the standard of athletics among both amateurs and professionals.

Before concluding, it is right that I should say one word upon that which may be called the moral aspect of athletics. That their practice tends to encourage self-control, self-reliance, without undue confidence, and a proper appreciation of other men's merits, there can be no doubt; moreover, they promote that spirit of good-fellowship which enables the beaten man to go up and honestly congratulate the victor who has conquered him; but, beyond this, as I have already said, the contests and gatherings offer the opportunity of making lasting friendships and connections which are often of the greatest value in after life. A reputation once earned by the boy or man in such pursuits follows him to other professions, and has more than once contributed in no small degree to early success in the work of life. To those who in the past or in the present have taken interest in athletic sports, or wish to know their history, or who feel, as I do, that they afford the opportunity of innocent and healthy pleasure, as well as of bodily development, I commend the study of these pages, compiled by one who has ample means of knowledge, and a ripe judgment with which to gauge the accuracy and authenticity of any records of the performances which he describes.

Richard E. Webster
Temple, October 1887.

1
The History of Athletic Sports in England

Hanc olim veteres vitam coluere Sabini,
... sic fortis Etruria crevit
Scilicet et rerum facta est pulcherrima Roma.

Running and jumping are so natural and so easy to the young, that in one sense it may be said they no more have a history than laughing or weeping. As long as there have been men on the earth it may safely be asserted that there have been running matches; and in every warlike nation feats of strength, speed, and endurance of the body have excited admiration. With but few nations, however, have athletic exercises formed an art and become a feature of national life; and where this has been the case there is a history, and an interesting history, of the practice of feats of strength and speed. To write such a history of English athletic sport is no easy task; for, as far as this writer is aware, it has never been seriously attempted before. The learned Strutt, whose work is such a mine of wealth to sporting antiquarians, contents himself with informing his readers that:

> it is needless to assert the antiquity of foot-racing, because it will readily occur to everyone that occasions continually present themselves which call forth the exertions of running. ... Originally, perhaps, foot-races had no other incitement than emulation, or at best the prospect of a small reward, but in process of time the rewards were magnified, and contests of this kind were instituted as public amusements – the ground marked out and judges appointed to decide upon the fairness of the race and to bestow the reward.

Such an *à priori* method of writing history will hardly account satisfactorily for the present form of athletic sport in England. The only other writer, as far as we are aware, who has attempted to explain the origin of English athletics to modern readers has given an excellent essay upon Greek athletics, and has then assured us that 'in one respect our position is like that of the Romans. Athletics are not indigenous with us.' It is our object in the present chapter to show with what success we can that competitions in running, jumping, and hurling of heavy weights are not only indigenous to the land, but have been one of the chief characteristics of both town and country life in England as far back as chronicles will reach; and that athletic sports, though they have had their days of waxing and waning, have always been a feature of life in 'Merrie England'.

It is difficult to obtain much information of the sports of the people in the middle ages as distinguished from the sports of the nobles. Just as the Roman historian expresses his opinion that the ancient Greeks were no better than the ancient Romans, the latter only suffering from the lack of eloquent chroniclers, so it is probable that the populace produced as good runners as Henry V and his Court; but in the days of chivalry the bards only chronicled the feats of persons of quality. The monarch in question 'was so swift a runner that he and two of his lords, without bow or other engine, would take a wild buck in a large park.' Long before his time we know that the youth of London had their summer as well as their winter sports. FitzStephen, the monk of Canterbury, born in London, writes in the reign of Henry II that the young Londoners had open spaces allotted to them near the City, where they practised, amongst other exercises, 'leaping, wrestling, casting of the stone, and playing with the ball.' No mention is made of running, but we can hardly imagine that leaping matches would be known and not running matches. FitzStephen is no mean observer of sport, and his description of 'sliding' on the ice in winter is almost as minute as that of Dickens in 'Pickwick'. The knightly youths, however, were taught to run, jump, and wrestle in the days of chivalry, as well as the citizens; but this was, of course, chiefly as a military training, the feats by which they earned the greatest glory, as well as the smiles of the fair, being performed on horseback, as befitted persons of equestrian rank. In the romance quoted by Strutt, called 'The Knight of the Swan', a certain duchess, Ydain by name, brought up her sons in 'all maner of good operacyons, vertues and maners: and when in their adolescence they were somewhat comen to the age of strength they were taught to runne, to just, and to wrestle'. Again, in the poem entitled 'Knyghthode and Batayle', written early in the fifteenth century, we find,

> In rennynge the exercise is good also
> To smyte, first in fight and also whenne
> To take a place our foemen will forerenne.
> And for to lepe a dike is also good,
> For mightily what man may renne and lepe
> May well devict and safe 'is party kepe.

Henry VIII throwing the hammer.

In another romance also quoted by Strutt, that of 'The Three Kings' Sons', it is said of a certain knight, 'The king for to assaie him made justes and turnies, and no man did so well as he in runnyng, playing at the pame, shotyng, and castyng of the barre, ne found he his maister.'

The running and weight-putting, to which the townsmen of London were so much addicted, were not always favoured by the kings of England, who were afraid that the practice of archery might fall into disuse; and we find Edward III especially prohibiting weight-putting by statute; but the statute, although never repealed, appears to have been more honoured in the breach than in the observance, for at the time of the decline of chivalry 'casting of the barre' was still a common pursuit. Henry VIII certainly in one respect chose his amusements better than some of his predecessors; while Edward II found his favourite amusement in 'cross and pile' (or, as it is now known, 'pitch and toss'), the much-married monarch, in his early days, was greatly devoted to this 'casting of the barre.' Even after his accession to the throne, his daily amusements embraced weight-putting, dancing, tilting, leaping and running. The example of a monarch has, it is well known, a most persuasive effect, and hence it is not astonishing to find from a contemporary writer (Wilson) that all active sports, both on horseback and on foot, including leaping, running and bar-throwing, became fashionable amusements.

In the succeeding age, however, we begin to find foot exercises less thought of by the upper classes. Richard Pace, the secretary to King Henry VIII, could advise noblemen's sons to pursue their sports, 'and leave study and learning to the children of meaner people'; but although his advice was, no doubt, followed by many of his readers, the 'new learning' gradually took hold of the upper classes, and cultivated minds began to be rather contemptuous of rough bodily exercises. Still, throughout the reign of Henry VIII gentlemen were accustomed to write in favour of pedestrian as well as of equestrian exercises. Sir William Forest, in his *Poesye of Princelye Practice*, holds that a prince should,

> In featis of maistries bestowe some diligence.
> Too ryde, runne, lepe, or caste by violence
> Stone, barre or plummett, or such other thinge,
> It not refuseth any prince or kynge.

About the same time that worthy knight, Sir Thomas Elyot, wrote the manual of education for a gentleman, *The Boke Called the Governour*, from which many succeeding writers borrowed largely without any acknowledgment. Sir Thomas, who was in many senses before his time, expresses himself strongly against the system of unnecessary flogging and in favour of a judicious mixture of athletics and learning for a boy. 'A discrete master,' he says, 'may with as much or more ease both to himself and his scholler lead him to play at tennis or shoote.' In the sixteenth chapter of his work he speaks of 'Sundrye fourmes of exercise necessarye for a gentilman,' and there are, he says, 'some exercises which with health join commoditie': 'Touching such exercises as may be used within the house or in the shadowe, such as deambulations, labouryng with poyses made of ledde, lifting and throwing the heavy stone or barre, playing at tennis and diverse semblable exercises I will for this time pass over,' and he exhorts his readers to study Galen De Sanitate tuenda upon the subject. What follows about running and jumping is curious, as it makes it plain that Sir Thomas knew that there were some people who decried these sports as being vulgar. He says, 'Rennyng is bothe a good exercise and a laudable solace' (we presume by solace he means pastime, and not consolation in the sense in which a certain well-known athlete of modern times stated that, whenever he was suffering from disappointed love, he took a walking tour to work it off). He defends running by the *argumentum ad hominem*, showing that Achilles, Alexander, and others were famous runners, and that Epaminondas not only ran but jumped every morning before breakfast for health and amusement. He goes on: 'Nedes must rennynge be taken for a laudable exercise sens one of the mooste noble capitaynes of all the Romans took his name from it' (meaning Papirius Cursor). In this argument he seems to us to be meeting the scholars of the 'new learning', who, while they studied the classics and classical models, were irreverent enough to decry athletics. That they did so there is no doubt from other sources. Roger Ascham, in his great book, 'Toxophilus', says roundly that 'running, leaping, and quoiting be too vile for scholars.'

However, although in the sixteenth century opinions were divided as to whether running, leaping and bar-casting were genteel or not, there is no doubt whatever that the common people were little affected by this, and went on with their amusements as before. A very few years after *The Boke Called the Governour* was published, we learn from one of the Harleian MSS that as the great football match which was usually played upon the Roodee at Chester became productive of much inconvenience, it was decided to substitute a footrace; and accordingly, instead of the shoemakers presenting the drapers, 'in the presence of the Mayor at the Cross on the Rodehee,' with a football of the 'value of three shillings and fourpence or above, by consent of all parties concerned the ball was changed into six glayves of silver of the like value, as a reward for the best runner that day upon the aforesaid Rodehee.' This affords a curious picture of sixteenth-century manners. Instead of the annual football match, 'Shoemakers v. Drapers,' the 'Championship of Chester' footrace is substituted.

Shakespeare, no doubt, saw some running matches both amongst gentle and simple folk. His own experiences of all kinds are reproduced in his pages, and 'private matches' and public competitions are alike mentioned by him. In the First Part of *Henry IV*, Act II, Scene 4, we have Falstaff offering to run Poins: 'I could give a thousand pounds I could run as fast as thou canst,' says the stout knight. In the Third Part of *Henry VI*, Act II, Scene 3, we have another allusion to foot-racing:

> Forspent with toil as runners with a race,
> I lay me down a little while to breathe.

We are, however, anticipating, for there is evidence nearly a century before Shakespeare of the fondness of the common people for athletic sports. Strutt quotes the following lines from Barclay's 'Eclogues,' first published in 1508. A shepherd says,

> I can both hurle and sling,
> I runne, I wrestle, I can well throwe the barre,
> No shepherd throweth the axeltree so farre;
> If I were merry, I could well leape and spring,
> I were a man mete to serve a prince or king.

A very curious piece of information given in Russell's *History of Guildford* has a bearing on the sports of the sixteenth century. In a certain law case to decide in 1597 the title to a field near the town, one John Durich, gentleman, figuring as 'the most ancient inhabitant,' who is common in such trials, said that he had known the ground for fifty years, and when a scholar at the Free School did 'runne there and play at cricket.' The most admirable description, however, of the popular sports of the sixteenth century is that often quoted from, the work of the younger Randel Holme or Holmes, one of the wandering minstrels and merry-makers of the North country. Speaking, it is believed, of the men of Lancashire, in lines which show him to be better as a sportsman than as a poet, he says:

> Any they dare challenge for to throw the sledge.
> To jump or leape over a ditch or hedge.
> To wrastle, play at stoole-ball or to runne.
> To pitche the barre or to shoote of a gunne,
> To play at loggets, nine holes or ten pinnes.
> To trie it out at football by the shinnes;
> At ticke-tacke, saw nody, maw and ruffe.
> At hot cockles, leap frogge and blind man's buffe,
> To drink the halfer pottes or deale at the whole canne,
> To play at chesse or pue or inkehorne,
> To daunce the morris, play at barley breake,
> At al exploites a man can think or speake,
> At shove-groate, venter point and cross and pile,
> At 'beshrew him that's the last at any stile,'
> At leapinge over a Christmas bonfire,

> Or at the drawing dame out of the myre,
> At shoote-cocke, Gregory, stoolball and what not.
> Pick point, toppe and scourge to make him holt.

It would require the length of an essay to explain all the above sports, many of which are still familiar under different names. 'Stool-ball' is the rudimentary form of cricket, the one player defending the stool while the other threw the ball at it. Probably, however, in one of the two lines in which 'stool-ball' is mentioned, it is a mistake for 'stow-ball' or golf. It is evident, therefore, that in the sixteenth century football and many other well-known pastimes were common. But for our purposes the verses are more useful as showing how the different forms of athletic sport were beginning to be systematised. In line 1 we have Throwing the Hammer, in line 2 the Long Jump and the High Jump, in line 3 running, and in line 4 'pitching' or 'putting' the weight, as distinct from 'throwing' the hammer with a sling round the head. Line 14 also describes a very curious kind of sprint-racing, which, we believe, was also practised by Roman schoolboys ('occupet extremum scabies'). A party of lads are together, and one suddenly starts off without any warning to run to a mark, which he names; the others join in and race to the mark. The last in pays a forfeit or gets a kick, as the case may be. It is one of the best tests of speed and quickness in starting, and is much like the common practice of modern sprinters of 'taking each other on at starts,' one starting when he likes and the other following him as best he can.

It is clear enough, then, that the common people had their regular athletic sports in the Elizabethan age, but that at this time people of fashion took little part in them. Pageants, processions, and masques were the amusements of Elizabeth's court, or bear-baitings or bull-baitings, and last, but not least, dramatic exhibitions. Nowhere in Robert Laneham's long account of the revels at Kenilworth, nor in Nichol's account of the 'Progresses of Queen Elizabeth,' are there, as far as we are aware, any allusions to pedestrian sports. In the 'succeeding reign the fashion turned again, as we shall presently see. Curiously enough, however, our best notion of the universal popularity amongst the lower classes of different forms of athletic sport is gathered from the Puritan writers, who were the bitter opponents of such pastimes. The Puritans, however, at the first did not oppose the sports themselves so much as the occasions upon which they were practised. What these occasions were is abundantly clear. The ordinary times for running, leaping, football and such like pastimes were Sundays and Church festivals, and the usual arena the churchyard; the greater and more uproarious festivities took place on the last days of the country fairs. The fairs, as being the more important, perhaps deserve attention first. The greater part of the trading of the country in the Elizabethan age was conducted by means of the fairs; horses, cattle, and all necessaries for the season were bought at them. In Harrison's *Description of England*, published at this time, a list is given of the 'more important' fairs, which mentions three or four hundred of these gatherings. It is scarcely to be wondered at, by those who know the peculiar faculty of the Englishman to combine business with sport, that when the business was over, or even before, sporting competitions should follow, the whole affair concluding, as the Puritan writers assert (and probably with some truth), with general orgies of intoxication and riot. Of the nature of the sports at these fairs, which, doubtless, continued in much the same form as long as the fairs themselves were held, we shall have to give some further account afterwards, but running, jumping, and weight-putting seem to have been invariable features of the programme. The Puritans, however, did their best to suppress all these sports entirely. John Northbrooke, writing as early as 1577, and demanding a Government supervision of fairs, alludes to the festivals in the following complimentary terms: 'There would not be so many loytering idle persons, ruffians, blasphemers, swingebucklers, tossepottes, etc. etc.' (there is a *crescendo* of abuse, and the extract must of necessity be Bowdlerised) 'if these dunghills and filth in commonweales were removed.' Stubbs, another Puritan writer, the author of the *Anatomic of Abuses*, expresses himself against the fairs in equally strong terms. His attitude to sport in general may be gathered from the fact of his speaking of 'tennise, bowles, and such like fooleries.' If the fairs, however, were 'dunghills', the practice of sports at the wakes, or Church festivals, and on ordinary Sundays, was still more shocking to the reformers. In 1570 one of them paraphrased into English, and dedicated to Queen Elizabeth, the foreign work of one Kirchmaier, who, as he wrote in Latin, adopted the name of Naogeorgus. The translator, Barnabe Googe, says of the people on Sundays:

> Now when their dinner once is done, and that they well have fed,
> To play they go, to casting of the stone, to runne or shoote,
> To toss the light and windy ball aloft with hande or foote.
> Some others trie their skill in gonnes, some wrastell all the day
> And some to schoole of fence do goe to gaze upon the play.

About the same time Thomas Cartwright, in his admonition to Parliament, asserts that the parson is as bad as his flock. 'He pusheth it over (the service) as fast as he can galloppe: for either he hath two places to serve, or there are some games to be playde in the afternoon.' However, we need say no more as to the Puritan efforts to suppress athletic sports. The merits of the Puritans can hardly obtain a fair hearing in a history of sport; they, no doubt, succeeded for a time in discountenancing it, and in putting down its practice very effectually upon Sundays, but when the Puritan government fell, its fall, to paraphrase Ridley's words, 'lighted such a fire' of sporting enthusiasm as has never yet been extinguished in England.

However, under the first two Stuart kings both the upper classes and such of the lower classes as were not converted to Puritanism showed an undiminished vigour for athletic sports. Peacham, who published his *Compleat Gentleman* in 1622, gives a list of the sports which a gentleman should practise. First of all comes, of course, riding. It is the 'great and most noble' sport, for 'kings have always delighted to ride'. Throwing the hammer and wrestling are low-class sports, 'not so well beseeming nobility but rather soldiers in a camp'; 'neither',

Sports in the time of Elizabeth I.

he goes on, 'have I read or heard of any prince or general commended for wrestling save Epaminondas and Achmat, the last emperor of Turkey.' This worthy, it appears, made a 'record' for hammer-throwing, and 'there was reared in Constantinople, for one extraordinary cast which none could come near, two great pillars of marble.' Our modern 'recordbreakers' receive a medal sometimes, but the event is not recorded upon marble pillars, because, perhaps, the recordbreakers are not emperors. Peacham, however, thinks highly of running, and in its praise he gives a shameful plagiarism from the book of Sir Thomas Elyot, to which we have referred before. Running is good because Achilles and Alexander were runners, and jumping is good because Eparhinondas and Alexander jumped before breakfast. However, he gives his own opinion that these exercises are 'commendable'. Whatever may have been the merits or demerits of the Stuarts, there can be no question that sportsmen owe a debt of gratitude to them. James I, though he was not an athlete himself, and though he objected to football, yet gave a general encouragement to sports, both by precept in his work, *Basilikon Doron*, and by practice in frequently acting as referee or judge. The following extract from the *Basilikon Doron*, which was a work of precepts to his son, is interesting:

> And amongst all unnecessaire things which are lawful and expedient I think exercises of the body most commendable to be used by a young prince. For albeit I grant it to be most requisite for a king to exercise his engine, which surely with idleness will rouste and become blunt, yet certainly bodily exercises are very commendable as well for baunishing idleness as for making the body able and durable for travell.
>
> The exercises that I would have you use, although but moderately, not making a craft of them [which means, we suppose, that a prince should be an amateur, not a 'pro'], are running, leaping, wrestling, fencing, dancing, and playing at the caitch, or tennise, archerie, pallemalle, and such like other fair and pleasant field games.

Both Peacham and his Majesty seem to despise hammer-throwing, the former expressing his dislike, and the latter saying nothing of it, from which it appears that fashion had clianged since the time of Henry VIII.

Although we can hardly fancy James I running or jumping, there is little doubt that athletic skill was honoured in his Court. In Arthur Wilson's life of James I, published in 1653, we hear of the royal favourite, the Duke of Buckingham, that 'no man dances better; no man runs or jumps better.' 'Indeed', remarks the sarcastic chronicler, 'he jumps higher than ever Englishman did in so short a time, from a private gentleman to a dukedom.' Another chronicler mentions the duke's fame as a 'leper,' which may or may not be another jest. What, however, is more interesting is the knowledge that not only the Court but the people at this time went on with their athletic matches in spite of Puritan opposition. From the *Annals of King James and King Charles*, published in 1681, we glean the following. As in the case of some of the preceding extracts, the sense is more obvious than the grammar is correct. 'The Reformers,' says the annalist, 'took exception against the people's lawful pleasures and holidays; and at last against all sports and publick pastimes, exercises innocent and harmless, such were leaping, dancing, running, or any mastery for to goal or prize. May-poles or Church ales as deboshed idle persons. In some of these pastimes several counties excelled, and to entertain community with their mirth the Court progresses took delight to judge of their wagers on their journeys to Scotland, which the people observing took occasion themselves to petition the King for leave to be merry.' The result of this petition was the issue by James I of the well-known *Book of Sports* in 1617, by which the people were permitted to have certain sports upon Sundays after church. The edict provoked little opposition at this date, but when it was republished by Charles I, in the eighth year of his reign, it formed one of the chief causes of complaint brought against him by the Puritan party. All the world knows that not long afterwards the Puritans proved stronger in the field; but we have something more than a suspicion that Cromwell's Ironsides must have been brought up in the national athletic sports, or they would not have displayed such skill and endurance. Indeed, their complicity in such criminal sports is rendered highly suspicious from the fact that a round cropped head is to this day the outward and visible sign of a pugilist or a pedestrian.

Before we deal with the sporting period of the Restoration, however, we must not omit to mention the account given of the common sports of the earlier part of the sixteenth century by Burton, the author of the *Anatomy of Melancholy*. Burton's book was not published until 1660; but he had then been dead twenty years, and had spent the twenty years or so previous to his death in compiling the work. If report be true, during the composition of the celebrated work he became so melancholy himself that nothing could extort a smile from him but listening to the ribaldry of the bargemen at Folly Lock, at Oxford; this specific never failed, it is said, to clear away his sadness for some time. His disposition, however, did not prevent his being a very keen observer of the country sports. He points out clearly the pastimes both of the gentry and of the people: 'Ringing, bowling, shooting, playing with keel-pins, tronks, coits, pitching of bars, hurling, wrestling, leaping, running, fencing, mustering, swimming, playing with wasters, foils, footballs, balowns, running at the quintain, and the like, are common recreations of the country folks; riding of great horses, running at rings, tilts and tournaments, horse-races and wild-goose chases, are disports of greater men, and good in themselves, though many gentlemen by such means gallop quite out of their fortunes.' He goes on to say that the country recreations take place at May-games, feasts, fairs, and wakes. This extract, backed by those we have already given, shows conclusively the universal prevalence of athletic sports in the early part of the seventeenth century.

That athletic feats were performed even under the Puritan government would seem to be the case if any reliance can be placed on the following piece of information, which is stated, in the *Gentleman's Magazine* of 1797, to be taken from a contemporary record. The whole account, however, is so obviously absurd, that were it not amusing it could hardly deserve for any other reason to find a place in an historical chapter. 'A butcher of Croydon' (says No. 147 of the *Weekly Intelligencer*), 'on December 1, 1653, ran twenty miles, from St Albans to London, in less than an hour and a half, and the last four miles so gently that he seemed to meditate, and not to ensult on the conquest, but did make it rather a recreation than a race.' At the present the best known record for twenty miles on a cinder path is 1 hour 52 min 44 sec.

With the Restoration, and the revulsion against Puritanism which led to the Restoration, came a great burst of athletic enthusiasm. Not only were the May-poles set up again, as every schoolboy knows, but the footballs were brought out once more into the streets and fields; the decision of pedestrian contests also became frequent, and attracted much popular favour. Indeed, one may almost say that from the reign of Charles II to the present time a complete and continuous history of pedestrianism could be obtained. So great was the relief in being able to resume the popular sports that even cripples took to foot-races.

In the second series of the *Loyal Protestant* we hear of a foot-race between two lame men, on Newmarket Heath, in the presence of the king himself. 'At 3 of the clock in the afternoon there was a foot-race between 2 cripples, each having a wooden

Cripples' race.

leg. They started fair' (a fact which even then seems to have deserved chronicling amongst pedestrians) 'and hobbled a good pace, which caused great admiration and laughter among the beholders; but the tallest of the two Avon by 2 or 3 yards.' However, there were plenty of contests more interesting than this, and Pepys makes frequent reference to them. On August 10, 1660, the diarist makes an entry: 'With Mr Moore and Creed to Hide Park by coach, and saw a fine foot-race three times round the Park between an Irishman and Crew, that was once my Lord Claypoole's footman.' On July 30, 1663, there is another entry which is even more significant of the popularity of foot-racing: 'The towne talk this day is of nothing but the great foot-race run this day on Banstead Downes, between Lee, the Duke of Richmond's footman, and a tyler, a famous runner. And Lee hath beat him; though the king and Duke of York, and all men almost, did bet three to four to one upon the tyler's head.' One cannot suppress the thought when hearing of such an 'upsetting of a pot,' and knowing of the wiles of professional sportsmen, that the 'tyler' upon this occasion found it more lucrative to lose than to win. Not only, however, were the 'professionals' busy with running at this time, but the amateurs were also to the fore. Two noblemen, my lords of Castlehaven and Arran (a son of my lord of Ormond's), rivalled the exploit of Henry V, and 'they two alone did run down and kill a stoute bucke in St. James's Parke.' This was for a wager, and came off in the presence of the king. These two, however, were not the only athletic noblemen. Pepys says of the Duke of Monmouth that 'he is the most skittish leaping gallant that ever I saw; always in action, vaulting or leaping or clambering.' Macaulay, in the second chapter of his *History*, has given the same picture of him: 'He mingled in, every rustic sport, wrestled, played at quarter-staff, and won foot-races in his boots against fleet runners in shoes.' Again one is tempted to make the reflection that in those days it was not 'good form' to beat a royal duke; for it is hardly credible that a man in jack-boots should be able to beat a 'crack' suitably attired. We know from Pepys that the courtiers played in this way at tennis with their monarch; and the old diarist, who says Charles was but a moderate player, calls their conduct 'beastlie'. This rough-and-ready way of handicapping by the weight of the boots seems long to have been popular. Most readers will recollect the foot-race in 'Humphry Clinker' between the lean author and the fat publisher for a bowl of punch. The former, as a handicap, borrows a great pair of riding-boots from his antagonist, and after a close race, when the publisher (running in his stockings) is getting 'blown', the impecunious author runs off with the boots on his feet, leaving only a pair of ragged shoes behind, and is seen no more. Monmouth, at any rate, never risked such a catastrophe.

No doubt it was about this time that the growth of a regular professional class of pedestrians was encouraged by the general custom of the fashionable gentlemen of the period who kept 'footmen' or 'running footmen' in their service. When gentlemen took to having town and country houses as well, and travelled about the abominable roads of the period, a running footman could travel much faster than the family coach, and could even go further in a day than a man on horseback. It is small wonder that, in an age given up to betting, matches should have been made by gentlemen between their footmen, and the footman of the period was

Monmouth in boots *v*. Soldiers in stockings.

often a professional pedestrian kept for the purpose. In any case a strong runner would easily find a footman's place, and his regular business of carrying messages on foot, or travelling in front of the family coach to make arrangements for the journey, would keep him in good fettle for such matches as his master might make for him. The good roads of the end of last century began to put an end to the running footman, and the railway system has completed his downfall; as a rule there is little in the footman of the present day to suggest that the original ancestor of the type performed marvellous pedestrian feats. A curious story which is told of the celebrated 'Old Q.' shows how a good runner could find his running powers available for procuring him service in a family. 'Old Q.' used to engage his footmen by a species of competitive examination. Every candidate for a vacancy was rigged out in the footman's uniform and given the regular staff to carry)', and then had to 'show his paces' by running up and down in front of the house. One abominably hot day 'Old Q.' reclined on a balcony, and a candidate was running so well that the nobleman made him go on running and running in the heat for the pleasure of looking at him. Finally he shouted to him from the balcony, 'You will do for me.' 'Yes', said the man, who had by this time resolved not to take service with such a master, 'and these things' (pointing to the gold-laced uniform) 'will do for me', whereupon he ran off with them, and was quite a good enough runner to outstrip pursuit.

From the time, therefore, of the rise of running footmen we find a regular line of professional runners, some in and some out of service; and accounts of the most important matches between the more famous of them are to be gathered from many contemporary records, while more occasionally one hears of the amateurs – that is, of gentlemen who back themselves to run against time or against each other for a wager. From the 'Luttrell Papers' it appears that in 1690 'Mr Peregrine Bertie, son to the late Earl of Lindsey, upon a wager, ran the Mall in St James' Park eleven times in less than an hour.' In the same records for the year 1699 there are several curious entries. Mention is made of William Joyce, the Kentish strong man, who pulled over a dray-horse in a tug-of-war, and could lift 20 cwt. He performed at the playhouse in Dorset Garden, the price of admission being, boxes 10s and pit 5s, from which he must have amassed something considerable. Another entry is also remarkable: a 'sporting man' was fined 9l 4s for swearing in the space of five hours. This the writer seems to consider a 'record' in the way of swearing.

One of the most graphic descriptions of a foot-race between two pedestrians, who were also 'running footmen,' is given in the diary of Sir Erasmus Phillips, who was an undergraduate at Oxford in the year 1720. The extract (which we gather from a correspondent to *Notes and Queries*) is as follows: 'Rode out to Woodstock: dined at the Bear (2s 6d). In the evening rode to Woodstock Park, where saw a foot-race between Groves (Duke of Wharton's running footman) and Phillips (Mr Diston's). My namesake ran the four miles round the course in 18 min and won the race, and thereby his master 1000l, the sum Groves and he started for. On this occasion there was a most prodigious concourse of people.' The alleged time is, of course, absurd, and shows that the distance cannot

Tug-of-war.

have been the full four miles, or that there was some other error in calculation; but the concourse of people to such an exceedingly 'out of the way' place as Woodstock is remarkable as showing the popular interest taken in the race.

But before we settle down to give any chronological sketch of the sport of pedestrianism and its regular paid exponents, it may be advisable to turn aside for the present, to show how far the nation still continued to indulge in running, jumping, and weight-throwing at country fairs and festivals. The Puritans had apparently succeeded in putting a stop to Sunday athletic meetings, but at the fairs and wakes the same sports went on as long as these fairs had any existence; while many of them, indeed, continued in one shape or another until they were replaced by the athletic meeting which is now almost invariably an annual affair in every country town. We have seen that, up to the time of Burton, the old country sports flourished with undiminished vigour. It is abundantly clear that they survived the Rebellion both in town and country. Stow, in his *Survey of London*, published in 1690, after quoting FitzStephen, says that the exercises mentioned by him have 'lasted to our time.' Strype, who published in 1720 another edition of Stow's Survey, mentions 'pitching the bar' amongst the pursuits of the lower classes of his day in London; while a later writer, Maitland, in his *History of London*, published in 1739, also describes footraces and leaping matches amongst the amusements of the lower classes. A paper in the *Spectator* tells the same tale as Strype and Maitland – that by the beginning of the eighteenth century athletic pastimes were considered low-class sports. In No. 161 of the second volume of the *Spectator*, Addison wrote a paper, professing to come from a country correspondent in the West of England, describing a 'Country Wake, which in most parts of England is the eve-feast of the Dedication of our Churches.' As a matter of fact, Addison is known to have been describing a festival which he had seen at Bath. The green, he says, was covered with a promiscuous multitude of all ages and both sexes. 'The whole company were in their holiday clothes, and divided into several parties, all of them endeavouring to show themselves in those exercises wherein they excelled.' There was in one place a ring of cudgel-players, in another a football match, in another a ring of wrestlers. The prize for the winners of these competitions was a hat, 'which is always hung up by the person who gets it in one of the most conspicuous parts of the house, and looked upon by the whole family as something redounding nauch more to their honour than a coat-of-arms.' One young fellow, who 'carried an Air of Importance in his looks,' appeared to have a reason for his pride, for 'he and his ancestors had won so many hats that his parlour looked like a haberdasher's shop.' The young maids also, it seems, took part in the diversions, for a farmer's son being asked what he was gazing at, says 'that he was seeing Betty Welch, his sweetheart, pitch a bar,' That running matches were also common at these wakes is clear from the comment of the *Spectator* upon the letter. He says that a country fellow who wins a competition is usually likely to win a mistress at the same time, and 'nothing is more usual than for a nimble-footed wench to get a husband at the same time she wins a smock.' A smock, or, as another writer says, 'a she-shirt,' was the regular prize for women at these rustic sports, and a hat for men, so that the pot-hunters and pot-huntresses of the day had less temptation to turn their prizes into money than comes to the winners of the silver and plated trophies of the present day.

Bath, however, was not the chief place in the West of England remarkable for its athletic meetings. Strutt, who wrote in 1801, gives an account of two important annual gatherings in the West Country, one on the Cotswold Hills in Gloucestershire, and the other upon Holgaver Moor, near Bodmin in Cornwall. To the first he says that:

> prodigious multitudes constantly resorted. Robert Dover, an attorney of Barton-on-the-Heath, in the county of Worcester, was forty years the chief director of these pastimes. They consisted of wrestling, cudgel-playing, leaping, pitching the bar, throwing the sledge, tossing the pike, with various other feats of strength and activity. Captain Dovej received permission from James I. to hold these sports, and he appeared at their celebration in the very clothes which that monarch had formerly worn, but with much more dignity in his air and aspect.

'I do not mean to say,' he goes on, 'that the Cotswold games were invented or even first estabhshed by Captain Dover: on the contrary, they seem to be of much higher origin.' Strutt then shows by a quotation from Heath's description of Cornwall, published in 1750, that a meeting of a similar nature was held near Bodmin. 'The sports and pastimes here held', says Heath, 'were so well liked by Charles II when he touched here on his way to Sicily, that he became a brother of the jovial society. The custom of keeping this carnival is said to be as old as the Saxons.'

There can be no question that the connection between fair and wakes and athletic sports was kept up well into the present century, and indeed in some out-of-the-way corners of England has lasted almost to the present time. But as the fairs decayed in importance, owing to improved facilities for travelling and trading, so did the glory of these popular athletic meetings depart with them. Still, side by side with the growing and flourishing profession of pedestrianism in the towns, these rustic sports kept their place, until finally, when the great athletic movement of recent years swept over the country, it renovated and rehabilitated these annual gatherings. The paper from which we have just quoted in the *Spectator* gives a very minute account of the one at Bath at the beginning of the eighteenth century. There is abundant evidence that their character did not substantially alter, although they undoubtedly diminished in number and importance. In the first volume of Hone's *Everyday Book* there is a communication from 'Mr Carter, the antiquary', describing the great 'May fair' held in the fields near Piccadilly at the end of the eighteenth century. The builder has covered the fields of Mayfair long since, and only the name survives to show what vulgar sports were held in that now fashionable quarter. There were shows of jugglers, a booth for boxers, another booth for cudgel players, a ring for fire-eaters, &c. 'The sports not under cover', says Mr Carter, who had been an eyewitness, 'were ass-racing, grinning for a hat, running for a shift, and an infinite variety of other similar pastimes.' Another correspondent of Hone's gives a similar account of Avingham fair in the North Country. After the dancing was over, the sports began in the presence of the mayor. Amongst the contests were 'foot-racing for hats, handkerchiefs, and she-shirts. The several races run, and the prizes distributed, they return to the last and gayest of their mirthful scenes, viz. evening dancing and drinking, finally departing "fu' blythe that night"'. In the same book there is a long account of 'Hungerford revel' in Wiltshire. The chief amusement at this festival was, of course, the cudgel-play which 'Tom Brown' has so well described for us. Besides this, however, the festival included in 1826 the following programme: (1) Girls running for smocks; (2) Climbing the greasy pole for bacon; (3) Old women drinking hot tea for snuff; (4) Grinning through horse-collars; (5) Racing between old women for a pound of tea; (6) Hunting a pig with a soaped tail; (7) Jumping in sacks for a cheese; (8) Donkey racing. There was another revel, called the 'Peppard revel,' earlier in the year, and the *Reading Mercury* of May 24, 1819, has an advertisement of the sports, promising eighteenpence to every man who breaks a head at cudgel-play, and a shilling to every man who has his head broke. One of the most interesting communications in the *Everyday Book* has reference to the North. A writer in 1826 regrets that in most of the great Northern towns the 'wakes' are dying out, 'although still held annually in nearly all the parochial villages of the North and Midlands.' The writer says, however, that in Sheffield (as we should naturally expect of this great home of pedestrianism) the 'wake' was still kept up. 'At Little Sheffield and in Broadlane the zest of the annual festivity is heightened by ass-races, foot-races (masculine) for a hat, foot-races (feminine) for a chemise, and grinning matches.' Perhaps the most interesting extract from Hone to an athlete is his account of the 'Necton Guild' in Norfolk, which was undoubtedly the first English athletic club. In 1817, Major Mason, of Necton, in Norfolk, determined to organise the local 'wake' into a regular athletic meeting. He allowed no stalls, stands, or booths for variety entertainments. Proceedings commenced with a procession headed by the Mayor of the Guild, and a circle was formed round a maypole. Then began the sports, which were as follows: – (1) Wrestling; (2) Foot-races; (3) Tingling matches; (4) Jumping in sacks; (5) Wheelbarrow-races blindfold; (6) Spinning matches; (7) Whistling matches; (8) Grinning matches; (9) Jumping matches. After the presentation of the prizes, the nature of which is not described, the dancing began, the strictest order and decorum being preserved by the beadles and other officers of the guild. This annual meeting, which commenced in 1819, was still being held in 1826, but we can find no further trace of its history. 'Numerous, respectable, and fashionable companies' generally attended the meetings of the Necton Guild, which appear to have been universally approved. Major Mason, of Necton, certainly deserves a niche in the temple of athletic fame for his institution of the guild.

These wakes were not confined to England alone. Hone tells us also of an Easter gathering at Belfast (which is to the present time the scene of an excellent athletic meeting), where running and jumping matches were the chief features of the day, and of another meeting at Portaferry, in County Down, where these amusements were diversified with 'kissing games'. 'The men kissed the females without reserve, whether married or single.' To clear the men, however, from the charge of rudeness, it should be said that the 'kissing is taken quite as a matter of course, without any coyness.' The author sagely remarks that 'tradition is silent as to the origin of this custom.'

We have, however, said enough of these fairs and the rustic athletic gatherings which took place at them. They doubtless grew rarer and rarer during the present century, but it is equally doubtless that some of them have survived quite up to the present day, although most of them have been replaced by regular athletic meetings held under modern and organised rules. The present writer, however, in the year 1885, witnessed a wake in a small Cornish town, where, besides the roundabouts, &c., there was in the evening an athletic meeting. The events were, running, jumping, a wheelbarrow race (blindfold), a sack race, and a greasy pole, and the prizes were either hats or garments, or of an edible or potable nature. From inquiry it appeared that the annual meeting was 'older than anybody could recollect.' We have little doubt that it was as old as the foundation of the town itself, as all the wakes were originally festivals of the foundation of the churches.

We have thus far followed the history of rustic sports up to the present tune, because there is no doubt that these meetings kept alive the athletic spirit throughout England, and each of them served as a nucleus for an athletic club and helped to create a centre when the modern revival of athletic sports came about. We have also been obliged, in a certain way, to anticipate matters, because through the eighteenth and earlier part of the nineteenth centuries there were two distinct streams of athleticism, the country wakes and the professional pedestrianism which began in time to rank as a branch of legitimate sport, in the same manner as the prize ring.

We have seen that there has been a regular history of professional pedestrianism ever since the Restoration, but it must not be supposed that both under the Merry Monarch and in the eighteenth century, given up, as it was, to wagering and betting of all kinds, there were no matches between amateurs. Thackeray, who knew the period he was writing about in the

'Virginians', and also understood something of the capacities of the human body for athletic purposes, tells of a match between Harry Warrington and Lord March and Ruglen, who jumped for a wager. The Virginian wins with 21 ft 3 in., beating his lordship, who could only cover 18 ft 6 in.; and Harry goes on in his letter to Virginia to state that he knew there was another in Virginia (Col. G. Washington) who could jump a foot more. Thackeray's correctness contrasts favourably with that of other writers of this century, some of whom, like Wilkie Collins in his *Man and Wife*, undertake to write of athletic feats without taking the trouble to acquire any knowledge of them. Such faults are possibly venial with writers who simply introduce them incidentally, though these latter sometimes make strange blunders. Scott, in his 'Lady of the Lake' (Canto V. Stanza 23), makes Douglas perform a ridiculous feat of weight-putting:

> Their arms the brawny yeomen bare
> To hurl the massive bar in air.
> When each his utmost strength had shown.
> The Douglas rent an earth-fast stone
> From its deep bed, then heaved it high,
> And sent the fragment through the sky
> *A rood beyond the farthest mark.*

We have some suspicion that Thackeray was thinking of this when, in his 'Rebecca and Rowena', he makes Coeur de Lion 'fling a culverin from him as though it had been a reed. It lighted three hundred yards off on the foot of Hugo de Bunyon, who was smoking a cigar at the door of his tent, and caused that redoubted warrior to limp for some days after.' There is another absurd feat, in the way of jumping, in the 'Lady of the Lake' (Canto III. Stanza 12):

> And from the silver beach's side
> Still was the prow three fathom wide,
> When lightly bounded to the land
> The messenger of blood and brand.

Eighteen feet for a 'standing long jump' is a 'record' which is hardly likely to be beaten (10 ft 9 in. is the best known at present at an athletic meeting). A list of such mistakes might be indefinitely multiplied, but we will only give one other here. Henry Kingsley, in *Geoffrey Hamlin*, makes his 'muscular Christian' curate run four miles in twenty minutes, then vault over a gate, take off his hat to a lady, and draw his watch out of his pocket to time himself; after which, being apparently not in the least out of breath, he enters upon a conversation about the benefits of athletics. No wonder this curate became a dignitary of the colonial church. He deserved the honour.

The annals of the eighteenth century are full of accounts of wagers for the performance of athletic feats, both sublime as well as ridiculous. The majority of the genuine athletic performances are those of professional pedestrians, amateurs only figuring occasionally in these wagers, and often in preposterous ones. Luttrell's *Diary* tells us of a wager made by a German of sixty-four years old to walk 300 miles in 'Hide Park' in six days, which he did 'within the time, and a mile over.' In 1780 the *Gentleman's Magazine* tells us that a man of seventy-five years old ran four miles and a half round Queen Square in 58 minutes. Eight years later a young gentleman, with a jockey booted and spurred on his back, ran a match against an elderly fat man (of the name of Bullock) running without a rider. The more extraordinary the wager the more excitement it often caused amongst the public. A fish-hawker is reported to have for a wager run seven miles, from Hyde Park Corner to Brentford, with 56 lbs weight of fish on his head, in 45 minutes! Another man trundled a coach-wheel eight miles in an hour round a platform erected in St Giles's Fields. Another extraordinary match was one between a man on stilts against a man on foot, the former receiving twenty yards start in a hundred and twenty yards. What is more astounding is that the man upon the stilts won the match.

A few examples may also be given of the many genuinely interesting matches which were brought off. As regards the alleged times, however, many of them are as obviously absurd as that supposed to have been done in the four-mile

Race between an elderly fat man and a man with a jockey on his back.

race in Woodstock Park, of which we have already spoken. An Italian is said to have run from Hyde Park Corner to Windsor in an hour and three-quarters. Another man walked from Bishopsgate to Colchester and back (102 miles) in twelve hours! In 1750 two well-known 'peds', Abron and Temple, ran a 4 mile match for 100 guineas a side, the former winning. In 1762 another man, for a wager of thirty guineas, walked seven miles just within an hour and five minutes on the Kingsland Road. Many of the matches (and these were the most popular ones) consisted of feats of endurance and long-distance matches against time. One Mr John Hague, in 1762, walked 100 miles in 23 hrs 15 min. How little notion the public had of the speed at which a good man could travel is evident from the nature of many of the matches which were made. A clerk, for instance, won a wager of fifty guineas by walking four miles in less than fifty minutes. This bet was made in 1766, and four years afterwards we hear of another man winning a wager by running a mile through the streets between Charterhouse Wall and Shoreditch Church gates in 4 minutes. In 1777 we hear of a performance in Yorkshire which is possibly correct in time: Joseph Headley, a pedestrian, running two miles in 9 min 45 sec. on the Knavesmire. The racecourse or the high road appears to have been about this period the usual arena of genuine pedestrian matches. In 1780 a pedestrian of Penrith walked fifty miles in 13 hours on the Newcastle racecourse. In 1785 one Woolfit, another pedestrian, walked forty miles a day for six consecutive days, between 6 a.m. and 6 p.m., on the high road. Soon afterwards a man named York ran four miles on the Egham racecourse in 24 1/2 minutes. In 1787 Walpole, a butcher from Newgate Market, ran a mile with a well-known pedestrian of the name of Pope, along the City Road, and beat him in the time of 4 min. 30 sec. – a good performance if true. In 1788 there was enormous excitement over a race between a pedestrian named Evans and Father Time at Newmarket, Evans being backed to run his ten miles within the hour. He is credited with covering the distance in 55 min. 18 sec., thereby putting 10,000*s* or thereabouts into the pockets of those who backed him. In the same year another pedestrian, named Wild, ran four miles in 21 min. 15 sec. on the Knutsford racecourse. The next year witnessed a remarkable feat of endurance, one Savagar, a labourer, walking 404 miles in 6 days along the road between Hereford and Ludlow, and going over a hill two miles long three times every day. All the stipulated reward for this feat was a sum of ten guineas, and he would, doubtless, have preferred to have lived in the time when Rowell, and some other pedestrians, a few years ago, netted many thousands by their long 'go-as-you-please' contests.

In 1791 we hear of some aristocratic amateurs on the path. Lord Paget, Lord Barrymore, Captain Grosvenor, and the Hon. Mr Lamb ran a race across Kensington Gardens for a sweepstake of 100 guineas. The spectators appear to have been numerous, and Lord Paget after a close race beat Mr Lamb, Captain Grosvenor being third. In 1793 another amateur. Colonel the Hon. Cosmo Gordon, appears to have assisted his friends to a good thing, as he undertook for a wager to walk five miles along the Uxbridge Road in an hour. He, however, was himself a true amateur, as he engaged,

Ready to start.

if he won, to devote the stakes to a fund for the relief of the widows and children of soldiers and sailors. The gallant colonel walked his five miles from Tyburn to Ealing easily within the hour – as well he might.

The greatest interest which was excited over pedestrian feats at this time always arose from long-distance competitions, in which endurance rather than speed or skill was exhibited. The most eminent athlete of all in this line (at any rate until the appearance of Captain Barclay Allardice) was Mr Foster Powell, a lawyer's clerk of New Inn, who may almost be said to have been the long-distance champion for a quarter of a century. He was born at Horseforth, near Leeds, in 1734, and was thirty years old before he performed his first celebrated feat, which consisted of running fifty miles on the Bath Road in seven hours, doing his first ten miles within the hour. After this he travelled abroad, exhibiting his feats of pedestrianism in Switzerland and France, and it was not until 1773 that for a heavy wager he performed the feat of going on foot from London to York and back in less than six days – to wit, in 5 days 18 hours – the distance being 402 miles. In 1777 he went from London to Canterbury and back (112 miles) in less than twenty-four hours, thousands of spectators watching him on the road and greeting his return. Eleven years afterwards, being then fifty-five years of age, he ran a mile match against a Mr Smith of Canterbury, who was too speedy for the elderly pedestrian, and beat him. At the age of fifty-seven Powell again went from London to York and back in 5 days 18 hours, and two years afterwards beat his own 'record' again by doing the same distance in 5 days 15 1/4 hours. It is hardly strange that so great a performer should have excited enormous interest, and the number of his recorded feats (the genuineness of which there seems no reason to doubt) would almost fill a book by themselves. 'Absurd as it may appear,' says an encyclopaedist in 1823, 'so desirous were people to have a sight of him that he was engaged at Astley's Amphitheatre for twelve nights, where he exhibited his pace in a small circle.' He died, however, soon after this, never having recovered from the effects of his last and most severe journey to York, and lies buried in the east corner of St Paul's Churchyard. From the contemporary accounts of his appearance he seems to have been of medium height and spare of person.

Probably the performances of Foster Powell did much to spread the popularity of pedestrianism as a sport, for we invariably find that one great performer brings a host of inferior imitators. In Powell's time pedestrianism 'boomed' again, and the waning popularity of the sport was again revived by the performances of Barclay Allardice. The feats of the latter pedestrian, indeed, called into existence a product which had never been known before – a book on pedestrianism. In 1813 a fellow-countryman of Allardice (who always ran under the name of Barclay) compiled a work, 'Pedestrianism, or An Account of the Performances of Celebrated Pedestrians during the last and present Century, with a Full Narrative of Captain Barclay's public and private Matches, and an Essay on Training.' It is from this work, published in Aberdeen by Mr Walter Thom in 1813, that we derive our account of many of the eighteenth-century feats which we have mentioned above. We can hardly blame Mr Thom for following the prevailing fashion of the age in his advice on training. The diet he recommends is beef, mutton, stale bread, strong beer, and Glauber salts; the exercise, constant morning walking and sweating. 'The patient,' he says, 'should be purged with constant medicines, sweated by walking under a load of clothes and by lying between feather-beds.' Fish, vegetables, cheese, butter, eggs, are strongly forbidden, and the use of an occasional emetic is suggested. Let modern athletes be thankful that they are trained upon a different system.

Mr Thom begins by stating that he had originally only intended to make an account of Captain Barclay, but then thought it advisable to add preliminary chapters upon the captain's more eminent predecessors in athletic fame. This preliminary part he divides into four heads – (1) matches of several days' continuance; (2) one day matches; (3) those which were performed in one or more hours, and required good wind and great agility; (4) those completed in seconds or minutes, which showed great swiftness. From this somewhat crude division it could only be expected that he would swallow a number of marvellous stories as to distance and time; but, in spite of these defects, the book is genuinely interesting.

It would be tedious to give a list of the long-distance performances recorded by Mr Thom and *The Sporting Magazine*, the best of them being those of Foster Powell; but it is worth notice that the performers are from every class of society – officers in the army, country gentlemen, farmers, labourers, butchers many of them being professional pedestrians and having no other occupation. Some of the more marvellous deeds are as follows: – Levi Whitehead, of Bramham, four miles on Bramham Moor in 19 minutes; Mr Haselden, of Milton, a private gentleman, ten miles on the Canterbury road in 53 minutes 'with ease'. This last performance was in the year 1809. In February 1808 Mr Wallis, a gentleman of Jermyn Street, two miles in 9 minutes 'in two starts', with a minute's interval between each start.

Though it is understood that the times are to be regarded sceptically, Thom's work gives a very vivid picture of the popularity of athletic sports during the twenty years preceding the publication of his work in 1813. Three pedestrians, Howe, Smith and Grey, appear frequently to have competed in twenty-mile and ten-mile races. In 1793 two pedestrians, Barrett and Wilkman, ran a ten-mile match on Kersal Moor, the former winning in 57 minutes. In 1805 Lieutenant Warren and Mr Bindall, an artist, ran a match of seven miles on the Uxbridge road, the artist winning by a quarter of a mile. Time given as 35 minutes. In 1805, James Farrer, for a wager of 200 guineas, ran against time on Knutsford racecourse, doing four miles in 20 min. 57 sec. One of the best-known 'pads' of this time was Abraham Wood, a Lancashire man, who, however, had his colours lowered in a four-mile race by Joseph Beal, a Yorkshire lad of nineteen, who beat the champion in 21 min, 18 sec. Beal is also credited with two miles in 9 min. 48 sec. on York racecourse in a match with another 'ped', Isaac Hemsworth, of Bolton, Lancashire.

In 1809 Captain Dane and Mr Davies ran a mile match in Bayswater fields, the captain winning by 'about 2 lengths', in 4 min. 56 sec. Two other amateurs, Lord F. Bentinck and the Hon. Edward Harbord, also ran a mile in 1804 for 100 guineas, the latter winning easily, and his lordship was shortly afterwards beaten by a Mr Mellish in another match over the Beacon course. In 1805 Mr Harbord tried sprinting in a match with Lord F. Beauclerk at 100 yards; the latter won by two yards. The winner afterwards met at the same distance the Hon. Mr Brand, and won easily, 'the latter gentleman becoming quite winded before he had run fifty paces.' Both these matches were brought off at Lord's Cricket Ground. Besides these, Thom gives the names of Colonel Douglas, Mr Lambert, Lieutenant Hankey, Captain Aiken, Lieutenant Fairman, and Captain Agar as being prominent amateurs about his time; and, indeed, it appears that the amateur pedestrians were chiefly officers in the army. This inclines us to believe the story which is often repeated, but for which we can find no sufficient verification, that about 1812 there was a regular annual athletic meeting at Sandhurst, which was afterwards discontinued.

Thom is of opinion that next after his pet hero, Captain Barclay, Abraham Wood, of Mildrew, in Lancashire, was the best runner of his time. His best reported performances were 20 min. 21 sec. for four miles over the York course, against one John Brown, who had previously beaten Wood over a similar distance on the Knavesmire. Wood, however, seems to have been a fair performer at shorter distances as well, as in 1809 he beat Shipley, of Nottingham, at a quarter mile on the well-known Knutsford course in 56 seconds. Sprinting appears to have been less popular than racing at longer distances at this time; but such sprinters as there were must have been marvellous men if the times recorded are accurate. Curley, the Brighton shepherd, ran a match against Grinley, a 'ped', in 1805, 'on the walk leading to the gate of Kensington Garden', Grinley winning by a head in 12 1/2 seconds. Next year Grinley again beat his antagonist on Hampton Court Green over 120 yards, upon this occasion doing 'level time'. Curley, however, beat another 'ped', Cooke, a soldier, over a sprint; but Cooke, for a wager of fifty guineas, beat Mr Williams, a gentleman, by a yard and a half. In 1808, however, Skewball, the famous Lancashire shepherd, ran 140 yards in 12 seconds at Hackney! This is perhaps the best specimen of the incapacity of the writers of that day to distinguish between possible and impossible times.

Captain Barclay Allardice is, of course, best known by his feat of walking 1,000 miles in 1,000 hours at Newmarket. The performance, no doubt, startled everybody at the time, although it has frequently been since surpassed. He was, however, a fine all-round performer. He was born in 1779, and had such an unextinguishable love for athletic sports, that when he was only 15 he won a wager by walking six miles in an hour on the Croydon road. When twenty-one he made a match of 5,000 guineas to walk ninety miles in 21 1/2 hours, and won it with ease, amidst the plaudits of thousands of spectators. He soon afterwards beat a Mr Ward a quarter of a mile in 56 seconds. In 1806 he again was matched at that distance against Mr Goulbourne, of the Royal Horse Guards, at Lord's Cricket Ground, and won easily in 1 min. 12 sec. He also won two mile races in matches with amateurs in 5 min. 7 sec. and 4 min. 50 sec, and was for the years 1796–1808, when he performed the 1,000 miles in 1,000 hours feat, the most prominent runner of the day. Nay, more, in the words of Thom, 'he ever evinced inflexible adherence to strict principles of honour and integrity, and whether as transacting with mankind individually, or as a public character responsible for his opinion and conduct at the shrine of his country, he always proved his sincere respect for the rights of others and his unfeigned attachment to the British constitution.'

Be that, however, as it may, he certainly deserves the thanks of modern athletes for his success in rendering athletic sports a popular pastime for gentlemen. There was, as is well known, no distinction in his time between professionals and amateurs, and gentlemen made matches with each other and with pedestrians as they pleased, and we find the great Barclay entering on a contest of endurance with Abraham Wood, and running him 'off his legs'. But throughout the first five-and-twenty years of the present century the ball which Barclay had started was kept rolling by plenty of successors; indeed, up to about 1825 so many amateurs made matches at Newmarket, or on the Uxbridge Road, or at Lord's Cricket Ground, and so much interest was displayed by spectators in these contests, that it seems wonderful that the system of athletic meetings for amateurs should not have arisen half a century earlier than was actually the case, though, as we have already stated, there is some evidence that there were regular meetings at Sandhurst early in the century. After about 1825, however, the popularity of foot races amongst amateurs appears to have waned, and we hear of few gentlemen engaging in matches. We believe, nevertheless, that of the amateur generation of the early part of this century there is still a survivor. The present Lord Tollemache (note: this was written in 1887 when the late Lord Tollemache was living), after running several sprint races, was backed by a friend to run any man in England over 100 yards. The challenge was accepted on behalf of a Mr MacNamara, and the match came off at the usual venue of Lord's Cricket Ground, Lord Tollemache again proving a winner. The late Mr Horatio Ross, who only died recently, also distinguished himself in his early years as a walker of long-distance matches. However, though there were fewer amateurs in the field, professional pedestrianism continued steadily to increase throughout the century, and we find a regular succession of celebrated short-distance and long-distance runners who challenged and wrested championships from each other in the same manner as the champions of the ring.

As the period to which we are now referring is almost a modern one, and as our business in this work is with athletic sports as a pastime for amateur and not with the business of professional pedestrians, we can hardly give here a history of the pedestrianism of the nineteenth century, for which such ample materials exist in the pages of the *Sporting Magazine* and *Bell's Life*. Some few memorable performances, however, claim attention as showing the steady progress of athletic ability. In 1825 James Metcalf (champion) gave J. Halton (ex-champion) 20 yards in a mile, for a stake of 1,000 guineas, on the Knavesmire, and the champion won in the time of 4 min. 30 sec.; but it is not for another fifteen or twenty years that we hear of this time being approached, and not until 1849 that we know of its being beaten by W. Matthews of Birmingham, who did his mile in 4 min. 27 sec. Between 1825 and 1838 or 1839 or thereabouts, although pedestrian matches at all distances were common enough, pedestrianism was hardly the popular sport that it became later on. We find that in the columns of *Bell's Life* it was the custom for many years to mention the future pedestrian fixtures at the end of that part of the paper which came under the heading of 'The Ring'. About the latter date (1838) *Bell's Life* began to give pedestrianism a heading to itself, and every week there is a list of some twenty or thirty events. Between 1840 and 1850 pedestrianism had another 'boom', and as usual when the sport was popular, the amateurs began to turn out again and make matches with each other or with the pedestrians. A curious instance of the difference of fashion may be seen from the varying practice of amateurs as to giving their real names in these contests. In 1838 *Bell's Life* gives an account of a cross-country steeplechase match got up by six medical students of Birmingham, who 'for several reasons' concealed their real names, and the account describes them under the pseudonyms of 'Sprightly', 'Rustic', 'Chit-chat', 'Neversweat', 'Vulcan', 'The Spouter'. The umpires selected a mile course, and, after an eventful race, 'The Spouter' won and 'Neversweat' was second. Five years afterwards the amateurs were running in their own names again, and the public were looking on at their matches with applause. Captain Hargraves and Mr Fenton attracted a large crowd to a mile match which they ran in 1843. It was not long after this that we find professional pedestrianism in what were almost its palmiest days. 'Billy' Jackson (the American Deer), J. Davies (the Lame Chicken), and Tom Maxfield (the North Star) ran a mile match upon the Slough Road, over what is still known as 'Maxfield's mile', amidst an enormous concourse of people and 'immense enthusiasm.' About this date *Bell's Life* had every week a list of nearly fifty fixtures of matches to come off, and pedestrianism as an institution was an accomplished fact. In 1850 'the major portion of the sporting population of Liverpool, Manchester, Newcastle, and the other great towns' turned out to see 'Tommy' Hayes beat 'Johnny' Tetlow, over four miles on the Aintree racecourse; and in 1852, when George Frost (the Suffolk Stag) won the championship belt at the old Copenhagen Grounds by a ten miles race, lithographs of the contest were published and sold by the thousand. Such was the popularity of pedestrianism at this period that it is hardly to be wondered that it should have aided other causes in setting the amateur movement going.

The 'Volunteer movement' is usually put forward as the explanation of the outburst of athletic spirit throughout the kingdom about this period. The more probable, and perhaps more philosophical explanation, of the impulse which undoubtedly began in the towns is that it was the natural product of the over-pressure of modern commercial and professional life. Hours of work being long, there comes a craving amongst adults for violent exercise, and that craving has led to the popularity of various athletic games, which are now so universally practised. Whatever may be the cause, however, of the 'athletic movement', there can be little doubt that the first amateur athletic sports were suggested by the performance of professional 'peds', and that whenever there was an unusual galaxy of pedestrian ability the amateurs began to imitate them. We have seen that, between 1845 and 1852, there was great public interest shown in pedestrianism, and it is accordingly not surprising to find that the first regular athletic meetings begin to be heard of about this time. In 1849 there was a regular organised athletic meeting at the Royal Military Academy, Woolwich, which was continued till 1853, when it was abandoned. In 1850 Exeter College, Oxford, started a meeting, which has been continued annually down to the present day. The following account of the first of these, which has been sent to us by one of the competitors himself, can hardly fail to be interesting to modern athletes; and the programme, which is probably the sole extant specimen, is in itself interesting enough to justify its reproduction in these pages:

Exeter College, Oxford, was one of the first institutions to start an athletic gathering, and it may not be uninteresting to give a narrative, collected mainly from the recollection of eyewitnesses, of the first set of sports ever held there, and of the gentlemen who were the originators and first performers.

The year was 1850. It was the evening after the College Steeplechase (vulgarly called the 'College Grind'). Some four or five congenial spirits, as their manner was, were sipping their wine after 'hall' in the 'rooms' of one, R. F. Bowles (brother to John Bowles, the well-known coursing squire, of Milton Hill). Besides the host there were James Aitken, Geo. Russell, Marcus Southwell, and Halifax Wyatt. The topic was the event of the day, and the unsatisfactory process of 'negotiating' a country on Oxford hacks. 'Sooner than ride such a brute again,' said Wyatt, whose horse had landed into a road on his head instead of his legs, 'I'd run across two miles of country on foot.' 'Well, why not?' said the others; 'let's have a College foot grind,' and so it was agreed.

Bowles, who always had a sneaking love for racing – born and bred as he was near the training grounds on the Berkshire Downs – suggested a race or two on the flat as

The History of Athletic Sports in England 53

well. Again the party agreed. The conditions were drawn up, stakes named, officials appointed, and the first meeting for 'Athletic Sports' inaugurated.

On the first afternoon there was to be a 'chase', two miles across country, 24 jumps, 1*l*. entry, 10*s*. forfeit; and on a subsequent afternoon, a quarter of a mile on the flat, 300 yards, 100 yards, 140 yards over 10 flights of hurdles 10 yards apart, one mile, and some other stakes for 'beaten horses', open to members of Exeter College only. The stewards of the 'Exeter Autumn Meeting' were R. F. Bowles and John Broughton; Secretary, H. C. Glanville; Clerk of the course, E. Ranken; and a well-known sporting tradesman in Oxford, Mr Randall, was asked to be Judge. Mr Randall is still alive, and though over 80 years of age, is a regular attendant at Henley, Putney, or Lord's, whenever there is a University contest.

Notice of the meeting, with a list of the stakes, was posted in the usual place – a black board in the porter's lodge. Plenty of entries were made, in no stake less than 10: for the steeplechase there were 24 who started.

Among the competitors were Jas. Aitken, J, Scott, Geo. Russell, Jnr Broughton, R. F. Bowles, D. Giles, H. J. Cheales, H. Wyatt, Jas. Woodhouse, C. J. Parker, P. A. Vilson, M. Southwell, H. C. Glanville, H. Collins, E. Knight, and some nine others.

The betting was – 2 to 1 *v*. Aitken, 2 to 1 *v*. Cheales, 8 to 1 *v*. Giles, 9 to 1 *v*. Wyatt, 10 to 1 *v*. Parker, 10 to 1 *v*. Scott, 12 to 1 *v*. Broughton, 15 to 1 *v*. Woodhouse.

The course chosen was on a flat marshy farm at Binsey, near the Seven Bridge Road: it was very wet, some fields 'swimming' in water, the brooks bank high, and a soft take-off, which meant certain immersion for most, if not all, the competitors. Twenty-four went to the post, not 24 hard-conditioned athletes in running 'toggery', but 24 strong active youngsters in cricket shoes and flannels, some in fair condition, some very much the reverse, but all determined to 'do or die'. Plenty of folk, on horse and foot, came to see this novelty (for in Modern, as in Ancient

Athens, men were always on the lookout for 'some new thing'), and in this instance, judging from the excitement, and the encouragement given to the competitors, the novelty was much appreciated.

As about half of the 24 starters left the post as if they were only going to run a few hundred yards, they were necessarily soon done with. Aitken, gradually coming through all these, had the best of the race until one field from home, when Wyatt and Scott, who had been gradually creeping up, ran level. They jumped the last fence together. Wyatt, who landed on firmer ground, was quickest on his legs, and ran in a comparatively easy winner; there was a tremendous struggle for the second place, which was just obtained by Aitken.

The time, according to the present notion of running, must no doubt have been slow, but the ground was deep, the fences big and all the competitors were heavily handicapped by wet flannels bedraggling their legs.

Of the flat races, which were held in Port Meadow, on unlevelled turf, no authentic record has been preserved of the winners of all the events. The hurdle-race was won by E. Knight, R. F. Bowles being second. The 100 yards by Wyatt, and he also won one or two of the other shorter races; but for the mile he had to carry some pounds of shot in an old-fashioned shot-belt round his loins, and ran second to Aitken, who won. Listen to this, ye handicappers of the present day!

Such is the history of the first set of athletic sports. But now a word or two as to the original patrons and performers, for we would not have the athletes of the present day think that the last generation were altogether 'unprofitable servants'.

Marcus Southwell, R. F. Bowles, and Geo. Russell (now Sir Geo. Russell, Bart., of Swallowfield), were perhaps more patrons than performers. But Southwell was a fine horseman, and could walk six miles in the hour without training: he, alas! was killed when on a tour in America by a horse falling on him. Bowles and Russell could both row, play cricket, and run a bit, and they perhaps were the most energetic in getting up the first edition of sports. There is a longer record of services against the name of James Aitken, beyond winning the mile race, and being second for the two miles. As a cricketer he played in the Eton eleven, at Oxford in the University eleven against Cambridge in 1848, 1849, and 1850, and was captain of the eleven in 1850. As an oarsman he rowed against Cambridge at Putney in 1849, was one of the Oxford eight and four that rowed over for the Grand and Stewards at Henley in 1850, rowed in the Oxford eight that beat Cambridge at Henley in 1851, and won the Goblets together with the present Mr Justice Chitty. He was ordained soon after leaving the University, and has had neither time nor opportunity for following up rowing or cricket to any great extent, but he has worked as hard and conscientiously in his parish as he did at No. 5 thwart in the University boat, and they say that even now, at lawn tennis, few of the young ones can hold their own against the Rev. James Aitken, vicar of Chorleywood, in Hertfordshire.

Halifax Wyatt, another of the performers, was born in the 'Duke's Country' – no doubt a point in his favour – and in his younger days was known to the noble editor of the Badminton Library, both in the hunting-field and on the tented sward, when I.Z. used to play at Badminton. At Oxford he won, as stated, the two miles and some of the shorter races in the sports. He played against Cambridge in the University eleven 1850, 1851, and in his college eleven in 1849, 1850, 1851. He rowed in the O.U.B.C. eight-oared races in 1849, 1850, 1851, in the O.U.B.C. fours 1849, and O.U.B.C. sculls 1850. Since leaving Oxford he has played a great deal of county cricket, in Gloucestershire, Devonshire, and Cheshire, and is an I.Z., M.C.C., Harlequin, &c. He did but little afterwards in running, but when quartered with the 4th Battalion Devonshire Regiment, at Limerick, he ran a 100 yards match for 50 feet against a Canadian in the 89th Regiment, and beat him. H. Wyatt retired from Devon Regiment as Lt Colonel, and has now for some years past managed the Earl of Sefton's extensive estates in Lancashire, and is a first-rate hand in 'looking on' at all those sports in which formerly he took such an active part.

This is a slight sketch of the men who 'set the ball rolling', but though their first meeting was evidently popular, the thing went slowly for a time. In 1851, Exeter College followed up the autumn meeting of 1850 with a summer meeting on Bullingdon, and we think that both a high and broad jump were introduced in the programme. In these sports both C. A. North and J. Hodges distinguished themselves, the latter, by the way, not long after for a wager riding 50, driving 50, and walking 50 miles in 24 consecutive hours. Lincoln College, Oxford, was the next to take up the idea and held some sports. Then a college in Cambridge. After this the thing went like wildfire, spreading simultaneously on every side; and after Colleges and Schools, first in London and then in the provinces clubs were formed for the promotion of athletic sports.

Kensington Grammar School began their regular sports in 1852, and we believe there are several other private schools round London which have had annual foot races and jumping matches since about the same time, which we have little doubt were suggested, or at any rate encouraged, by the interest taken by the boys' parents in 'The American Deer', 'The Suffolk Stag', 'The Greenwich Cowboy', and other pedestrian worthies of the same kidney. In 1853 Harrow and Cheltenham both started athletic meetings; and Durham University also had a gathering which however, appears to have died a natural death.

Undoubtedly there were races at several of the public schools before this date, but they can hardly be called athletic meetings. The pastime of 'hare and hounds', as an amusement for schoolboys, is quite as old as any other English athletic pastime, Strutt gives a quotation from an old comedy, written towards the close of the sixteenth century, in which an 'idle boy' says:

> And also when we play and hunt the fox
> I outrun all the boys in the schoole.

This is no doubt an allusion to 'hare and hounds,' and Strutt himself, writing in 1801, gives the following account of the pastime which he calls 'hunt the fox' or 'hunt the hare': 'One of the boys is permitted to run out, and having law given him – that is, being permitted to go to a certain distance from his comrades before they can pursue him – their object is to take him, if possible, before he can return home.' The Crick Run at Rugby appears to have been founded in 1837, and at Shrewsbury there is known to have been a school steeplechase a very few years afterwards, while in 1845 Eton started an annual steeplechase, sprint races and hurdle races, which came off on the road all on different days. Curiously enough, this is the first mention that we can find anywhere of short hurdle races. (Note: In 1837 and 1838 we had hurdle races at most of the tutors' and dames' houses at Eton, as I know from the fact of having run in and won races of the sort there in those years. One hundred yards over ten hurdles was the usual course.) Hurdle racing, now so popular amongst amateurs, is almost entirely an amateur sport. In 1853 *Bell's Life* has an account of two amateurs competing in an 'all round' competition, which included the following events: A mile race, walking backwards a mile, running a coach wheel a mile, leaping over fifty hurdles, each 3 ft 6 in. high (the present regulation height), stone picking, and weight putting; and in the same year the *Times* contains an account of a match between Lieut. Sayers and 'Captain Astley' in a flat race and a hurdle race. All the school meetings, which began about 1852 and 1853, as we have seen, included hurdle racing in their programmes, and even up to the present day the chief homes of hurdle racing are the public schools and universities. The pastime of hurdle racing, however, can hardly be entirely modern, as Professor Wilson ('Christopher North') appears to have been an adept at something of a similar nature early in the century. The Professor of Moral Philosophy had so distinguished a reputation as an athlete that his name should not be omitted from a chapter on athletic history. Hone has an anecdote of his 'taking down' a brother private in the militia at Kendal. The latter boasted that he had never been beaten in a jumping competition, and Wilson accordingly challenged him to jump for a guinea. The unbeaten champion could only cover 15 feet, Wilson clearing 21 feet, to his opponent's amazement.

About 1852, then, it came to be considered a recognised and reasonable form of sport for a school or college to devote a day or an afternoon to a meeting for competitions in the old English sports of running, jumping, and throwing of weights; but the notion of open competitions, championships, or contests between the Universities in athletic sports, in the same way that they were already competing in cricket and boat-racing, was still far from dawning on the English mind. Races and jumping matches were still considered school pastimes like 'tag' or 'prisoner's base', and even at the Universities their progress towards popularity was very slow. The following is the information given as to this progress by the writer of *Modern Athletics*:

> At the two Universities there were no athletic sports of any description until 1850, when Exeter College, Oxford, took the initiative and held a meeting, which has since been repeated annually. In 1856, and even in 1858, *Bell's Life*, in its report of these sports, styles them 'rural and interesting revels', and again, 'a revival of good old English sports'. Exeter College was alone until 1855, when mention is first made of any sports at Cambridge, St John's College and Emmanuel taking the lead. At Oxford, Balliol, Wadham, Pembroke and Worcester followed the example of Exeter in 1856; Oriel in 1857, Merton in 1858, Christchurch in 1859, and in 1861 separate college meetings had become general. At the close of 1860, the Oxford University sports, open to all undergraduates, owed their foundation to the exertions of the Rev. E. Arkwright, of Merton College. At Cambridge the University sports had already been founded in 1857, but annual meetings of the separate colleges were not frequent as at the sister University until 1863.

How suddenly the importance of athletics increased at the Universities in 1864, the first year of the Inter-Varsity meeting, may be gathered from some remarks of Sir Richard Webster made at the annual dinner of the London Athletic Club in 1886, when he said that for winning half-a-dozen strangers' races in one year he had received a few pounds in coin, while the next year a friend whose performances had been of the same order received about 40s worth of prizes from the silversmiths.

Soon after 1860 these athletic meetings had become a regular feature of school and college life. Trinity College, Dublin, instituted a meeting in 1857, which has since had a continuous existence and undiminished popularity. In England, Rugby School held its first regular meeting in 1856, Winchester in 1857, and Westminster and Charterhouse in 1861. By this latter year all the public schools, as well as the Universities, were holding sports, and there is little doubt that the growth and popularity of the public school system has done much not only to foster but to spread the spirit of athletic competition throughout the kingdom. Lads who have gained health, pleasure, and reputation from athletic pursuits at school are hardly likely to drop their tastes as soon as school is left behind, and it is certain that the athletic movement was largely aided by the impetus it received from the return of the old public school boys to their homes throughout the country.

While, however, the schools were beginning to take up athletic sports in a tentative way soon after 1850, it is not until more than ten years afterwards that we begin to hear of a class of amateur athletes, as distinguished from professional 'peds', holding meetings of their own. The pages of *Bell's Life* during this period occasionally show us that amateurs were matching themselves against the professionals, and we find not only records of amateur matches where the contestants are described as amateurs (as in 1853 one between Mr Green and Air. Martin at 150 yards), but also cases of amateur meeting 'ped' (as in the preceding year the match between Green, 'the amateur', and Michael Turner). The time, however, was getting ripe for amateurs, as we find even the highly respectable *Times* newspaper recording matches like the one mentioned above between Lieut. Sayers and Captain Astley, and another between Mr Whaley and the Hon. Arthur Wellesley, who ran a match for 150 guineas on the Donnybrook Road in 1854. Something was, however, wanting to set athletic meetings going outside schools, colleges, and bodies such as the Honourable Artillery Company, which held its first fixture for its own members in 1858, and the required impetus was probably given by a renewed burst of public excitement over professional pedestrianism in 1860 and the following years. In 1860 L. Bennett, better known as 'Deerfoot', a Canadian Indian, appeared on the scene in England, and there began a series of matches between him and the best English pedestrians, which excited the public interest even more than the great period of ten years or so before. The performances of Bennett, Lang, Sian Albison, Teddy Mills, Jack White, and a score of other celebrities of this period set the public talking again about foot-racing, and in the winter of 1861 the West London Rowing Club held an athletic meeting, thinking that their rowing men might like some hard work and exercise to keep them in training during the winter season. As far as we can discover, the first 'open race' for amateurs was held in the summer of 1862, when Mr W. Price, a promoter of pedestrian handicaps, decided to offer at the Hackney Wick grounds a 'handsome silver cup' to be competed for by 'amateurs only', thinking doubtless that this would prove a new attraction to sightseers. The report of this open amateur handicap, which took place on July 26, 1862, shows that as a means of provoking speculation in the betting way it was rather a failure; but to amateurs the race is interesting for other reasons. In the first heat the reporter says that the betting was 6 to 4 in favour of Mr Green, who beat Mr, Johnson, but that 'not much was done'. In another heat Mr Spicer (who belonged, by the way, to the Honourable Artillery Company) started off at mark with Mr Chinnery, who was afterwards to make so great a name as a holder of many championships. On this occasion, however, Mr Spicer outlasted Mr Chinnery, and beat him.

On August 30 in the same year Mr Price offered prizes for two more open races at a quarter and three-quarters of a mile. In the former, Mr Martin, whom athletes will perhaps be surprised to hear was no other than the veteran Civil Service walker, Mr C. M. Callow, was one of the competitors, as also was Mr Walter Rye, afterwards champion walker, who, however, appeared in his own name. Another of the competitors was Mr C. H. Prest (afterwards a celebrated amateur, but of somewhat doubtful 'amateurity'), who ran under the name of Baker. There was at the time a prevalent idea that an amateur athlete should conceal from the world his taste for athletics, as the report of this meeting in a sporting paper mentions the runners who had appeared in the mysterious style as Mr R., Mr N., and so forth. Possibly, however, the reporter, acting on the principle *omne ignotum pro magnifico*, thought to lend importance to the budding amateurs by thus throwing an air of mystery over their names. At this second meeting at Hackney Wick, Mr Chinnery, in the three-quarter mile race, had again to succumb to the redoubtable Mr Spicer, although receiving ten yards' start from him.

It is not until the next year that the stray London amateurs made any effort to form themselves into a club. In June of the year 1863 certain gentlemen, including in their numbers some of those who had figured at the West London Rowing Club meetings and Price's handicaps, founded the Mincing Lane Athletic Club, calling the club after that well-known trade centre, in which the majority of the founders were engaged in business. In 1864 they held their first meeting at the West London grounds at Brompton on April 9, but so little attention was paid to it that we cannot find that a report of the meeting appeared in any paper. Another meeting was held on May 21 of the same year, in which Mr Chinnery won the mile race, and on that occasion a full report of the proceedings was published in all the sporting journals. During the year two challenge cups for 220 yards and 10 miles walking races were presented to the club, which has ever since been a flourishing institution. In the spring of 1866 the club changed its name, and became, as it now is, the London Athletic Club.

It is from the year 1864, indeed, that amateur athletic sports as an institution may be said to date. Not only did a regularly constituted athletic club begin in that year to hold open races, but the same season witnessed the institution of the Inter-University sports. Negotiations were carried on in 1863 between the two Universities as to the holding of an Inter-Varsity contest; but before anything could be arranged, the summer term with its cricket and boating arrived, and it was found impossible to get the athletes together. However, on March 3, 1864, the Cambridge men came over and met their Oxford brethren on the Christchurch Cricket Ground. On this occasion neither side won the 'odd event', for the excellent reason that there was no 'odd event' to win. The programme consisted of eight contests, and four were won by each University. Since then it is hardly necessary to say that the meeting has been annual, although the University athletes did not come to London until 1867.

The same year, 1864, saw the Civil Servants hold their first meeting – a meeting which still is an annual and important event; but it wanted yet a year or two before amateur athletics became general throughout the provinces as well as in London. In 1865 several football and cricket clubs promoted meetings, but it is not until 1866 that we hear of athletics being generally practised throughout the kingdom. By this time the amateurs had decided to have nothing to do with the professional 'peds' of the day, owing to the 'roping' and 'squaring' tactics of some of them which were notorious. At the beginning of 1866, when the Amateur Athletic Club was formed by some old University and London athletes, the prospectus announced that the club was formed to 'supply the want of an established ground upon which competitions in amateur athletic sports might take place, and to afford as completely as possible to all classes of gentlemen amateurs the means of practising and competing against one another, without being compelled to mix with professional runners.' The newly formed Amateur Athletic Club held a championship meeting in the spring of 1866, which was a conspicuous success, and this was the first of the long series which are still being continued under the management of the Amateur Athletic Association. The intention of the founders of the Amateur Athletic Club was no doubt to place their club in the same position with athletes as the M.C.C. stood to cricketers, and the design at first seemed to promise well, for the championship meetings were very successful, and in two years' time the club opened a splendid running ground for amateurs at Lillie Bridge, which immediately became the headquarters of amateur athletics. The active athletes, however, continued to ally themselves more with the L.A.C. than the A.A.C., and the latter club soon ceased to hold any meetings but the championship.

It is hardly necessary, however, to pursue the history of athletics since the year 1866. By that year sports had been instituted in most of the large provincial towns as well as in many rural districts, 'The Athlete', a record published in 1867, gives an account of nearly a hundred meetings held in England, and the same publication for the ensuing year shows that the number had then swelled to nearly a hundred and fifty. The progress of amateur athletics has since been rapid and continuous, and there is now hardly a single town throughout the country which does not have its annual athletic meeting. But by the year 1866 amateur athletics had definitely taken their present form, and though clubs have waxed and waned, and popular favour has ebbed and flowed at intervals, a generation of Englishmen has recreated itself with athletic sports in the same shape. The system of sports which had its growth in England has been successfully transplanted not only to Canada, Australia, and other British colonies, but to the United States; and it is now no rare event to find Englishmen, Irishmen, Scotchmen, Americans, and colonists competing together in the championship meetings of the Old Country.

2
A Modern Championship Meeting

In the foregoing chapter we have shown how the pastimes of running, leaping, and hurling of weights, which have always been followed by Englishmen as a means of amusement and for the display of rivalry, began rather more than a quarter of a century ago to be developed into a systematic sport, and have come at the present time to be considered, like racing and cricket, as national institutions. As regards social attention, athletic sports were probably at their zenith from 1870 to 1875, for at that time the 'masses' had not begun to appear as amateur athletes upon the running-path. So far as wide-spread popularity amongst all classes is concerned, athletics have reached a height at the present time, from which they may possibly fall, but which they can hardly exceed. As every pastime has its day, and it is possible that another age may know no more of athletic sports than the present age knows of cambuc or the quintain, it may not be out of place at the present time to try to present to the uninitiated reader such a meeting as may be witnessed to-day, so far as the pen can avail to describe a stirring scene of life and movement. Every pursuit has its classic days – days which are vividly impressed upon the memory of those who study the sport. One of these was the Oxford and Cambridge meeting of 1876, when M. J. Brooks, the Dark Blue President, jumped 6 ft 2 1/2 in. in height, when there was scarcely a foot of standing room at Lillie Bridge, and over 1,100*l*. was taken from the fashionable crowd that thronged to see Young Oxford compete against Young Cambridge. Another classic day was the championship meeting of 1881, when 12,000 people went to the Amateur Championship meeting at the Aston Lower Grounds, Birmingham, to see the pick of the English. Irish, and Scotch athletes meet the Americans, Myers and Merrill, for the English championship titles. Yet another such was the championship meeting of 1886, held on July 3, at the London Athletic Club grounds at Stamford Bridge – a gathering which for more reasons than one deserves to be preserved in accurate recollection.

The first event upon the programme is fixed for three o'clock, and by that time some two thousand spectators have assembled. About five or six hundred of these are at the lower end of the ground in the open walk reserved for the 'shilling public'; the remainder are near the stands and on the gravel at the head of the ground. They have paid two shillings for admission, and by a glance at them you can see that many hail from the country, and that all have come for pure sport. There may be, perhaps, a hundred ladies on the ground, but not more. The championship is a 'business' meeting, and the majority of the spectators know thoroughly the form of the men competing, and are already discussing the chances. All open betting is forbidden by the rules of the Amateur Athletic Association; but where there are sporting men, some will have their fancy, and betting there will be, but for small and often trifling amounts, and almost entirely between friend and friend. The day is a perfect day for athletics, very warm, so that men's muscles are supple and without a trace of stiffness, and with a slight breeze blowing up towards the stands, so that the times of the runners in the sprint races and hurdles are sure to be fast.

And now, before the runners come out, let us take a glance at the centre of the ground. On a large table facing the grand stand, but within the railings, are set out the handsome silver challenge cups, which each winner holds for the year of his championship only, but of which he can never obtain the absolute possession. Between the cups as they stand on the table are spread the gold, silver, and bronze medals of the Association. Each winner is to receive a small gold championship medal, which, let us hope, will remain an heirloom in his family. The second man in each race has a silver medal to keep. The bronze medals are for a different purpose, and may be regarded more as certificates of merit than as prizes. In most of the competitions, when a man is placed neither first nor second, but has done a performance which is of championship merit – for instance, has finished his half-mile under 2 min. 2 sec, or his mile under 4 min. 30 sec. – he is awarded the 'standard' medal. (Note: The standards are not the same for every year. They are fixed by the championship committee of the A. A. A. for each year, and the general tendency has been to raise them to accord with the gradual improvement in times and performances.) No standard medals are given for the hundred yards or hurdle races, from the difficulty of satisfactorily fixing a standard and timing men to see whether they are within the standard time. Close by the winning post are gathered the reporters and the officials, while the rest of the greensward enclosed by the railings and cinder track is bare; for the orders are strict that none but the recognised representatives of leading papers and the officials are to be allowed inside the enclosure. There are about a dozen reporters, therefore, inside the track with the officials. The judges, who have in athletics, as well as in all other work, arduous and delicate work, are all tried men. The first on the list is A. J. Puttick, an old runner of the London Athletic Club, whose gigantic form is always to be seen at a gathering at Stamford Bridge, sometimes, as now, in a frock coat and glossy hat, and at others in that quaint sesthetico-athletic garb which marks his double character of amateur athlete and amateur violoncellist. Close by him is 'Jack' Reay, who a few years ago was champion hurdler, and the best flat race runner in the Civil Service. These two, together with G. P. Rogers, the Secretary of the London Athletic Club, and C. H. Mason, of the same club, once amateur champion at a mile and ten miles, are four of the men who have led the athletic movement in the metropolis for the last dozen years, and are, perhaps, the four best judges in London. The two last named are both on the ground to-day as members of the committee, but are not judging. The two other judges are E. B. Holmes, one of the best of the well-tried officials of the Midland district, and H. Beardsell, of the Huddersfield Athletic and Cricket Club, whose sound sense and judgment make him as able a judge as he is a debater on the councils of the Amateur Athletic Association. Besides the judges there is a referee, who has absolute discretion to decide when judges differ; but when the judges are up to their work, as on this occasion, the referee's position is an honourable sinecure. Then there is the starter, R. Cameron, of Liverpool, well known to stand no trifling from the runners. For some years the starter at these meetings has been the professional 'Tom' Wilkinson, of Sheffield, but Wilkinson being otherwise engaged on this afternoon, the popular voice pointed out Cameron as the best starter amongst amateurs. The starter is helped by a 'marksman', who places the men on the scratch, so that the starter may not have to move from the position he has once taken up, and may fire his pistol when he likes. The marksman of to-day is C. V. Hunter, one of the leading spirits of the Blackheath Harriers' Club, who is to be seen upon every Saturday afternoon officiating in some capacity at an athletic meeting. The remaining officials are the timekeepers – three in number – for in these days of 'record-breaking' there must be no doubt about times. After each race the three are to compare their watches and then announce the official times. All have 'fly-back' stop watches marking the division of the second into fifths. If all agree upon one time that is the official time; if all three differ, the middle time is given; if one watch differ from the other two, the 'verdict of the majority' stands as the official time. Besides the official timekeepers, there is another timekeeper, who, with the assistance of a 'standard judge', decides who have got within the standard times. The 'standard timekeeper' stands at the elbow of the 'standard judge', and when, as for instance, in the first race, the half-mile, 2 min. 2 sec. has been reached, the timekeeper, keeping his eye upon the watch, says 'Now', and the judge, with his eyes fixed on the line, sees what runners have got within the standard, and will win the 'standard medal'. Last, but not least, are the two 'clerks of the course', whose business it is to call out the names of the runners in the dressing-rooms, and see that they come out upon the course up to time. In a club meeting, where there are many handicaps with large entries, the 'clerks of the course' have the hardest, as well as the most responsible, part of the day's work, as if they fail, or get behindhand, the whole meeting becomes demoralised. Here, there, everywhere, now on the track, now in the dressing-room, now soothing the feelings of this or that grumbler (for an athletic meeting is seldom without some competitor or spectator with an imaginary grievance), is Mr Herbert, the energetic and courteous secretary of the A.A.A., who has had all the burden of preparing for the meeting upon his shoulders.

The first race upon the programme is the half-mile, for which there were ten entries; but five of these fail to turn up at the post, Bryden and Nalder keeping themselves for the mile and the others making no appearance at the meeting. And here let us say that the championship meeting has since 1880 been absolutely open to any competitor of any station in life provided he has not run for money or run against a professional in public; so that the old 'gentleman-amateur' who enters for a championship knows that he may have to run a mile against a postman or put the weight against a blacksmith. The five starters for the half-mile are Haines, a countryman from Faringdon, in Berkshire, who runs gamely, but with a stiff, awkward action at the hips, which must waste his strength. Then there are the two crack Londoners, both members of the South London Harriers' Club, E. D. Robinson and Stuart Howard, of whom the latter was for some time thought the coming champion until he was beaten by Robinson in a level half-mile at the Croydon sports. Robinson is a tall bony-looking athlete, with a tremendous and rather slouching stride, which always induces the spectator to think that he is going more slowly than is actually the case. Stuart Howard has decidedly a more taking style than his club-mate, as he runs with his chest thrown back and erect, and his legs shooting straight out; but a high action is often more taking than successful. The field is made up with two other Londoners, J. A. P. Clarke and Bessell, neither of whom is much in the hunt to-day, though Clarke has done some fine times at a mile. When the pistol fires Haines dashes off with the lead at a hot pace but with laboured action; Robinson hanging close behind him. The first lap (half the distance) is completed in 55 2/5 sec., Haines moving by this time with greater effort than ever. When another hundred yards are passed, however, Robinson spurts by him, and going up the back stretch seems to have the race at his mercy. Meanwhile Howard is creeping up, gets to Haines' shoulder at the top of the ground, and when the three enter the straight, 120 yards from home, Robinson is half a dozen yards in front of the other pair. Howard shoots away from Haines in pursuit of the leader and gains slowly upon him, but Robinson, who is clearly tiring, can still keep his long stride, which brings him home a couple of yards in front of Howard in 1 min. 59 sec. A fine race and a fine performance is the opinion, for both men are clean run out, and to beat 2 min. is what only some eight or ten amateurs have ever been able to do. Next come the heats of the 100 yards race. Ever since 1868 at the championship meeting the track has been roped off with iron posts and cords, so that each runner may have a clear course to himself. Just now sprinting is watched with peculiar interest, as there are four runners on the path, Cowie, Ritchie, Wood, and the new celebrity Wharton, of each of whom his friends aver that he is 'the fastest man who ever put on a shoe'. Cowie, for the three last years champion at this distance, has unfortunately broken down in training by a sinew giving way, to the intense disappointment of the public, who, however, are looking forward to seeing Wharton, of Darlington, who is a 'coloured gentleman'. The first heat, with Cowie absent, attracts little attention, and is won by Shaw, of Hereford. In the next heat Ritchie, the Bradford crack; Wood, who trains on his farm in Norfolk; Levick, a speedy little Londoner, and Peter James, from Sydney, New South Wales, are the competitors. Ritchie gets away a trifle sharper than Wood, and when both are moving the Yorkshireman is half a yard ahead. With this distance between them they rush over the hundred, and Ritchie wins by a short head in 10 1/5 sec., Levick being outpaced, and the colonial nowhere. Both Ritchie and Wood are well built for sprinting: the former is of middle height, has a tremendous chest, bull-head and large thighs. Wood is almost a giant, being heavily built all over, has a 40-inch chest and scales over twelve stone. The third heat is known to be a moral for Wharton, but there is intense curiosity to see him move. When at the post with Bassett, of Norwood, Nicholas, of Monmouth, and an unknown C. S. Colman, he is seen to shape well, standing like a rock with his feet close together. At the crack of the pistol he is off like lightning, running in a wondrous fashion. Sprinting of many kinds has been seen: some sprint bent forward, some with the head and shoulders thrown back, but here is a man running away from his field with body bent forward and running almost on the flat of his foot. There is short time for wonder, however, as Wharton is half a dozen yards in front of Bassett when he bursts the worsted – for a worsted stretched between the posts breast-high has long since replaced the old-fashioned tape at athletic meetings. There is a hush in the crowd, while the three timekeepers put their heads together; for it is seen that the winner has done a fine performance. All three watches agree in marking 10 sec. or 'level-time', and when the telegraph board shows the figures a cheer bursts from the crowd, for at last after years of struggling and disputing a genuine 'level-time' performance has been accomplished. Half an hour later Wharton comes out for the final to meet Shaw, Ritchie, Wood, and Bassett (the last two of whom as 'seconds' in the two fastest heats run again), and he is once more greeted with a cheer. In the final Wharton is not off so fast, and at ten yards Wood and Ritchie are in front of him; then the foreigner rushes ahead and is leading by two yards twenty yards from home. This time, however, he appears to tire a little – and no wonder, for sprinting is a violent effort and leaves the bones and muscles aching; Wood and Ritchie close on him a little, and Wharton wins by a good yard, with Wood this time a foot in front of Ritchie. The time again is 10 sec., 'level-time' twice in an afternoon – a marvel indeed!

Meanwhile between the heats and final of the hundred a gigantic Irishman, J. S. Mitchell, of the Gaelic Athletic Club, from Emly, County Limerick, has won the hammer throwing (a 16 lb hammer, four feet long, thrown from a 7 ft circle), with a throw of no ft 4 in., his opponent, J. D. Gruer, of the London Scottish R.V., making but a poor show this year; and the two heats of the 120 yards hurdle race have been run off. In the first, C. F. Daft, of the Notts Forest Football Club, and S. Joyce, of the Cambridge U.A.C., are first and second, while in the other heat (from which Croome, the Oxonian, who won the Inter-Varsity Hurdles, is an absentee), G. B. Shaw (note: Shaw left England for New Zealand, where he won the championship, and returned to England again, and during the years 1891, 1892 and 1893 was the best English hurdler. In the latter year he once covered the usual distance well inside 16 sec. In 1891 and 1892 he was beaten in the championship by D. D. Bulger, a very speedy Irishman. In 1892 he was only beaten by a few inches in 16 sec., the third man, Batger, the New Zealand champion, being only a foot behind Shaw. Never did three such good hurdlers meet in one race before, and of the three I think Godfrey Shaw was the best upon his best day.), of the Ealing Harriers, and S. O. Purves, another Cantab, fill the first two places. Then comes the pole jump, in which F. G. F. Thompson, of the L.A.C., fails at 10 ft, and Tom Ray, of Ulversion (who so far has never been beaten at this sport, and holds the present record of 11 ft 4 1/4in.), wins his fifth championship with a leap of 11 ft. A marvellous jumper is Ray. He is a tall, rather heavy man, of fine proportions. Grasping the pole about its middle, he takes his leap, and when the pole is perpendicular, poises it almost at a standstill, raises himself clear up it by sheer force of arm, and shoots himself over the bar. Sometimes he poises the pole too long, and the present writer can once recollect, when he was acting as one of the judges at the Northern Counties Championship, seeing the pole and jumper, after a moment of suspense, fall (to his great relief) upon the other judge. Then comes the final heat of the hurdle race. Daft, last year's champion, and Joyce, the Cantab, have another rattling race. For the first eight hurdles they rise together; at the ninth Daft has the slightest possible advantage, and as neither man is rising an inch too high, or thus wasting an ounce of strength, it is evident that the 'run in' will decide the race. Over the tenth hurdle Daft again has a shade of advantage, and, running on faster, wins by a yard in sixteen seconds, another 'record' – the second during the afternoon. Next comes the quarter-mile race – won last year by Myers, the flying American, but by this time Myers, like W. G. George, another amateur champion, has joined the professional ranks. There is little chance of another record being done in this event, for since first Myers in America cut into the old record of 50s (done both by Colbeck in 1868 and J. Shearman in 1877), he has more than once beaten 49 seconds, and done times which probably no man, either professional or amateur, has ever touched. The race this year is set down for two heats, but as Cowie is *hors de combat* and four others do not put in an appearance, the six runners are sent off in one heat. This is lucky for Wood, as he has two 'hundreds' out of him, while Lyle Smith, the Civil Service 'crack', comes up fresh for this race. The other four starters are Wharton, whose phenomenal performance in the sprint makes people wonder what he is going to do in the quarter; E. D. Robinson, who is nearly as good at this distance as at a half-mile; W. Lock, of Windsor, and Norman Jones, who are good men, but hardly good enough for their company. When the pistol fired for a moment everyone held his breath, for Wharton was seen to be flying off almost at top speed with the same extraordinary flat-footed action. Wood, who knew by experience how fast his opponent could travel, was determined not to let him get away, and so the pair ran away from their field down the long straight of nearly 300 yards, upon which the first part of the quarter is run at Stamford Bridge. But when a little more than 300 yards had been run it was evident that Wharton had shot his bolt; he died away and stopped, and Wood was left a hundred yards from home with a ten-yard lead; but upon him, 100, it was evident that the pace had told, and it seemed doubtful whether he could last to the end. Slowly but surely Lyle Smith and Robinson, who were coming up behind, gained on the leader, and nothing but pluck and condition brought Wood in two yards in front of Smith, a yard behind whom was Robinson, the winner's time being 49 4/5 sec. – a great time, for there are but few men like Myers, and no one until he showed the way ever got within 50 seconds. Here, as is always the case, the fast time was due to the pace-maker, as, besides the first three, Jones and Lock finished within the standard of 52 sec.; and five men in one race finishing within 52 sec. is almost a phenomenon.

The quarter being over, the mile, which is usually considered the race of the day, succeeded. For this there are eight entries, of whom seven are going to the post, and certainly they are a good representative lot. T. R. Bryden, of the Clapham Rovers F.C., was looked upon early in the season as a probable champion as soon as last year's champion. Snook, of Shrewsbury, was adjudged by the Amateur Athletic Association to have forfeited his claim to rank as an amateur. Then there is F. J. Cross, the Inter-Varsity runner, who in the spring showed himself good for 4 min. 27 sec. on any day. Haines, of Faringdon, is also having another try for a championship at another distance, and there is the dark horse from the West Country, T. B. Nalder, of Bristol; it is rumoured, indeed, that a good many West countrymen have come up to put their money upon him. Besides these, Mabey, of the South London Harriers, has shown some good form of late, and Hill and Leaver, of the same club, are also starters. The race itself, however, is hardly in doubt from the start. Nalder gets off briskly with a lead, and is followed by Haines, Cross, and Bryden. The West countryman is a small thick-set man, with a fine free action and a good workmanlike style, running without effort, and with a long springy stride. For half a mile the positions are unaltered, but in the third lap Cross, who looks a bit heavier and rather less fit than he was at Lillie Bridge in the spring, takes the lead and keeps it until three laps have been completed. Beginning the last lap Nalder spurts to the front again in easy fashion, evidently having the race at his mercy; and, although Cross, who is a tall and strong youngster, chivies him gamely up the back stretch, Nalder gradually gets further away from his taller rival, and, coming down the straight looking very fresh, wins easily by twelve yards in 4 min. 25 2/5 sec. – a fine performance, as it is evident that he had a bit in hand if wanted. Cross, finishing gamely, just stalls off Bryden at the end, and beats him by two yards for second place, both Bryden and Mabey, who finishes fourth, beating 4 min. 30 sec., and gaining the standard medal. Four men inside 'four-thirty' is rarely to be seen, and when it was done ten years ago by Slade, H. A. Bryden, L. U. Burt, and T. R. Hewitt, it was thought that such a feat would never be repeated. However, that was at the time when 4 min. 26 2/5 sec. was the record, and not 4 min. 18 2/5 sec., as it is now. Then the next hour is taken up with the Seven Miles Walking Race. Walking races are hardly so satisfactory now as ten years ago, for judges are lenient and walkers aspire to fast times; consequently most of the walking seen on the running-path is of shifty character, and, if not absolutely a run, is more like a shuffle than a fair heel-and-toe walk. The walking race to-day is also to be marked with an unfortunate incident. C. W. V. Clarke, of Reading, starts at a great pace, when he unfortunately loses a shoe, and Jervis, of Liverpool, a very doubtful goer, leads at the end of a mile, which is finished in 7 min. 15 sec. At two miles Clarke has caught

Walking race.

Jervis again (14 min. 57 1/4 sec.), and at three miles (22 min. 59 1/5 sec.) the pair are still together. Before the fourth mile is reached, however, Clarke has shaken off Jervis, and as the latter has been cautioned by the judges for moving unfairly, he decides to leave the course. Clarke, however, begins to go very queerly, and finally, just before the fifth mile, staggers and falls from sunstroke, and has to be carried off the course. As most of the other competitors have by this time retired, J. H. Jullie, who is still plodding along in the rear, is left, by the retirement of Clarke and Jervis, with the lead, and he eventually carries off the race in the poor time of 58 min. 50 1/5 sec. For the High Jump, which followed, Ray, the pole jumper, E. J. Walsh, Nuttall and Purves, two old Cambridge blues, and Rowdon, from Teignmouth, in Devonshire, are the competitors. They jump off turf over a lath placed between upright posts, and not off cinders, as is sometimes done at sports, and as is better on wet days when the grass is slippery. The Devonshire man, a slim, boyish-looking athlete, takes but a short run and then goes straight over the bar. He easily beats his opponents, and wins with 5 ft 11 1/8 in., the exact height being afterwards measured from the centre of the lath to the ground. The Weight Putting takes but a short time, There are two competitors, and Mitchell, who won the Hammer Throwing, wins the other heavy weight competition with a 'put' of 38 ft 2 in. The weight (16 lbs) is 'put' from the shoulder, the men being placed in a seven-feet square of cinder, marked off by boards projecting an inch from the ground. Within that square they can swing their bodies as they like, but if they 'follow' their throw outside the charmed square the judge cries 'No throw', and no measurement is taken. The Long Jump is also a moral for one jumper – J. Purcell, of Dublin, last year's champion. The men have a long run of fifty yards or so (if they like to run so far) over cinder, and the 'take off' is from a board about an inch wide fixed level in the ground. Beyond the board the ground is hollowed out, so that if they over-run the mark the jump is sure to be abortive. It requires, however, much skill and practice not to 'take off' before the mark. Purcell, who in his six tries four times gets over 22 ft, wins with 22 ft 4 in. E. Horwood, of Brackley, being second with 21 ft 7 1/4 in.

These last three events have been going on in the centre of the ground, while the long walking race is being held on the track. Next comes the Steeplechase, an event which did not appear in the championship programme until 1879. Two countrymen – Harrison from Reading, and Dudman from Basingstoke – oppose Painter, the best representative of the metropolis. There are four circuits, over hurdles, mounds, and a water-jump, to complete the two miles. This contest also introduced a surprise, as Dudman and Painter, making a race between them, ran each other off their legs 600 yards from home; and Harrison, who had seemed out of it, sailed by them as if standing still, and won anyhow. The last race of the day, however, produced another fine performance. Six of the best metropolitan cross-country runners had to meet E. D. Rogers, of Portsmouth, a runner who was little known until he made a good show in the Southern Counties Cross-Country Championship at Sandown Park in the early spring. Rogers is a stiff, ungainly runner, but apparently with tremendous strength; and, taking the lead from the start, he lurched over the ground at a great pace, completing his first mile in 4 min. 50 1/5 sec. and the second in 9 min. 50 2/3 sec. in itself a very fine performance. By this time he had the race at his mercy, having run W. H. Coad – the best Londoner – off his legs. In the third mile, in 15 min. 25 3/5 sec., Rogers did little more than keep his lead, and he finally won with great ease in 21 min. 1 4/5 sec., not in itself a first-class performance, but the winner's two miles showed of what stuff he was made. So ended a great day's racing; and as the winners came up to receive their prizes it was only natural that most of them should have received a hearty welcome from the crowd.

The day's sport was remarkable in itself for more than one reason. For one thing, the average of merit shown by the winners was greater than had ever been seen before at a single meeting. The Hundred in 10 seconds; the Hurdles in 16 seconds; the Quarter in 49 4/5 seconds; the Half in 1 min. 59

sec.; the Mile in 4 min. 25 2/5 sec.: no such performances had ever before been done together upon one day by amateurs. But the meeting was also significant for another reason, though whether for good or evil to the sport it is hard to say. In the early days of the championship sports, from 1866 onwards, the majority of the events were carried off by the University athletes; and for the first ten years the struggle was between the Varsity runners and the old Public School men, the gentlemen amateurs from London and elsewhere who came forward to try conclusions with the Inter-Varsity runners. Of later years, since the championship in 1880 was altered from the spring to the summer, fewer of the Varsity runners have competed, partly, no doubt, because it is awkward to train in the summer terms at Oxford or Cambridge, but partly, too, from the fact that the Varsity cracks are often not good enough to meet the highly trained and seasoned athletes who are the pick of the amateurs of the present day. At the championship of 1886 it became clear that the supremacy of the path had passed away for the present from the metropolitan to the provincial runners. The difference between the old style of London athlete, or the Varsity athlete, and the modern athlete from the provinces is not one of locality nor yet of degree; it is a difference of class, of which we shall have to speak again; but the Stamford Bridge championship of 1886 shows that, until another development takes place, three-quarters of our amateur champions will be drawn from the masses.

3
Running and Runners

All must agree that running, walking, and leaping are the most simple and genuine of all competitions. When a Derby is won it is always a point for argument whether the greater credit is due to the horse or to the jockey; and when Cambridge is badly beaten over the Putney course there is always the critic to say that the Oxford weights were better arranged, that erratic steering threw away the race, or that the losers were underboated. The athlete who wins a big race owes nothing to his apparatus, and his success can only be due to his own excellence or his opponent's shortcomings. And even if running be more unsociable than rowing, it has the counterbalancing advantage for the individual that his success cannot possibly be ascribed to others. In every eight on the river there is said to be one duffer, and every one of the eight can be certain that someone considers him to be the man. In athletics a 'duffer' can only win by the help of a handicap; the cause of his success is then evident, and if he gets the prize he takes little credit with it. When the athlete has got a pair of the best shoes, a zephyr, and a pair of silk or merino drawers (called by courtesy knickerbockers) just *not* coming down to the knee, so as to leave that useful portion of the leg free, he has got all the stock-in-trade required to win half-a-dozen championships. The science of athletics, then, consists in the scientific use of the limbs; the tools of the athlete's trade are the thews and muscles of his own body, which God has made and man cannot refashion. Of the athlete, therefore, it can be said, more than of any other sportsman, *nascitur non fit*. Much, no doubt, can be done by training and practice, but no amount of either can make a man with small thighs a sprinter, or a man with a short 'fore leg', that is leg between knee and ankle, a high jumper. To acquire excellence in these branches of sport demands knowledge of how to utilise the natural advantages of the body. Many men possessed of great natural excellences have, by a careful system of self-exhaustion, neutralised their gifts; some others have also within our knowledge appeared almost to have acquired fine form from mere practice; but these latter are very rare examples. Of runners and the art of running – in so far as there is an art in running – we propose in the ensuing pages to offer some reflections and reminiscences, without actually going so far as to elaborate an actual manual of training. Of books on training there are already numbers, more or less valuable and more or less harmful, but books on training must always tend to fail in proportion as they are elaborate, because the end to be acquired is perfectly simple – to become hard and muscular, and at the same time to be in perfect and robust health, and sound in every organ, and no rigid rules can possibly suit all persons alike. Just as every man over thirty should, it is said, be his own doctor, so every man who has been a couple of seasons 'on the path' should be able to train himself. At the same time there are certain general rules which help a man to attain his best form, and these we shall not fail to enumerate.

First of all, then, before a man begins to train for any event of any kind he should have a good substratum of health and strength to start upon. If the would-be athlete is very badly out of condition, and fat and flabby from laziness and high living, it will do him no harm to take a Turkish bath to start with. Some smart five-mile walks followed by a good rubbing down with a rough towel on returning will soon make him fit to begin his training, if he has in the meantime kept regular hours and lived on a modicum of good healthy food of the kind to which he is usually accustomed. Without this preliminary care, not only will the runner get stiff and jaded by beginning violent exercise too quickly, but he will incur the greatest possible chance of straining or snapping a muscle, and thus placing himself hors de combat for a season. Granting, however, that our novice is, from the effects of football, walking, tennis, or cricket, in fair ordinary condition, we will follow his course through the different branches of athletics. And first as to sprinting.

Sprinting, or Sprint-running, is the technical name given to the running of those short distances over which a man can spurt or 'sprint' at top speed without a break. The rough-and-ready experience of the last generation, which almost stereotyped the distances and conditions of racing, decided that 300 yards was the limit of sprinting distance, and that the next distance for racing purposes – the quarter of a mile – was something *sui generis*, and distinct from sprinting. Probably for the generality of runners the old and popular division of distance was right, but those who saw Myers and Phillips race for the English championship at Aston in 1881, or saw the American crack win his quarter-mile handicap at Lillie Bridge in 1884, when he ran round his field and came in a winner in 48 4/5 seconds, can hardly help arriving at the conclusion that with some phenomenal runners a quarter is only a sprint 'long drawn out' But whatever be the limit of sprinting powers, sprint-running, which is always the most popular of all kinds of athletic sports with the public, is certainly something entirely different both in the action and in the essentials of success to the running over longer distances. In sprinting, the front muscles of the thigh, which bring the leg forward, are the most important factors for speed, as it is on the rapid repetition of the stride that the main result depends; in running of longer distances the back muscles of the thigh, which effect the propulsion, bear the chief strain. Both sets of muscles are of course used in every race, but the longer the distance the less important the front muscles become. And here we may perhaps give vent to a reflection which must often occur to those who consider a meeting of foot-races far superior in point of interest to a set of cycling matches. At a cycling meeting the same man who wins the mile race will probably win the five or ten mile races, and may even, like H. L. Cortis during his time, hold all the records from one to fifty miles. The reason is simply that, although there are differences of degree in staying powers with cyclists, the same muscles are used for every race, while between the sprinter and the miler there is a difference not of degree but of kind. At a meeting of foot-races there is an infinite variety of different kinds of excellence. It is common for a runner to manage two distances well; he may be able, like F. T. Elborough or Colbeck, to run any distance between 100 yards and half-a-mile, but the man who can beat his compeers at every distance has not yet been found, and is not likely to be.

But to return to our subject of sprinting. The rapidity of motion, we have said, is derived from the front muscles of the thigh. The push comes from the back muscles of the thigh and from the small of the back. To convey to an uninitiated reader a notion of what real sprinting includes, he may be reminded that in longer races a man who wishes to pass an antagonist makes a rush or spurt for a few strides. Sprinting consists in a continued rush or effort at high pressure, and as such is far more exhausting than it seems. The foregoing reflections may serve to explain in some measure the many surprises and anomalies that a consideration of sprinters and sprinting suggests. Sprinting ability consists in the capacity to make a violent effort in the way of speed. It is therefore not a paradox to say that it requires as much cultivation as a capacity for any other kind of athletic sport. You may find the capacity in men who appear of all shapes and sizes to a superficial observer. Certainly your sprinter may be tall or short, may be of any weight up to thirteen stone, though he is rarely a feather weight. He is more often inclined to be fleshy than to be thin, and may be of any height, though he rarely is over six feet. Of some famous sprinters the unspoken reflection of many a spectator must have been, 'Well, you are the last man I should ever have thought could run fast'. When Junker, the Russian, who won the Hundred Yards Championship in 1878, first appeared at an athletic meeting, a patriotic and jocose journalist described him as a 'bulky foreigner'. Another well-known sprinter, also a champion at the same distance, was advised by a competent authority to try some other distance, as he was too fat to run fast. Another curious thing about sprinting is the varieties of action in which good performers indulge. Junker sprinted as if he were badly bandy-legged, although we never knew that he was so. Lockton, of the L.A.C., who in his day was, we think, even faster than Junker, ran in the style most affected by professional pedestrians, with his body low and well forward. W. P. Phillips, who managed to beat Lockton for the championship in 1880, ran almost erect, looking even more than his full height of six feet. Trepplin, one of the fastest of the many fast sprinters who have hailed from the Universities, was a vision of whirling arms and legs. Junker was flatfooted and erect; Wharton, the champion of 1886, is flatfooted, yet manages somehow to bend his body far forward as well. Yet many and various as are the forms which sprinting ability takes, there are one or two signs by which a sprinter can be recognised. Whether his legs be short or long, he has large muscular thighs and a broad back. A sprinter, too, to use a cant phrase of pedestrianism, 'strips big' – i.e. looks bigger stripped than he does in his clothes; or, in other words, is a heavier man than he appears to be in his ordinary life.

But, before we discuss the best forms of sprinting and its exponents, we must say something of the practice and exercise which a sprinter should take in order to reach his best form. The best practice for a 100 or 120 yards race is to have continual bursts of thirty yards or so with another man, who is about as good or rather better than yourself. If practising with a man who is inferior, you should give him a short start in these 'spins' and catch him as soon as you can. Such practice both helps a man to get into his running quickly and 'pulls him out', to use a trainer's expression; that is, the striving to keep pace with a better man, or to catch a man in front whom you can catch, involuntarily forces a man to do a little better than his previous best if he is capable of it. A man should never practise sprinting alone; he becomes sluggish, and can never really tell whether he is doing well or ill. If he is simply training for a 100 or a 120 yards race, after half-a-dozen of these spins he should take a few minutes' rest and then run the full distance, or at any rate a burst of seventy or eighty yards, before he goes in to have a rub down and resume his clothes. If he is training for 220, 250, or 300 yards he must, of course, accustom himself to longer trials; but in general, even for the longest of these distances, it is quite enough to run 200 yards at full speed. In fact, as a general rule, for all practice it may be laid down that a man should very rarely run a trial for more than two thirds of the distance for which he is training. In writing this we know that to many trainers such an opinion will be considered a rank heresy; but that it is a sound rule, at any rate to amateurs who have other daily avocations to attend to, which must occasion more or less fatigue, is our firm conviction. The great point in every race, and especially in a sprint or in a quarter of a mile, is to come to the scratch fresh. Our experience of amateurs is that two out of three of them come to the scratch in a big race a little bit overdrawn; but of this we shall have something more to say anon.

In the short sprints the start is, of course, almost half the battle, and a man should be continually practising a start and a ten-yards run – and very trying to the back the performance is. It is, of course, advisable to get accustomed to start from a pistol, but if there is no friend handy to fire a pistol or say 'Go' without any warning, it is not a bad device to fling a stone over one's head in the air and start as soon as it is heard to fall to the ground. Some men we have known to improve a yard or even two by frequent practising at starts, and most hundred-yard races are lost or won by less than a yard. We need, perhaps, hardly describe the right attitude of the body for a start in these days when everyone has seen an athletic meeting. The runner should be on his toes, with the right foot seven or eight inches behind the left foot, which is on the line, and so that the chest is almost parallel to the line and bent slightly forward. Some in starting stretch their right arm forward so as to bring the chest completely straight to the line, but this is not adopted by all, and if overdone is, we think, a great mistake. The body should be balanced on the toes with the weight pressing slightly upon the right or rear foot, so that a good kick may be obtained from it with the slightest possible delay when the pistol-shot is heard.

Little more need be said of practising on the path for sprints. It must not be forgotten, however, that the sprinter wants to keep himself hard and fit during the time that all his racing practice consists of hard bursts for very short distances. A few miles' walking during the day is always good for health, but great care must be taken by the sprinter never to get stiff, for he has no time during his race to run off even the slightest stiffness. A trot once round the track at a moderate pace with a springy action to stretch the legs is also a good thing; but in these trots the sprinter should never let himself 'get off his toes' – i.e. run so that his heel touches the ground; when his heel begins to come down on the ground it is a sure sign that he is getting jaded, and he had better leave off and walk back to the dressing-room.

The problem, therefore, which a sprinter has to solve, is how to get strong and muscular without getting stiff or slow from too much exercise. One aid to the solution of the problem is of a kind which would hardly be suspected by the uninitiated. It is to have a rubber. We do not mean that the sprinter should cultivate the study of whist (although we are sure that, if he is

Started.

sensible, he will do so), nor do we mean that he should wear a golosh and use the American name for that article. A rubber is a man, occasionally a friend, usually a hireling, generally one's trainer, who sometimes with a glove or towel, but mostly with his horny hand, rubs you all over the body, but chiefly over the legs and back, until you are as muscular as a gymnast and as smoothed-skinned as an infant. Well can we recollect the vigorous rubbings of Bob Rogers and the cast-iron hand of old Harry Andrews at Lillie Bridge and the delicious glow and feeling of 'jumpiness' with which we used to stride out of the dressing-room after the operation was over. Well also can we recollect how a kindly fellow-undergraduate, now a muscular Christian, and himself, we hope, in training for a bishopric, essayed to keep the present writer in training when laid up for a fortnight by a sprain, by vigorous vespertinal rubbings. But your amateur rubber is too perfunctory in his ministrations, and cannot vie with the professional exponent of the art.

The old professional trainers were strongly prejudiced against the use of cold water applied externally. A bath they thought weakening and relaxing, but though we cannot altogether agree with them in this dogma, we thoroughly concur in their belief in the efficacy of the 'dry rub'. It prevents any chance of stiffness, minimises the liability to catch colds, and its effect in hardening the muscles can only be known by those who have tried it. Most well-advised athletes now take their shower-bath first and have their rub afterwards. Some men we have seen combining the maximum of rub with the minimum of wash in the following manner: The rubber fills his mouth with water from a glass, blows it in fine rain over a portion of the victim, and then proceeds to polish that portion first with a towel and then with his hand. The process may be efficacious, but we never felt inclined to try it.

Although a hundred yards takes a very short time in running, a good many amateurs have earned a long and lasting reputation by their performances over the distance. We have heard many speak of W. M. Tennant, of Liverpool, who won the championship in 1868, but to this generation of runners he is but a name. A contemporary of his was

In condition.   Out of condition.

E. J. Colbeck, undoubtedly the best amateur of his time, but scarcely so good at 100 yards as at 300 yards or a quarter of a mile. We can recollect Colbeck running a dead heat at Lillie Bridge in a hundred yards with A. J. Baker, who won the championship in 1870, and who was probably the fastest Londoner over the distance until quite recent times. Colbeck was a very tall, heavy man, who sprinted with his chest thrown back, and he owed his speed, we think, more to his tremendous stride than to any true sprinting capacity to make a rush. Baker was a sprinter pure and simple, and, as far as we recollect, 'ran low', in what is to our mind the best and most workmanlike sprinting style, with his body bent well forward. Whether a man can change his sprinting style is, we think, rather doubtful; but it is obvious that, if the chest be not thrown well forward, the stride must be shortened by the drag which the weight of the trunk will put upon the legs. This, we think, the pedestrian trainers must well know, as nearly all, and even the mediocre, pedestrians 'run low' when sprinting. The trainers also, we think, believe in the efficacy of their craft and of coaching to completely alter a man's style, for we know on good authority that a Sheffield trainer came up and accosted one of the London heavy-weight sprinters, whom he had seen running at a Northern meeting, and told him if he would learn to run a bit more forward he would beat ten seconds in a month. We have, however, seen so many men get over sprinting distances with all sorts of actions that we feel doubtful about the wisdom of interfering with a man's natural action as far as sprinting is concerned. As a rule, when the sprinter has settled down to his practice and is improving in pace, his style involuntarily begins to approximate in a greater or less degree to the best model.

From the year 1869, when J. G. Wilson, Worcester College, Oxford, scored his first win in the Inter-University Hundred Yards, to the year 1879, when E. C. Trepplin, of B.N.C., Oxford, scored his last win at the same meeting, it is hardly too much to say that the pick of the best amateur sprinters came from Oxford and Cambridge. With Trepplin the race of University sprinters seems unaccountably to have reached an end, for from 1880 to the present there has been no really fine sprinter at the Universities, although there have been plenty of fine performers at longer distances. Of these University sprinters, Wilson, who won in 1869, 1870, and 1871, and secured the championship in 1869 and 1871 (Baker being the winner in 1870), was perhaps the pick of the lot. He was a well-made man of medium height and weight, and ran in irreproachable style with a free stride, his body slightly forward and chest perfectly square. After Wilson's retirement, W. A. Dawson, a Cambridge athlete who won both the Inter-University and Championship Hundred Yards, was decidedly the best runner of the next year. Dawson was a shorter man than Wilson, but ran in much the same style, and though a small man was thick-set with a strong-looking chest and back. Of the succeeding University runners, Urmson, of Oxford, a tall thin man with a very long stride, who was a capable performer at any distance from 100 yards to a mile (a rare phenomenon), was better at a quarter-mile than a sprint. As with some others, his speed came from his long stride more than from a rapid repetition of the stride; and he was an inferior man at a sprint to Trepplin, the last and perhaps the best of the Oxford sprinting celebrities. Trepplin, who won at the Oxford and Cambridge sports in 1877, 1878, and 1879, had a *contretemps* at the start of the Hundred Yards race at the championship meeting in 1877, and declined afterwards to compete at the championship meeting. He was over six feet in height and weighed close upon thirteen stone, being big and muscular all over. His style was anything but pretty, for, although he bent his body well forward when sprinting, he had a great deal of ungainly arm action, and until fit found it difficult to run as straight as an arrow on his course, as most sprinters do naturally. Strangely also, though possessed of great muscular strength, he was quite incapable of staying any distance, and though he could, when trained, run 150 yards in a level 15 seconds, could not rely upon himself to run 220 yards, and was unable to stay home in any longer sprint than 150 yards. Had Trepplin competed in the championship of 1878, however, he could hardly have beaten the Russian, L. Junker, who was the Hundred Yards champion of that year. Junker, like Trepplin, never attempted anything but the shorter sprints, and was only once beaten in his brief and brilliant career upon the running-path during the season of 1877 and 1878, when in July 1877, in a level Hundred Yards race at Birmingham, he ran third to J. Shearman and H. Macdougall, both of whom, though sprinters of the first class, were lucky enough on that occasion to meet Junker on one of his off days. Junker was 5 ft. 9 in. or 5 ft. 10 in. in height, and had a very stiff action, running almost on the flat of his foot; but though ungainly he was of great strength in the legs and back, and to these qualities his speed was doubtless due. The story of his introduction to the running-path in England is rather a quaint one. On one occasion he appears to have been 'chaffed' by some business acquaintances in the City as to his clumsiness and slowness. Upon this he remarked that he was a good runner – a remark which was followed by a roar of laughter. The Russian thereupon waxed warm and volunteered to run one of the mockers for a bottle of champagne. The match was made and came off at Stamford Bridge, when Junker beat his opponent, who was a fair athlete, by the 'length of the street.' The result was that he joined the L.A.C. After winning a few handicaps he soon found himself at scratch, and able to win from that position; and, as was noticed above, was only once beaten. Unfortunately he did not meet Trepplin during his year of supremacy upon the path, but Bob Rogers, the ground-man of the L.A.C., who trained both athletes at different times, was strongly of opinion that in a match between them there would have only been one in it, and that one Junker. Indeed, the opinion of Rogers was that Junker would have found a more dangerous opponent in C. L. Lockton, who was undoubtedly the best sprinter of 1879. Lockton had a very long career upon the path, having been something of an 'infant phenomenon'. When a schoolboy of fifteen he was quite able to hold his own amongst good company, and was only sixteen when he won the Long Jump championship in 1873. He soon seemed to deteriorate from overwork, but in 1875 again he cleared over twenty-two feet in his school sports at Merchant Taylors', and was then almost the best sprinter and hurdler in England. Some unlucky accidents kept him from the path, and he was not really seen at his best until 1879, when, at one of the rival championship meetings, he won the Hundred Yards, Hurdles and Long Jump in the same day. Lockton was, we think, the most beautifully proportioned runner we ever saw on the path, and would probably have been first class at any distance he chose to take up. Unfortunately he left behind him, as some others have done, the reputation of being a 'fine runner but a poor racer'. In practice his trainer timed him to do level time over a hundred yards day after day, but on more than one occasion he succumbed to his inferiors, notably in the championship of 1880, when he was beaten by a few inches by W. P. Phillips and Massey. Lockton both sprinted and hurdled in a very graceful and taking style, and the contrast between him and Phillips when they ran together was most marked, Lockton running low and Phillips perfectly erect. For the next three years (1880, 1881 and

1882) the Championship Hundred Yards was won by W. P. Phillips, the best English amateur at a quarter mile before Tindall's day, whose untimely death from heart disease in 1883 came as a shock to the athletic world. Phillips, who was over six feet, was, like Lockton, a model of manly strength, and was a splendid oar as well as runner. From 220 yards to a quarter-mile he was unrivalled, but a hundred yards was hardly long enough for him. His three championships were each won by a few inches, and in each case a lucky start had something to do with his victory. His runner up in 1881 and 1882 was J. M. Cowie, who afterwards took the championship at this distance for three years, and was possibly superior, and certainly not inferior, to Lockton and Junker and the older cracks. Although only of medium height and calibre, he, like the other celebrities, was very strong in the back and thighs, and his superlative form was in a great measure due to years of persistent and careful training; for though he was of first-rate ability as long ago as 1880, it was not until 1884 or 1885 that he showed his very best form. The other celebrities of the day at sprinting, Wharton, Ritchie, and Wood, have been previously described. But it is always an unsatisfactory task to attempt to compare the athletes of past and present days in any branch of sport, and, although in longer races the time test can be applied satisfactorily, the conditions of wind, weather, and ability of timekeeper prevent timing in short sprints from being an absolutely certain guide. As far, however, as any line can be taken through times, there seems to be but very little difference between the merits in sprinting of the chief cracks during the last fifteen years.

The next distance beyond the 300 yards sprint which is regularly run is the quarter of a mile, although managers of athletic meetings who desire a novelty, or ambitious competitors who flatter themselves that they will obtain some credit by making a record over a distance which no one has ever tried before, occasionally promote a race at some intermediate distance. As a general rule, however, it may safely be said that the experience which decided what distances should be regularly run was not at fault, for of the distances of 220 yards, a quarter-mile, half-mile, and mile, each brings forth a totally distinct class of runner, who may excel at his own single distance and at that alone. Generally the quarter of a mile is a most interesting race, as it gives an opportunity both to the man who has real sprinting pace and to the man who has stay and strength. As an example of how much reliance can be placed upon the popular manuals of sport, of which so many are published, we may perhaps quote with advantage the sapient remarks contained in one of these publications which is now before us. 'The quarter-mile race', says our author, 'is about the severest course that can be run; it requires both pace and stamina.' So far he is doubtless right, for runners have been known to 'run themselves blind' before reaching the tape in this race; that is, have been so exhausted that they could finish and feel the tape, and yet were unable to see anything. After stating, however, how severe the 'course' is, the practical directions given for preparation for the race are that the athlete 'should run the racing distance only once a day'. A moment's reflection should show even the uninitiated how absurd this advice is; for it practically amounts to this: 'To make a man fresh and strong, to give him both spurt and reserve of energy upon an approaching day, you should make him thoroughly exhaust himself at least once a day.' It is advice of this sort which sends athletes into the hospitals or to an early grave, while, if they had passed their youth in a sensible and rational course of training and practice, they would have laid in a stock of health and strength which would have rendered them independent of a doctor's advice for the rest of their lives.

It may seem a paradox, but it is, we think, true, nevertheless, that there are two entirely different ways of preparing for a quarter-mile race. The reason is this, that the distance is a common ground for two entirely different classes of runners. On the one hand, the best quarter-miler of the day is often the man who is the best sprinter as well, and has found that this distance is not beyond his sprinting powers when he is very fit. On the other hand, the sprinting quarter-milers sometimes find themselves outclassed by a runner who is of nothing more than second-class sprinting ability, but whose stay and strength enable him to keep his stride from shortening up to the very end of a quarter-mile or even farther. To take some examples from the present day. To Cowie and Wood the quarter is really a sprint, and nothing else. But a pair of Cambridge runners, W. H. Churchill and R. H. Macaulay, occur to our mind who were indifferent sprinters, and yet could beat 51 seconds for a quarter-mile, and could probably have reached 50 seconds if pressed; while H. R. Ball is another example of the same class. Even Myers, the best quarter-miler by a very long way who ever appeared in the amateur world, was of no particular account at any distance shorter than 200 or 220 yards. The first class of quarter-miler can rarely (if ever) attempt any distances over the quarter, even the 600 yards race being beyond his powers. On the other hand, the second class is often seen at the top of the tree at 600 yards or half a mile as well, as were Colbeck, Elborough, and Myers. With regard, then, to training for a quarter-mile, it is easy to understand that the two classes of runners should not prepare themselves for a quarter upon exactly the same system. To lay down a short and comprehensive rule for the first class, we should say that the sprinter who trains for a quarter-mile should train for it in the same way as he does for a sprint. His trial spins should be over longer distances up to 220 or 300 yards, and his stretches round the path or the grass – we mean the slow stride round upon the toes which we have already described – should be longer; but, being a sprinter, he should recollect that it is upon his speed and freshness that he must rely to win, and he should on no account let his practice jade or exhaust him. Once and once only (if at all) should he run the full distance of the quarter at full speed, and after that should take a day of almost complete rest. A hard quarter-mile run out is likely to exhaust and impair the energies for a long while, and if once a man in training gets a bit stale, it is a far harder task to bring him back to fitness than to make him fit in the first instance. A personal reminiscence may perhaps avail to point a moral while this subject is under discussion. The writer and his brother were both training for the Amateur Championship in

1878. Unfortunately they were ill-advised enough to run two matches before the event to find out for certain which was the better man, but in the second race they were so closely matched that they ran each other to a standstill. This was a week before the race, and the consequence was that on the day of the race both were utterly and hopelessly stale. From the result of the race it became evident that their only two opponents were in an equally 'weary, flat, stale, and unprofitable' condition, for the race was won in the slow time of 52 4/5 seconds. When such a fact occurs as the only four entrants for a championship race coming to the scratch overtrained, it may be gathered that a warning against doing too much work is not unnecessary.

The sprinter then who trains for a quarter-mile should take his starts and short sprints daily, and finish up two or three times a week with bursts of 200, 220, or occasionally 300 yards, and at the same time should from time to time take his practice strides upon his toes more frequently than if he were merely training for 100 yards; but he should never forget that he is a sprinter training for a sprint, and that his speed must be retained at all cost. The same reflection should be present in his mind when he is in the race. It will be the height of folly to try and make the race slow in the hopes of his sprinting; powers bringing him in at the end. At the end he may be jaded and unable to utilise his speed, and if he be not near the front then his chance of winning is gone. His right course is to use his speed while he has it, and in the first 100 or 150 yards he may have made a gap of five yards between himself and his slower opponents, who are relying on their staying powers. Then let him slacken if he likes, but only to go off again when his opponents are again at his heels; and if he be not overtrained, his speed and reserve of energy will serve to bring him up to the finish first.

Most of the advice given by books and by trainers as to the practice for a quarter-mile race comes down from the times when it was thought that 300 yards was the limit of a sprinter's powers, and sprinters accordingly did not think of attempting so long a distance. The result is that an amateur training for a quarter of a mile is usually persuaded to overwork himself, and he not only runs himself stale, but may perhaps impair his health. All this evil arises because trainers, and those who rely upon books and precedents more than upon their own common sense, act as if the desideratum must always be the reduction of weight and the acquisition of staying powers.

The second class who are found competing for quarter-mile races are those who have moderate sprinting ability, and owing to a naturally long stride and good staying powers never flag over the distance and finish as strong as lions. These runners can, no doubt, stand a good deal more work than the mere sprinter. They can run their quarters without that amount of exhaustion which is felt by the runner the limit of whose tether is the quarter, and they may doubtless run their trials over the whole distance half-a-dozen times during their month of training without doing themselves anything but good by such a large amount of exercise. They must not, however, on any account neglect their speed, and frequent starts and short spins must be practised in addition to their longer trials; for some time or another during the race, if a quarter-miler of this class is to win, he must spurt past his speedier opponents. Even with these, however, our own experience has shown us that more men come to their rare overdrawn than unfit. As it is with diet, so it is with exercise; each man must be treated in the preparation for a race with that amount and that quality which will suit his individual case, and the mistakes that are made come from following a system with unreasonable subservience without recollecting for what ends the system was originally adopted.

In considering the performances of celebrated sprinters we have seen that it is hard to say whether those of the present or the past day are better, but in coming to the quarter-mile and longer distances there can be no doubt that the runners of the last few years have done better times over these courses. The reason is not only that the men are better trained, and that out of the larger number of competitors there is more chance of finding a veritable champion, but there is this further consideration, that it is only by slow degrees that athletes have discovered of what amount of speed and stay the human body is capable.

In the early days of athletics a quarter-mile was often treated by good runners as a waiting race, and the times of good races were accordingly very slow. For the first two years after the establishment of the championship in 1866 the quarter-mile race was won by Ridley, an Eton boy, who certainly must have been a phenomenon, as in 1867, while still at school, he won the Hundred Yards and Quarter-Mile Championships in the same day. The times, however, can show nothing of his real ability, as they were as follows: in 1866, 55 seconds; in 1867, 52 3/4 seconds. In the following year, when Kidley was at Cambridge, he showed something of his true powers, for in the Inter-University meeting of that year he won the Quarter-Mile in 51 seconds, winning with some ease. That year, however, he was not destined to be champion, for it was then that E. J. Colbeck appeared in his best form. Colbeck is one of the first great figures that stand out in the history of amateur athletics. Few could beat him at 100 yards, while from 220 yards to half a mile no one was in the hunt with him. He was a tall, strongly built man, with a tremendous natural stride, to which and to his strength he owed his remarkable success. Unfortunately, he, too, like W. P. Phillips, whose performances in some sense recall those of Colbeck, was doomed to find an early grave. The tale of Colbeck's celebrated quarter-mile at the championship meeting at the old Beaufort House grounds in 1868 is one that has been often told. Coming along at a great pace, he led all the way round the ground, and was winning easily when a wandering sheep found its way upon the path and stopped still there, being presumably amazed at the remarkable performance which the runner was accomplishing. The athlete cannoned against the sheep, broke its leg, and then went on and finished his quarter in 50 2/5 seconds. This time was never equalled until J. Shearman in 1877 covered the distance in exactly the same time at Lillie Bridge, and was never surpassed in England by an amateur until Myers paid his first visit to England in 1881. Since that time Myers has shown what can be done by running a Quarter-Mile handicap at Lillie Bridge in 484 seconds, and since 1881 several English amateurs have shown themselves capable of beating 50 seconds. Probably, what might have been learnt from Colbeck, and what was not really learnt by English amateurs until Myers put the Englishmen to shame, was that it is possible for an amateur to make a sprint of a quarter-mile and rush at full speed over the whole distance. However, none of the subsequent times can take away from Colbeck the honour of having made a record (and certainly under unfavourable circumstances) which stood its ground for thirteen years during times when every other record made by Colbeck's contemporaries had been long since surpassed and forgotten. Furthermore, it is evident that Colbeck was by no means rendered hors de combat by his wonderful performance, for upon the same afternoon he won the Half-Mile Championship in 2 min., 2 sec., then a record and at all times a fine performance, and made a good show in the Hundred Yards against the winner, W. M. Tennant. If there ever was an English amateur able to hold his own with Myers, Colbeck was probably the man.

The next pre-eminent performer at a quarter-mile after Colbeck was R. Philpot, of Cambridge. Curiously enough, while Oxford was for so long famous for her sprinters, Cambridge produced a long line of famous quarter-milers. Pitman, Ridley, Philpot, Churchill, and Macaulay all came near to Colbeck's time, but could never quite approach it. Of this line, as far as it is possible to judge between men who were not contemporaries, Philpot, by general consent, was the best; indeed he was credited with having beaten 50 seconds at Cambridge, although the sporting authorities could never be induced to accept the record. At his first appearance at Lillie Bridge he was beaten by R. V. Somers-Smith, of Oxford, as well as by his colleague, A. R. Upcher, the winning time being 50 4/5 seconds under exceptionally favourable conditions. However, in the Inter-University meeting of 1871, Philpot, upon a cold and windy day, covered his quarter in 50 3/5 seconds, running Colbeck's time very close, and in 1872 he won the same race again as well as the championship. Philpot, though not so tall as Colbeck, was of the same style, tall and strong, and was a good enough sprinter to run J. G. Wilson to a yard in 1871, but he was *par excellence* a quarter-miler, that distance being his real *forte*. Philpot, however, at that time would have found no mean opponent in J. C. Clegg, of Sheffield, who during the summer season in the provinces could almost count on sweeping the board at any meeting of all events from 100 to 600 yards. Clegg was a very tall man, hardly so thickly built as Colbeck or Philpot, whose pace, as with Colbeck, came from his stride, but as most of his performances were over grass, the times show nothing of his merits. In 1874 another of the great figures of athletic history, F. T. Elborough, appeared upon the scene, and before his appearance another provincial runner, W. I. Clague of Burslem, somewhat unexpectedly displayed in London an extraordinary performance at a quarter-mile. Starting in a handicap at Lillie Bridge in 1873, in which he was unable to get nearer than third, he undoubtedly covered his distance, untimed, in something well under 50 seconds. Clague originally made his appearance as a hurdler, and, as a rule, in sprints and quarters used to be unable to beat J. C. Clegg, but at the time of which we speak, when he appeared in London, he struck us as one of the finest natural runners we ever saw. He was of medium height and weight, but ran with his body low, and with the smallest possible appearance of effort, although his stride was very long for his height, indeed the length of stride seemed in no way due to length of leg. He took long and easy bounds over the ground, and both in build and style of running was not unlike Cowie, although the latter had not that peculiar ease and light-footedness which distinguished Clague. Unfortunately, Clague never met Elborough, who was the leading figure amongst amateur runners of short distances, during the three seasons of 1875, 1876 and 1877, and who during that time divided with Walter Slade, the miler, the reputation of being the most famous amateur upon the planet.

Elborough was well above the medium height, being quite 5 ft 10 in., and weighing, we believe, about 11 st. in training. Although not so strong physically as Colbeck, who must have been a couple of inches taller and a stone heavier, in his capacities he was a second Colbeck, as his long stride made him a sprinter hard to beat at 100 or 150 yards, and invincible at 220 or 300 yards. As a quarter-miler he had no one to extend him, and as, although he trained assiduously, he was somewhat fitful and fanciful in his appearance on the path, he did no performance at this distance at all worthy of his reputation. A line, however, can perhaps be drawn by collateral form which would show his powers. In two quarter-mile races in two successive years at the Civil Service Sports a handicap of seven yards brought Elborough and J. Shearman together. The latter was doubtless an improved man when in 1877, in a match with H. H. Sturt, he covered the quarter at Lillie Bridge in 50 2/5 seconds, but at any time Elborough at his best could, we think, have given five yards to the elder Shearman. Indeed, his trainers and the public never doubted that Elborough, had he been wound up for a quarter, could have got well inside 50 seconds. In those days, however, the feverish desire for making records (which we think the athletes have caught from their cycling brethren) was not raging, and runners like Elborough liked to win their races and their championships without troubling to scamper over so many yards of cinder a shade faster than some predecessor. In style Elborough ran very erect, shooting his legs out in front of him. He was cleanly but not strongly built, and his excellence as a runner must be set down to his perfect proportions. Up to the spring of 1876 we believe he never attempted more than 600 yards, and was in traming for the Hundred Yards and Quarter Championships of 1876, but being dissatisfied with his speed, altered his mind at the last moment, and started for the Half Mile and the Quarter, winning both with great ease. Ultimately he proposed to extend his practice to mile running, but being beaten in the provinces in the summer of 1877 at 1,000 yards by C. Hazenwood, he never afterwards made a show upon the path.

In 1880, W. P. Phillips, who had been doing some fine performances at 220 yards, turned his attention to quarters, and had he run with a little more judgment in his initial attempt in the championship of that year might have earned the title upon the first occasion he ran a quarter in public. Phillips, however, who was a very fast sprinter, seemed by some fatality bound to make a *fiasco* of all his attempts to win the Quarter-Mile Championship, and, although undoubtedly capable of a better performance at this distance than any Englishman since Elborough, either from nervousness or bad judgment, invariably spoilt his chances by running too slowly in the early part of the race. Thus he was beaten in 1880 by M. Shearman, in 1882 by H. R. Ball, and in 1883 by Cowie, although he was undoubtedly a better man than any of the three over this distance. In 1880, after racing off fast, he slowed in the middle until he had allowed the winner to get seven or eight yards away from him, and then was only beaten by two yards at the finish. In 1881, when he met Myers, who was undoubtedly too good for him, he pushed the American crack along the whole way, was not shaken off until 100 yards from home, and then only finished three yards behind the winner in 48 3/5 seconds. The Aston track, upon which this race was run, is certainly very fast for a quarter, the last 300 yards being downhill; but whatever the time was, Phillips showed his extraordinary excellence by being the only man who could ever make a race with Myers at this distance. In 1882, therefore, with Myers out of England the Quarter Championship seemed a moral for Phillips; but, to the intense astonishment of everybody, he started as if he were going for a mile race, and never had the least chance of catching H. R. Ball, who sprinted throughout, and won in the fine time of 50 1/5 seconds. Probably Phillips, who was certainly not deficient in pluck, as his race with Myers showed, suffered all along from the 'weak heart' from which he suddenly died in the next year, and to this must be ascribed the disappointing form he displayed on some occasions.

During the last few years, Cowie, Wood, Ball, and Tindall, the old Cambridge 'blue', have all done performances equal to or better than 50 seconds for a quarter. Probably, however, the improvement in quarter times since Myers appeared in England is due to the lesson taught by that runner, that to run a good quarter one must be prepared to 'spin' all the way, and there will very likely yet be seen some further developments in the way of fast quarters in the next few years.

Our survey of famous quarter-milers may aptly be concluded with some notice of Myers. There is very little doubt that this runner, while in his best form, some years ago, could have approached very near to 48 seconds in his quarters, a performance which it is improbable that any other runner, amateur or professional, could have compassed. Myers, in more senses than one, was a phenomenon; his physical conformity was somewhat marvellous, and of a kind not likely to be soon met again. Although about 5 ft 8 in. in height, his weight was only just 8 stone, and from a glance at a photograph which we have before us of the American in running costume one fact strikes the eye at once: that his legs are disproportionately long as compared with his body. According to his own account his mother died young of consumption, and Myers himself, although not appearing in the least consumptive, certainly was not troubled with an ounce of superfluous flesh. Being, then, little more than a long pair of wiry legs, with a very small and light body upon the top of them, it is hardly surprising that he should have made a very good running machine. Certain it is that Myers' extraordinary times over a quarter and a half mile arise from the fact that, as he begins to tire and labour in his running, his stride appears to lengthen instead of shortening. Those who have noticed him running quarters have seen that about the middle of the race, when the English heavy-weight sprinters take their first breather, Myers is enabled to shoot away and place a gap of half-a-dozen yards between himself and the second man without an apparent effort. Having, in fact, no weight to carry, no distance under a mile can tire him, and this it is, we think, which enables him to run right away from any opponent at any distance where staying power is a necessity as well as speed. Certainly Myers is unlike any of his predecessors at this distance; whether another will ever appear like unto him it is hard to say.

A very favourite distance at athletic meetings is 600 yards; but, although the race is so common, it can hardly be considered a distance in itself, as it is very rarely that the winner who can manage 600 yards is not capable of doing a half-mile as well. The fine sprinter, who may be able, by a certain amount of staying power, to make a first-class quarter-miler, cannot, as far as ordinary experience goes, manage 600 yards. In fact, at any distance over the quarter, one may say that staying powers are more important than speed. The man who can run 600 yards comfortably can probably do any distance whatever creditably, while many sprinters could hardly cover a mile as fast as a schoolboy. In a 600 yards race, therefore, the sprinting quarter-milers are found conspicuous by their absence. It is a race which cannot be won by the winner rushing off fast and making use of his pace while he has it. In a word, the man who can run 600 yards comfortably may safely train for a half-mile as well, and it is not necessary to consider the runner of 600 yards apart from the half-miler.

The medium distances, however (600 yards, half-mile, 1,000 yards), produce a distinct type of runner, who must be trained in a distinct way. Many men, like the Hon. A. L. Pelham, H. W. Hill, of the L.A.C., and T. E. Wells, the Oxonian, were half-milers pure and simple. The half-miler is sure to be good at a quarter and good at a mile, for he must have speed and stride, and must have as well good wind and staying powers; but many and many a runner can only find his true distance at half a mile or 1,000 yards, and until he trains for these distances misses his real vocation upon the cinder-path. The system of taking exercise for races changes completely as soon as sprinting distances are left behind. The man training for medium distances will, of course, do himself all good and no harm by sprinting to improve his speed, but his sprinting is only an accessory, and not the essential, to success. He has got to improve his legs, wind, and all the muscles of his body in strength, and the way to do this is not gradually to lengthen the distances of practice so much as gradually to increase the pace over those distances. As we have said before, the man who is training for half a mile will do enough to take his trials over 600 yards, or thereabouts. As he gets fitter he should accustom himself to go faster over his spin. Once or twice before the race he may have 'a full-dress rehearsal' – a veritable trial over the whole distance, that he may know exactly what he has to do in the race, and the more walking he can get in the day the better, as there is nothing so healthy, and so little exhausting, to a man in training as brisk walking in fresh air.

Suppose, then, the half-miler has got himself into the state of preliminary fitness, and is going to give himself three weeks of training for a race. On the first day he will do with a steady equable 600 yards. On the second day a brisk 600 yards, which will stretch his limbs a bit, and remind him that running is not all pure enjoyment. On the third day he may take it easy again, and do a very slow, steady half-mile, without making any attempt to spurt, or quicken, or push himself along at any part of the course. On the fourth day he can do the brisk 600 yards again; on the fifth a steady and slower 600; on the sixth a rather brisker 600 yards than he has done before; and then, if he takes a good walk on the intervening Sunday, he will feel himself at the end of his week a good deal more like a runner than he was at the beginning. A similar programme will do for the remaining three weeks of training, but his full trial should be at least a week before the race, and for the last few days before the event he should take no spin at all that can possibly exhaust him. Indeed, on the day before the race a sprint or two will be quite sufficient to maintain him in the state of fitness to which he has arrived. Above all, if on commencing practice any day he feels that he has not got over his yesterday's exertions, he should make a point of having a light day's work upon that occasion, as it is always better to do too little work than too much. But the runner, while practising, should never forget that the main object of all his practice is to improve the even pace which he can accomplish over the distance. In medium and long-distance races the runner must accustom himself to run at an even pace, and at as fast an even pace as he can command over the distance, keeping his spurts for when they are wanted, either to pass an antagonist or to get in front at the finish; so that, in training for these distances, it is of importance to know how fast one is going. It is wise, therefore, to be timed from day to day by a trainer, who will tell the man what pace he ought to go for the distance he is running for the day, and whether in the actual spin he has got inside it or not.

A word might here be interposed as to the tactics of a race. In medium or long races an immense deal in the way of success depends upon the judgment with which a race is run. If you decide to pass an antagonist you had better spurt to do so, and not try to pass him slowly, as this may end in his shaking you off again. If you spurt by an antagonist you may possibly take the heart out of him, and he may shut up 'like a telescope' on the spot. Another reflection which a runner should always bear in mind is, that when the dreadful thought occurs to his mind that he is 'done', it should be succeeded by the reassuring idea that his opponents are probably equally 'done' also. If this latter rule were always bear in mind we should not see, as we often do, cases in which the race does not fall to the swift but to the plucky. As a corollary to the two practical rules given above we may mention an anecdote which aptly illustrates them. We saw a match at Oxford between two cracks at 600 yards. The distance was rather beyond both runners, who were really quarter-milers. Before the run home was reached both parties had shot their bolt. The one in the rear, feeling himself 'done', decided that a desperate state of affairs required a desperate remedy, and pulling himself together, rushed clean past his antagonist with a spurt. The antagonist immediately shut up, but the winner was so much done that he could hardly crawl home in very slow time. We have since seen many important races where it has struck us that, had the beaten man made another effort, he could have turned the battle; but he has allowed himself to be defeated by some plucky 'cutting down' tactics of an inferior opponent. In the spring championship of 1879, M. R. Portal, the Oxonian, a beautiful mover and a magnificent runner, was cut down at the end by E. Storey, who won in 51 2/5 seconds at a time when Portal was quite equal to doing time a second better. In justice to Portal however, of whose merits Bob Rogers thought unutterable things, it must be said that he came to the scratch far from fit on that day. Want of condition is an admirable thing to breed irresolution in a race, and while it is easy to be game when one is fit, it is far harder for a jaded man to keep his gameness and a good head upon his shoulders. One game little runner, E. A. Sandford, the Oxford miler, certainly won both his Half-Mile Championships in 1874 and 1875 from faster men by pluck and judgment.

Although the half-mile has always been an event at the championship meeting since its foundation in 1866, the half-mile races were usually competed for by the long-distance runners alone, until Colbeck won the Half-Mile Championship in 1868; indeed, in 1867 an Oxford runner won the Half-Mile Championship with a time of 2 min. 5 sec., which is what any moderate performer can now achieve. Colbeck's successor in the championship for two years was R. V. Somers-Smith, the Oxonian quarter-miler, after which the Hon. A. L. Pelham attained the honour. Pelham was the tallest man whom we ever recollect to have seen figure on the running-path. He made his first appearance in London while, we believe, he was still a schoolboy at Eton, and being as long and leggy as a colt and some three or four inches over six feet, excited great astonishment by his prodigious strides. At Cambridge he was a contemporary of G. A. Templer, who was also a fine quarter-miler, and who ran in 1872 a dead heat for the Half-Mile Championship with T. Christie, the Oxford miler, in what was then the unbeaten time of 2 min. 1 sec; but in a race at Cambridge soon afterwards Pelham eclipsed the performance by beating for the first time 2 minutes over Fanner's path, finishing in the race in front of Templer. Pelham, with his prodigious stride, was too tall and leggy to spurt, and accordingly was not a first-rate performer at a quarter, and at the same time had not sufficient staying powers for a mile, so that he never made a good show for his University, as there is (more's the pity) no half-mile race in the Oxford and Cambridge programme. He was purely a half-miler, and undoubtedly the best of his day, and no one until 1876 contrived to repeat his performance of finishing the distance within 2 minutes. A year or two later H. W. Hill appeared in his best form, and showed himself, when thoroughly fit, to be as good at a half-mile as any of the champions, although he occasionally had to succumb at this distance to Waher Slade, the miler. Slade in 1874 was holding undisputed sway over every distance from half a mile to four miles; but twice in the races for the L.A.C. Challenge Cup was beaten by Hill in the autumn. Hill, strangely enough, seemed never to be able to get fit until late in the summer, and, indeed, his running excellence apparently was quite as much due to persistent practice as to natural ability). Still, however Hill's speed and stay were obtained, he was certainly a magnificent performer at half a mile and 1,000 yards. He was of about medium height, and weighed, we suppose, less than 10 stone, but, although not a sprinter, ran with the greatest dash and determination, and being faster than Slade, when he could beat him, won by sheer pluck in running the mile champion off his legs by forcing the pace. Strangely enough, about this time another famous runner, who, like Hill and Pelham, was a half-miler and nothing more, appeared upon the scene in Ireland – L. H. Courtney. On two occasions Courtney met and beat Slade at this distance in Ireland, although he was by no means Slade's equal at a mile. Courtney was taller than Hill, and ran like Clague and some other fine natural runners, with a springy action, bounding over the ground with a very light foot. However, at the end of 1875 Courtney retired, and early in 1876 Slade appeared to be the best half-miler left upon the path, as he had managed to beat Hill in the spring of that year, while Pelham had also apparently retired. In this year Slade again did some fine performances in Ireland, once beating 2 minutes in Dublin, and at Belfast soon afterwards beating 1 min. 59 sec. over grass. By this time great things were being whispered about of Elborough's capabilities at this distance, and by a happy thought the committee of the L.A.C. managed to get together all the four cracks of the day – Elborough, Slade, Hill, and Pelham – to compete for the L.A.C. challenge cup at the autumn meeting in 1876. The meeting attracted an immense crowd and produced a race the recollection of which can never be effaced from the memorj'of anyone who witnessed it. Pelham, bounding away in front with his gigantic strides, led by several yards until the first quarter had been completed, when the others began to draw upon him, Slade being in front of Hill and Elborough acting as whipper-in. Along the top stretch, 250 yards from home, Slade closed upon Pelham and took the lead into the straight. Once well into the straight Hill made his effort, however, rushed past the pair, and took a lead of several yards. Then came the shouts for Elborough; the champion was seen striding up to Hill, and a hundred yards from home he took the lead. Hill, however, ran with the greatest determination, and chased the winner home, being only beaten by about three yards. Half-a-dozen yards or so behind Hill came Slade, and about an equal distance behind Slade came Pelham, all four finishing within 2 minutes, Elborough's time being 1 min. 57 1/2 sec, Hill's 1 min. 58 sec., and Slade's and Pelham's a shade inside 1 min. 59 sec. and 2 min. respectively. Here, as in other cases when good men meet, they serve to extend each other, and some fine performances are the result.

In 1877 Elborough was beaten at 1,000 yards by C. Hazenwood, a Northern runner, who afterwards came to London. The latter, like the others we have mentioned, although a fair miler, was only first class at the medium distances. Of his powers while still a provincial runner many tales are told, and he is freely credited by some of his admirers with having done 1 min. 56 sec. or thereabouts in practice. He was a small man, with by no means a taking style, and after he came to London certainly never displayed any remarkable performance. We believe that when he defeated Elborough he was better trained than any amateur before or since; for, according to one enthusiastic admirer, he was so fit that his face and skin absolutely shone.

In 1881 when Myers paid his first visit to England he met the best English cracks at half a mile at Stamford Bridge in June, and after forcing the pace for three-quarters of the distance left the others as if standing still and won at his ease in 1 min. 56 sec. That Myers could have knocked off a second or two from this record if pressed we have very little doubt, and his easy win was hardly wonderful. What is more wonderful was that the second and third men, S. H. Baker and S. K. Holman, both sterling good runners, but who had never got within 2 minutes before, were so far 'pulled out' by having the pace forced by a better man that both, we beheve, finished the distance well within 1 min. 59 sec. Neither Baker nor Holman, however, was in our opinion so good at half a mile as William Birkett, the champion of 1883, who was a veritable half-miler, being too heavy in build to be as successful at a mile. Birkett was a tall, broad-shouldered man with much stay and strength, and was probably better than any of the half-milers who have run during the last few years, with the possible exception of George, whose semi-professional training even while he was an amateur made him too good even at the shorter distance for any other amateur under ordinary circumstances. Had Elborough, Courtney, and Birkett been trained to the pitch that George attained, we have no doubt they would have been capable of better performances at this distance.

In training for long-distance races, in which category we should place those at a mile and upwards, improvement of speed is of course the object of attainment as in every other race, but the improvement is that entirely which comes from increased staying powers and wind; and for the purposes of training it is these latter alone which must be cultivated. The system of training, therefore, is substantially the same in kind as that we have recommended for the half-mile runners; and as the miler is necessarily one who is possessed of natural stamina, he is able to bear the increased amount of exercise and longer spin, which he must necessarily get through to acquire the requisite strength of muscle and lungs. The system for all training for long distances, to describe it shortly, is to take continual and daily spins of half a mile and upwards, the pace being gradually increased as the man finds he can stand it. If the runner takes a long spin or a very fast spin one day and finds upon turning out the next day that he feels slack from the previous day's exercise, he will do well to take an easier day's work on that occasion. The same system in the main will apply whatever the distance to be run, only if it be a very long distance the daily spins must be lengthened correspondingly. One runner may of course be at his best at one mile, another at four, and another at ten miles, but all the three are runners of the same class, bring into exercise the same muscles, and require in varying degree the same essentials to success. The exercise they need is such as will get the limbs hard and the wind abnormally good. All will do well to walk as much as they can without making themselves stiff; when they start their running on the path in earnest they must get over a daily spin of half or two-thirds of the distance, and when they run the full distance should aim not at spurting from time to time, but at discovering what is the best even pace they can maintain over their full journey. It is hardly necessary, therefore, to point out what essential assistance is given by a 'watch-holder', who can tell the runner at what pace he is doing his laps, so that he can know whether he is keeping up the speed he wishes. In these longer distances it is hard to give advice as to the actual daily work which should be undertaken. The following table is supplied to us by two successful distance runners who used it:

One Mile.
First day. – Two-thirds of a mile at steady pace.
Second day. – Half-mile.
Third day. – Slow mile.
Fourth day. – Fast half-mile.
Fifth day. – Six hundred yards at steady fast pace.
Sixth day. – A fast three-quarter mile.

Four Miles.
First day. – Two miles slowly.
Second day. – A mile.
Third day. – Three miles.
Fourth day. – A mile, faster.
Fifth day. – Two-thirds of a mile steady fast pace.
Sixth day. – Two miles steady fast pace.

On the seventh day, wind and weather permitting, each runner would take a brisk Sunday walk, of from six to ten miles, taking care not to catch a chill, and to be well rubbed down after the walk as well as after the runs.

To the statement that the miler and ten-miler are all of the same class, there is one important qualification. The long-distance runner is rarely over middle height or middle weight, and frequently is undersized. Whatever his weight is, the runner has to lift it all at every stride, and consequently all the weight of the body, except that of the muscles which are actually used for travelling over the ground, is simple dead weight which has to be carried. As the distances are lengthened, the heavier man gets more and more handicapped, and at ten miles, or in long cross-country races, the smaller and lighter men come more and more to the fore. The crack long-distance runner rarely weighs more than ten stone, and a man of the calibre of Walter Slade, six feet high, and weighing over 11 stone, is rare on the path. There are occasional exceptions; thus Deerfoot was, we believe, a very heavy man for his height, which was medium. Some of the best professionals, however, were very light men; Jack White, who at the time of writing still holds the five-mile record (24 min. 40 sec.), weighed 7 stone 10 lbs; Howett, of Norwich, 7 stone 8 lbs; while Lang and Cummings were both under 10 stone. Indeed, on comparing crack amateurs at shorter and longer distances, the difference is striking; Colbeck, who was a six-foot quarter-miler, weighed over 12 stone; Slade the miler, who was of the same height, was more than a stone less.

And at this juncture, we feel inclined to offer a respectful suggestion to our brothers, the 'coaches' on the river. It is a constant occurrence for the newspapers to record how the coach, after taking the crew for a long course, afterwards took out Nos. 5 and 6, the heavy weights, for some tubbing practice. Apparently then the coach believes that Nos. 5 and 6, being the biggest and most muscular of the crew, can stand the greatest amount of work. This may be so: there are no invariable rules as to physique and stamina; but it is abundantly proved from military, as well as athletic, experience, that the biggest men are not those who can stand the most work. In average cases, then, the coach had much better give some extra work to bow and No. 2 than to Nos. 5 and 6. We should not offer the advice if we had not seen so many big men trained stale, and then abused for laziness, in every branch of sport.

The supremacy of a sprinter is sometimes short-lived, as a man's best pace often leaves him when he is still young and perhaps only a year or two over his majority. The long-distance runner, however, rarely rises to the top of his profession until he has been a season or two upon the path, and then remains the acknowledged champion for years. The first Inter-Varsity Mile Race was won by C. B. Lawes, then at Cambridge, a magnificent all-round athlete who stroked the Cambridge boat, besides winning the Inter-Varsity and Championship Miles in different years. In the following year, 1865, another Cambridge man, R. E. Webster (a gentleman who has since risen to the top of the legal profession, and has been Sir Richard Webster, Attorney-General), was without doubt the best distance runner of that year. Webster's opponent in the Inter-Varsity Mile of 1865 was the Earl of Jersey, then at Christ Church, Oxford. Both Sir Richard Webster and Lord Jersey are still popular figures in the athletic world, the former being always received with rapture by the Varsity athletes of the year when he presides at the annual dinner which follows the sports, while Lord Jersey has been President and Trustee of the Amateur Athletic Association and an active worker for its benefit since the foundation of that society in 1880. We never saw either of these athletes run, but are told that Webster was a great man at a spurt, and was very active and bustling, and indeed, we believe that Sir Richard lays claim to having possessed sprinting abilities – a claim, however, which at this lapse of time we have been unable to verify. We have recently seen a very interesting cut, which appeared in the *Illustrated Sporting News* of April 18, 1865, representing the Inter-Varsity sports of that year. The explanatory letter-press at the foot of the picture is 'The Mile Race – Mr Webster putting on a spurt opposite the Grand Stand'. Mr Webster is represented as spurting gaily away from Lord Jersey, who appears to be in difficulties. The portraits of both seem to be fairly good ones, and the cut certainly does justice to Mr Webster's freshness and vigour. The Oxford men of that day, however, aver that Webster was not as good a runner as J. W. Laing, of Oxford, who won the Mile and ran a deadheat with C. H. Long, a Cantab, in the Two Miles Race at the Inter-Varsity sports in 1866. Laing did not start in the Championship in 1866, and that race fell to C. B. Lawes, who had been unplaced in the Inter-Varsity Mile. The third man in the championship of 1866 was destined to eclipse the fame of all his predecessors. This was W. M. Chinnery, of the L.A.C, still well known as an active patron of all sorts and conditions of sport. Chinnery won his first championship in 1868, and his last in 1871, and in '68 and '69 won both the One and Four Miles Races at the championship meeting Although in the latter years of his career he was run very close by J. Scott, of the same club, he managed to beat that athlete in a mile at one of the L.A.C. meetings in 1870, this being, we believe, the only occasion upon which they met at that distance. During his career, Chinnery was the leading figure at all long races: he was tall, weighed, we should say, over 10 stone, and ran with a long easy stride, but with very little dash. Probably he was so seldom pressed that he got into a monotonous way of running, relying on his stride and stay, and not on any other tactics. His opponent, Scott, was thought to be better at four miles than a mile, although we think that both he and Chinnery were capable of beating 4 min. 30 sec. at the latter distance when put to it; and at that time 4 min. 30 sec. was considered an almost superhuman performance, as the runners usually went off slowly, and waited upon one another until half-way. Scott was a shorter and slighter man than Chinnery, and ran with a much lighter tread, holding himself more erect than his great rival, and shooting his legs out in front of him. Another sterling good man, who was a contemporary of Chinnery's, was Sydenham Dixon, of the Civil Service. Dixon, although a lighter weight, had, we think, greater pace than Chinnery, but the latter could outstay the Civil Service runner. From 1868 to 1871 inclusive, Dixon won the Civil Service Mile, his usual pace-maker being C. J. Michod, the best steeplechaser of the time. Michod, with great regularity, would make the pace year after year, only to be cut down by Dixon at the end; but in 1873 Dixon found the tables turned upon him by G. F. Congreve, who played him exactly the same trick, and just managed to shoot him upon the post, amidst the wild indignation of the crowd, who thought Dixon had acquired a vested interest in the race after so many wins from year to year. Scott would, we think, have done a fine performance at ten miles, but in his day four miles was the utmost limit ever run by amateurs, and at this distance he made, in the championship of 1871, a very fine time (20 min. 38 sec.), which was never beaten until the famous match in 1875, between Walter Slade and J. Gibb. In the Four Mile Race, Scott was running quite alone, and winning with inconceivable ease, so that it is most likely he was capable of very great things. The same remark applies to the celebrated Oxonian, J. H. Morgan, who (as the historians say) 'flourished' circa 1868–1870. No one could ever get near him in the three miles race at the Inter-Varsity sports, and in one of his races he trotted in 200 yards in front of the next man, in 15 min. 20 sec. Morgan was a short strong man, a light weight with a good deep chest – the best type of runner for long distances.

When Chinnery had retired from the path Scott was not left for long in undisturbed possession of the field. In the summer of 1872, a tall strong healthy-looking lad who had not long since left Tonbridge School began to astonish the handicappers by the number of races he was

Steeplechase – the water-jump.

winning. However far Walter Slade was put back he always managed to win, so rapidly was he improving, until one fine day at some sports of the Thames Hare and Hounds, at Wandsworth, it was discovered that Slade, who had fifty yards or thereabouts from Scott in a handicap mile, had come in considerably more than fifty yards in front of him. This at once settled Slade's position as a 'crack'. As Scott soon afterwards left the path we do not think the pair ever met level at a mile, but from this time onwards until he left the path in 1877 Slade was never beaten at the mile.

Slade, as we have said before, was a tall man, about six feet in height and weighing over eleven stone when in strict training, and he ran heavily, crunching the cinders as he sped over the path. In 1874 he lowered the amateur mile record to 4 min. 26 sec. when he won from scratch the Open Mile at the Civil Service Sports in this time. The Strangers' Open Mile at these sports has always, indeed, been one of the classic handicaps of the year. In 1868 Chinnery won this race in 4 min. 29 sec., then a record; after Slade's time W. G. George, the now famous professional, won the same race from scratch in 4 min. 19 2/5sec, and the year afterwards W. Snook won the same race from scratch in 4 min. 20 sec. In 1875 Slade eclipsed his previous performance by covering his mile in 4 min. 24 sec. at a meeting of the L.A.C. at Stamford Bridge in a celebrated race when he met H. A. Bryden and L. U. Burt, both the others being, like himself, tall men. Bryden, who ran in beautiful style, had, however, little dash, or he might, perhaps, have lowered Slade's colours; while L. U. Burt was too tall and heavy to hold his own in such company, unless very highly trained. On this occasion of lowering the record, all three covered the distance within 4 min. 30 sec.

Another contemporary of Slade's deserves notice for his mile performances. This was W. H. Seary, who, at the time of his zenith on the path, was an Oxford scout, and if report be true, used to utilise, for training purposes, his journeys across 'Tom' and 'Peck' quads, and stride across the gravel in great style. Any way he was a superb runner, with a long stride and light of foot. His entry was, we believe, refused at the championship meetings and in London, but he often figured at the provincial gatherings, and had he met Slade would have had a good deal of money put on him by the Northern enthusiasts. On the only occasion when he and Slade were entered together at Widnes, the meeting was postponed on account of wet weather, and at the adjourned meeting Slade was unable to be present. Another fine miler, in the years 1876 and 1877, was E. R. J. Nicolls, of Christ Church, Oxford, who won the Inter-Varsity Mile in 1876 in 4 min. 28 sec. Nicolls was in even better form in the succeeding year, but a family bereavement prevented his taking part in the Inter-Varsity and championship sports of that year. Unlike most runners, Nicolls seemed to delight in running as a pastime, but to have little ambition to take part in a big race, although this was certainly not from nervousness, as his performances were chiefly due to dogged perseverance and pluck and most careful training.

Slade was beaten in the Four Mile Championship of 1875 by James Gibb, a pretty runner with a short stride and of light weight, who was seen at his best in longer distances than a mile. A match was afterwards made at four miles between Slade and Gibb, which came off at Lillie Bridge on the evening of April 26 of that year in presence of a large crowd, nearly the whole of the Stock Exchange (or at any rate the younger members of that institution) turning out to support Slade. After a close and magnificent race, Slade, who hung at his opponent's shoulder all the way, rushed past and won in 20 min. 22 sec., Scott's old record being disposed of by this performance. Besides Gibb, however, Slade had several famous contemporaries at longer distances, chief of whom was James (better known as 'Choppy') Warburton, a North-countryman of much the same build as Slade, whose weight and style of running made him more successful over a grass course than over cinders. Warburton, as the hero of a hundred fights on the running path, reaped a large harvest of prizes, and, after the manner of his kind, became a Boniface, and used to exhibit himself in costume, together with his trophies, for a small fee to an admiring public. He afterwards turned professional runner, an example which has been followed by several of his more famous successors.

Another fine performer, who had a very long career on the path, was C. H. Mason, a good light weight who won the Mile Championship in 1872, before Slade's appearance on the path, and the Ten Mile Championship in 1879 and 1880, long after Slade's retirement. Mason always ran with consummate judgment, and had a fine turn of speed in the middle or at the end of a race, as well as a great deal of dogged pluck. In one ten-mile handicap, where he started at scratch with W. E. Fuller, he was compelled to stop over and over again from stitch, but with undaunted perseverance he refreshed himself with nips of brandy, and eventually getting rid of his enemy, went off again at a great pace, overhauled Fuller, and passed him with ease. In the Four Mile Championship of 1876, however, Mason met another runner of similar staunchness, Albert Goodwin, of Oxford. Goodwin had made a great reputation in early life as a sprinter, hurdler, and jumper, and went to Oxford late in life as a married man with a family. His age and matrimonial condition, however, did not prevent his becoming the best three-miler Oxford ever sent to Lillie Bridge up to 1876. In the Four Mile Championship there was a fine race between Goodwin and Mason, and each, knowing that he could sprint at the finish, waited upon the other; but the Oxonian was a bit too fast for Mason at the end, and won in slow time.

In 1879 the Spring Championship was won by B. R. Wise, of Oxford, and the Summer Championship by W. G. George. As George was for many years before the public as amateur and professional, he hardly needs a description. He is a tall, thin man with a prodigious stride, which arises from his bringing his hips into play more than any distance-runner we have ever seen, and years of training and practice have cultivated his staying powers to an extraordinary degree. During his career as an amateur, which lasted from 1879 to the end of 1884, he had only two serious rivals on the path at a mile or upwards. In 1882, he started very unfit for the Mile Championship, having only just recovered from illness, and was beaten by Wise. The latter, not a strong man, was a tall light weight with a springy stride, a successful runner from the fact of his knowing exactly what amount of training would suit his constitution. He took no hard practice at all, going only short spins, and sometimes knocked off work altogether. As a result he came to the post in all his races fresh and confident; and on the occasion when he beat George ran with wonderful judgment, steadily increasing his pace all round the last lap at Aston, until he had his man settled at the top of the straight, when he came away and won in 4 min. 24 2/5 sec. Wise, who was a man of great enthusiasm for athletics, was the first Vice-President of the Athletic Association, and that body lost much by his return to his native country, New South Wales, in 1883. He has since held the post of Attorney-General of that colony.

George's other great rival was W. Snook, of Shrewsbury, a runner of very remarkable physique. A short, thick-set man with tremendous legs, shoulders, and chest, he certainly looked most unlike a runner of long distances; but he, too, like George, trained his strength and staying powers to an extraordinary pitch of excellence, and although most unlike George in build, resembled him in striding straight from the hips, and thus covering more ground in each stride than would have been thought possible from his height and make. When at his best Snook was very little inferior to George at any of his distances, and George's amateur record for a mile of 4 min. 18 2/5 sec. was made after a hot race with Snook in the championship of 1884. In one year (1883), when George was again a bit off colour, Snook was too good for him in the Mile and Four Mile Championships, but on all the other occasions when matches were made between the pair, and both were fit and well, George proved himself the better man. Still Snook, when he won the Civil Service Mile from scratch in 1883 in 4 min. 20 sec. was certainly not pressed at the finish, and a hard race on that day would, we think, have made him do an astonishing performance. Since George has turned professional he has in a match with Cummings completed a mile in 4 min. 12 3/5 sec., and this seems to set at rest for ever the question which, in spite of George's victories, was always being debated – who was the better man upon his best day.

Although steeplechases were popular in the early days of athletics, they fell into disuse at important meetings for many years, and were not included in the championship programme until the summer meeting of 1879. In the very early days of athletics something of the nature of a steeplechase or long hurdle race was always included in a programme, and naturally so, for the impromptu races and matches from which the sport arose were often from point to point over a piece of country. But as athletics began to reach the artificial stage, and the natural runner was unable to keep pace with the trained athlete in his spiked shoes on a cinder-path, steeplechases began to drop out of fashion, except where they were retained to please spectators; for the British public, in the true style of those who rejoice in gladiatorial shows, like to see somebody or something coming to grief or rendered ridiculous. The result was that for many years the steeplechase was considered as forming the comic part of the entertainment at a meeting, and the managers of sports made huge water-jumps which it was impossible for anyone to clear, so that the lookers-on might see runner after runner tumble into a filthy pool and emerge muddy, bleeding, soaked, and groaning. However, not even these silly exhibitions could spoil a sport in itself admirable; for nothing can really be a prettier or surer test of a combination of staying power, agility, and pluck than a race of some distance over hurdles or obstacles which are not too high or broad to prevent the runners from having a chance of clearing them. As soon, therefore, as the paperchasing movement, which is described elsewhere, had taken firm hold of the athletic public, steeplechases at athletic meetings began to regain popularity, the distances selected being from three-quarters of a mile up to two miles, but seldom over the latter distance. We are sorry, however, to see that the old form of steeplechase, with impossible water-jumps and prodigious prickly obstacles, is still retained at some meetings, in order that the public may laugh while the miserable performers wallow in the mud or make ugly faces when they may happen to fall back into the brambles or furze, and we must confess to thinking still that the best steeplechases are those across well-selected country, and not round an artificially prepared and enclosed course.

The good steeplechaser must, of course, be a long-distance runner, as no one without staying powers can hope to last the distance; he must be a good jumper as well, and in addition there is a very great art in clearing the obstacles which can only be learnt by constant practice. The object of the clever steeplechaser is to exhaust himself as little as possible over the jumps. He therefore takes the hurdles of ordinary height according to the regular hurdling manner in his stride, never rising an inch higher than is absolutely necessary. The waterjump has to be taken in a different way. The regular practice is for a high hurdle studded with furze branches to be placed on the edge of the water. If the water is too broad for his powers the runner makes no attempt to clear it, but jumps carefully so far into it that, by leaning well forward, his hands may immediately seize the bank, and he then pulls himself cleverly out without losing time. If, on the contrary, he thinks he can clear it with a kick, he gets one foot on the top of the hurdle and thence gets a kick off, which takes him over the water; but this is a very clever piece of jumping which requires great practice. Some runners, especially in the shorter steeplechases, come with a rush and a bound clear over the hurdle and water, and this bit of 'gallery' is always enthusiastically applauded; but, as a rule, it is a waste of strength in the long run, and the old hands are seldom seen to indulge in such display. As the obstacles may be of all sorts of height and stiffness, however, it is difficult to lay down any general rules to suit all runners and all obstacles, but in no case should the 'chaser alight on both feet from a jump, as he then comes to a dead stop. Most runners take their spring from the right foot, and get over their obstacles a bit sideways with the right leg in the rear.

A steeplechase of two miles was one of the events in the first Inter-Varsity gathering on the Christ Church cricket-ground at Oxford in 1864, when R. C. Garnett, of Cambridge, proved himself too good by six yards for the present Attorney General, of whom, as a runner, we have already spoken. In the following year, however, the event was changed to a two mile flat race; and there have been no more steeplechases at Inter-Varsity gatherings. For the four or five years before 1875 the few steeplechases that were included in meetings round London were nearly all won by C. J. Michôd, a Civil Service runner, who was very clever over the obstacles and water-jumps, and would have been a fine distance-runner had he been gifted with a little more pace for a spurt. We can recollect on one occasion Slade starting at scratch with Michôd in a steeplechase at the Richmond Cricket Club Sports; but the crack miler blundered so much over the hurdles, banging his shins, and occasionally falling prostrate, that Michôd before long sailed away from him, and eventually won the race outright, Slade giving up. In the summer championship of 1879 a two-mile steeplechase was included in the programme, and was won by H. M. Oliver, an old London paperchaser, who for some years previous to that date had settled in Birmingham and become the leader of the athletic movement in the midlands, and founder of the famous Moseley Harriers Club. Oliver was only a moderate performer on the flat, but was certainly a very clever jumper, never wasting an ounce of his strength, and he beat, in 1879, C. L. O'Malley and the other Londoners by the clever way in which he got upon the top of the hurdles and jumped from them clean over the water-jump without an effort. Of late years the best steeplechasers have nearly always been the bestpaperchasers of the day, the ordinary flat-race runners having little opportunity to practise jumping without taking part in crosscountry runs. The best Londoners have been C. L. O'Malley, who, however, never, we believe, figured as a paperchaser, and J. T, Wills, an old Oxonian, who was good on the flat also. Strangely enough, as the sport is a very genuine and interesting one, steeplechasing is quite unknown at athletic meetings at the Universities; and what makes this still more strange is that in hurdle-racing – a kindred sport –

the Varsities uniformly produce some of the best men in every year; indeed, of the twenty-nine hurdle-racing champions up to the date of writing, seventeen have hailed from Oxford or Cambridge.

Hurdle-racing. – In the early days of amateur athletics hurdling and steeplechasing were considered as kindred sports, the former being a test of short-distance running *plus* jumping, the latter of long-distance running *plus* jumping. So much was thought of this judicious combination that the first Inter-University meeting at Oxford, in 1864, had two hurdle races and a steeplechase out of eight events, the remaining items being three flat races and two jumps. The two hurdle races were at 120 yards and 200 yards, each having ten flights of hurdles. The former distance, however, soon became the more popular; and the committee who drew up the programme for the first championship meeting settled the future of hurdleracing by fixing upon 120 yards race with ten flights, the hurdles being 3 ft 6 in. high, at even distances of ten yards, with fifteen yards between the start and the first hurdle, and a similar distance between the last hurdle and the finish. As soon, however, as the distance between the hurdles became stereotyped the runners were not long in finding out that in the race invented to test running and jumping powers in combination the more running there was, and the less jumping, the faster the time over the distance would be. Experience soon taught that three strides would take a man from hurdle to hurdle, and that he could spring off one leg and alight on the other, taking the hurdle in his stride. The result was that hurdle-racing over the recognised distance soon became a very difficult and pretty but highly artificial performance. The 'crack' hurdler takes every stride of exactly the same length, rises exactly the same height at every jump, and moves with the regularity and precision of clockwork. Some jump off the right, some off the left, foot; in either case, when the spring is taken the front leg is jerked up enough to enable the runner to get his shin or knee over the bar; that leg then is dropped again, so as to enable him to alight on the ball of his toe; meanwhile the hind leg is lifted in similar style over the bar and straightened at once as soon as the bar is cleared, and directly the other toe has alighted the next stride is taken almost without a pause. It will be obvious how slight a delay is caused by clearing the hurdles when it is considered that men who are equal to little better than 12 3/4 seconds over 120 yards on the flat have covered 120 yards over ten hurdles of 3 ft 6 in. high in 16 seconds. The sport is a pretty one, requiring great skill, speed and agility, and a 'light foot', but we cannot help expressing a wish that in addition there might be seen other short hurdle races at meetings where the runners should not know the exact distance between each hurdle, and the exact height of the jump, and so would be unable to calculate the precise length of the stride and the precise amount, to the smallest fraction, of the power required to lift them over the hurdle. Running is nothing if not natural, and graceful as hurdling is, in our opinion it has been brought to too high a pitch of artificiality. We have seen H. K. Upcher, one of the best of the Oxford hurdlers, take two spins over hurdles, when in each spin his feet fell in exactly the same track (and we may add the same part of his shin scraped the top of the hurdle in exactly the same spot), so that a Red Indian following him by his tracks would hardly have seen that he had been twice over the same ground.

The hurdle-racer must, as we have seen, have a light foot, and so he is rarely a heavy man, but he must also have a strong back and thighs, so as to take his spring and his fresh start without any pause. Thus he is always one who runs in a 'springy' style, but a good high jumper is rarely of any use as hurdler, as he has a natural inclination to jump too high and waste time in his spring into the air. Hurdle-racing and long-jumping ability more often go together. Indeed, the main point in hurdle-racing is not to learn to jump well over the hurdle, but to learn not to jump too high. The best way to attain this is, in our opinion, to practise over hurdles the top bar of which is loose. It may seem a paradox, but we think it is true, that the runner can best learn by having no fear of coming to grief by crashing into the top bar. Upcher, of whom we have spoken, probably took as much care over his practice for hurdling as any man has ever done, and so fearful was he of getting into the habit of rising too high, that when he began, whether the hurdles had a loose top or not, he would crash through half-a-dozen of them, leaving a track of desolation behind him. His shins certainly suffered in the performance, as he was in the habit sometimes of carefully bumping them against each hurdle to see that he was going all right. The hurdles at the Old Marston running-grounds at Oxford, over which so many cracks practised, had loose tops which came off when struck by the leg, but recently the Oxonians have practised over ordinary hurdles, it being thought by some that the 'loose-top' system encouraged rashness, and led to catastrophes at Lillie Bridge.

The beginner always finds himself unable to do the regulation 'three stride' with any success over hurdles of full height, and either has to practise over low ones placed the proper ten yards apart, or to slope the obstacles forward so as to make the height less and the jumping more easy. The secret of success lies more in assiduous practice than in anything else. Probably any athlete with fair abilities at sprinting and long jumping can with practice make himself a good hurdler if he be not too heavy-footed, and so unable to recover from the spring. The really brilliant hurdler, however, is always a clean built man with little weight at the buttocks to drag him backward, and the heavy-weight sprinters who try hurdling are usually failures. Some of the best hurdlers have been small men who have found their natural stride long enough for the three-stride system, while a man with too long a natural stride can hardly reduce it with success. Great strength of back is naturally required for the rise to the hurdle, and the hurdler not only needs assiduous practice, but must come to the post very fit and without a trace of stiffness. As regards the amount of exercise and practice, he must train in much the same style as the sprinter, taking great care over starts and spurts on the flat in addition to his daily spin over the timber. We need scarcely say that it is not in the least necessary to cover the full distance every day in practice. The hurdler probably benefits quite as much as the sprinter by the rubbing process which we have before described.

Hurdle-racing is undoubtedly more popular at the Universities than anywhere else. The University element in London brought the sport forward in the metropolis very early, but until quite recently it was very rare to find a good hurdler, except from Oxford or Cambridge. It is not too much to say, indeed, that only two first-class hurdlers have hailed from London – Reay and Lockton – and hardly any of note from any other part of the country except Nottingham, which of late years has been quite a centre of hurdling ability. After all it is hardly surprising that hurdlers should only be found in a few places, for the sport cannot well flourish in any locality where there are not great facilities for its practice.

The first champion at the 120 yards hurdle race was a Cambridge man, T. Milvain, a gentleman who has since passed the post first in several contested parliamentary elections at Durham. The third man in the race was C. N. Jackson, the well-known treasurer of the O.U.A.C., and also treasurer of the A.A.A. since its foundation. Of Mr Jackson's services to the cause of athletic sport at Oxford, as well as elsewhere, it is almost unnecessary to speak, but his reputation as a hurdler while he was still an active athlete may fitly be mentioned. In the year 1867 Jackson was the winner of the Oxford and Cambridge hurdle race, and but for a *contretemps* would, no doubt, have been champion in that year as well. In his heat he disposed of Milvain with great ease, but in the succeeding attempt there was a dead heat between R. Fitzherbert, of Cambridge, and J. B. Martin (the present president of the London A.C.). The result was that a fifth hurdle was added in the final heat, upon some ground which, we believe, had not even been mown. In the draw for places Jackson unluckily found the rough ground allotted to him. and was unable to make any show in the race. His great performance, however, had been done previously in the autumn of 1865, when he covered the distance in what is still the record time – 16 seconds. Jackson was a strongly-built light weight of rather over medium height, the most successful type of hurdle-racer. In 1868 and 1869 the championship went away from the Universities, falling in the former year to W. M. Tennant, of Liverpool, the sprinter, and in the latter year to G. R. Nunn, of Guy's Hospital. In 1870, however, with J. L. Stirling, of Cambridge, began the long line of University cracks which has continued almost without interruption until the present time. Stirling made his first and only appearance at the Oxford and Cambridge Sports in 1870, when he won with ridiculous ease by half-a-dozen yards, in 16 3/5 seconds. In the same year he won the championship, a performance which he repeated in 1872. He was, we believe, never defeated in a hurdle race, and, if our recollection is right, was a taller and heavier man than the successful hurdler usually is. He ran also in a style somewhat different from that of many of his precursors, his right leg not being doubled back at all, but hanging behind him, as he strode clean over the hurdle. The best University hurdler of 1871 and 1872 was E. S. Garnier, who ran with great dash, but was a trifle too heavy to fly over the sticks. Garnier, who was a thick-set man, also represented his University at hammer-throwing – an unusual circumstance, hammer-throwing and hurdling being almost the opposite poles of athletic sport. Garnier won the championship in 1871, but in the following year he met Stirling at Lillie Bridge, and the Cambridge runner beat him. In the following year Upcher made his first appearance, and probably he was as good as Stirling. He was a strong muscular man, but not heavy in spite of his strength, and was a fine natural broad jumper, being able to leap over hurdles, hedges, and other obstacles with great agility when in boots and great-coat. He practised hurdling exclusively upon his own system, and was in his time regarded as the best exponent of the art ever known. He won the Inter-Varsity and Championship Hurdles in 1873 and 1874, and so great was the behef in his powers that the astonishment was unbounded when, at the Inter-Varsity meeting of 1875, a Cambridge man, A. B. Loder, was seen to be holding Upcher in the hurdle race. Neck and neck the pair raced over the jumps and reached the tape apparently together, but the judge decided that Loder had won by a few inches, amidst the wild cheers of the Cambridge partisans. Three days afterwards the pair met over the same course in the championship, when another neck-and-neck race resulted in a six-inch victory for Upcher. This, we believe, was Upcher's last appearance on the path, and the next year Loder had matters all his own way at both meetings. Loder was a trifle taller than Upcher, and was a trifle faster than his opponent over the flat, but the Oxonian was, we think, a bit cleverer over the hurdles. In 1877 the hurdle race at the Oxford and Cambridge Sports fell to the Oxonian S. F. Jackson, who was yet fresh at the game, and unable to make a show with J. H. A. Reay, the Londoner, who won the championship this year. Reay was a fine all-round athlete and excellent hurdler, who had for some years been unrivalled in London, but was unlucky in appearing during the days of Upcher and Loder. He ran more in the Stirling style than the other pair, trailing his leg well behind him, and so jumping slightly higher than was necessary. In the following year S. F. Jackson ran a greatly improved man, being only beaten a foot in 16 2/5 seconds by S. Palmer, of Cambridge. Palmer was a 'converted sprinter', that is to say, a sprinter of first-class merit who took to hurdling after trying sprinting for a year or two first. His success at the latter sport may be gauged from the fact that he won four championships, and was credited with 16 seconds in his championship of 1878. Palmer left Cambridge in 1878, but was frequently seen on the path for the next five years. Wonderful as his success was, he was probably more of a sprinter than a hurdler, being wonderfully fast between the sticks but rather clumsy as a jumper, giving his shoulders a twist as he cleared each obstacle. He was not, we think, quite so good as the Oxonian G. P. C. Lawrence, who was champion in 1880 and 1881. Lawrence was a tall slight man, a good all-round jumper and runner, who for some years, until he conquered his inclination to jump too high over his hurdles, had no great merit. As soon, however, as he had learnt to skim instead of leap over his jumps he became the best hurdler of modern times, having a peculiar nervous power (although not physically strong) of making a prolonged spurt. In the championship of 1881 he decisively defeated Palmer, having in the previous year scored an equally decisive victory over Lockton. The latter was undoubtedly the best hurdler the metropolis ever produced. Of his wonderful capacities as a sprinter we have already spoken, and when, as sometimes happened, he took part in hurdle races when the hurdles were a few inches below the regulation height, his speed over the obstacles was something extraordinary. At a hurdle handicap at Catford Bridge, at the meeting of the Private Banks, we saw him start 24 yards behind the scratch man, and clear the 144 yards and ten hurdles (below the regulation height) in 18 seconds. In the championship of 1880, however, Lockton probably lost his head, and came to grief in the Hurdles, besides failing in the Hundred Yards. Lockton was never in his best form again after 1880, and when Lawrence retired Palmer again won the championship in 1882 and 1883. For the last few years the Universities have not produced a hurdler of the calibre of Lawrence or Palmer, and the centre of hurdling activity for some years shifted to Nottingham, which has produced in turn three fine performers – F. F. Cleaver, C. W. Gowthorpe, and C. F. Daft, twice champion. Cleaver for some years, in the absence of the Varsity cracks, used to sweep the board at the chief provincial meetings, being very fast, although a bit clumsy in his jumps. After his retirement and that of Palmer, Gowthorpe, like Cleaver a member of the Notts Forest Football Club, won the championship of 1884, and Daft, the champion of 1885 and 1886, also represented the same club. Here, as at the Universities, is seen the value of a 'tradition' in producing skilful performers. There were good hurdlers in Nottingham long before Cleaver, one of them, S. W. Widdowson, having earned a great reputation in the provinces a dozen years ago.

Occasionally in the provinces there are hurdle races of 300 yards or a quarter of a mile where the runners have the opportunity of showing their natural and not artificially cultivated abilities in contests which combine sprinting and jumping. Such races, however, are unfortunately so few and far between that they can hardly be said to give scope to a special class of runner. Perhaps a new fashion may someday call into existence a class of short-distance steeplechasers.

4
Jumping, Weight-Putting, etc.

JUMPING

In no branch of athletics have practice and cultivation led to such an extraordinary improvement as in high and broad jumping. At the first Oxford and Cambridge meeting in 1864, the High Jump was won with 5 ft 6 in., the Long Jump with 18 ft, and even at the present day foreigners hear with incredulity that men can jump more than 6 ft in height, and clear more than 23 ft on the flat. The improvement is perhaps more marked in long jumping than in high jumping, but even in the latter, careful training and assiduous practice has shown that the human body is capable of greater feats than were thought possible before jumping became an organised sport. Probably 'Christopher North' would have found it as hard to believe that M. J. Brooks jumped 6 ft 2 1/2 in. high in 1876, as did Donald Dinnie, the Scotch 'professional', who, on seeing an account of Brooks' jump, promptly wrote to the papers to show that, upon *à priori* grounds, such a feat was impossible.

Perhaps nothing is so pretty and interesting as a High Jump, and a light-weight jumper who leaps straight over his obstacle and alights on the balls of his feet is almost certain to be graceful in his movements. Still there are a variety of different styles of high-jumping, and some successful performers get over the bar sideways with a crab-like motion which is more effective than beautiful. The muscles used for the spring are those in front of the thigh which pass down to the knee-cap. The knee is bent when preparing for the spring, the muscles are contracted, and from the sudden and violent straightening of the leg with a jerk, the impetus is given. A high-jumper, therefore, must have these muscles not only strong but naturally springy and elastic, and from this it follows that in a certain sense the high-jumper, like the sprinter, is born, not made; for though muscles can be hardened and strengthened by practice, nothing but nature can make them elastic. As a matter of fact the high-jumper is nearly always short-thighed, with a well-shaped knee, a rather long leg from knee to ankle, and with an ankle, like the knee, cleanly and delicately shaped.

Halfway over.

Well over.

It is always said, and with some show of truth, that a high jumper is fanciful and uncertain. The reason is easy to see, for not only will a touch of cold or stiffness in the joints spoil a man's form, but the greatest possible difference is made by inability to take off at exactly the right distance from the bar. Thus, if the 'take off' is a little up-hill, a little down-hill, or so slippery as to make the jumper nervous of falling, he may rise from the wrong place, and jump into the bar instead of over it. It is sometimes amusing to act as judge in a high jumping contest. One man wants to jump with the sun on his right, another with the sun on his left, one likes to alight upon the mattress which is always kept for the purpose, another is put off if he sees the mattress in front of him; another sticks a bit of paper into the ground to guide him as to his take-off, while yet another hangs a blue handkerchief on the bar to show him where he is to jump to. To all this a courteous judge can raise no reasonable objection, but the competition in consequence becomes unduly prolonged and wearisome to the public, as each competitor has three tries at each height, and the mattress, handkerchief, and paper have to be shifted about at each jump. Luckily, even the most obliging officials cannot be asked to put a curtain over the sun for the jumpers' convenience.

The jumper has to get himself fit in the same way as the sprinter. He must become strong, light, and hardy without becoming stiff. As a bye-play, then, he will do no harm if he indulges in a bit of sprinting and takes exercise canters, being careful to keep upon his toes; and the more he avails himself of the services of a rubber the better. For his main practice he must jump over the bar daily, being cautious not to overdo himself any day, and if he be wise he should learn to take off both against the wind and with it and under all sorts of atmospheric conditions, as he will then be less likely to be 'put off' when he appears upon a strange ground to take part in a competition.

Of late years it has been the practice to put the posts upon the cinder-path or to have a 'take off' of cinders for the jumpers. Some of the performers, however, prefer taking off from grass under any circumstances, and no doubt they are right in thinking that good dry springy turf is better than cinders. At the same time we have plenty of rain in England; the grass is sometimes too slippery for fair jumping, and in such a state that even a sprinkling of cinders or sawdust is insufficient to get it into condition. The managers of a meeting should be careful, if they intend their jumps to be upon the grass, to cover up their 'take off' for a day or two beforehand. At the same time the jumper will be wise if he can get the opportunity to practise both upon cinders and turf, and he will thus be prepared for all emergencies.

The usual practice in competition is for the bar to be raised one inch each time, and not more, when the jumpers are beginning to approach the end of their tether; but they are usually given a few jumps at lower heights to start with to get their legs into form. In the championship the bar is usually placed at first at 5 ft, then raised to 5 ft 2 in., then to 5 ft 4 in., and then to 5 ft 6 in. if all the competitors agree, but if any object, after 5 ft 4 in. the bar is raised an inch each time. Although the jumping was very poor at the first two Inter-Varsity competitions, the first championship meeting in 1866 brought out two fine performers, both Cantabs, T. G. Little and J. H. T. Roupell, who tied at 5 ft 9 in., a height which remained the 'record' for the next five years. In the next year Little again won the championship with a tie, his partner on this occasion being another Cantab, C. E. Green. In 1868, however, the Varsity men were no longer in sole possession of the field, for in this year that wonderful athlete R. J. C. Mitchell, of Manchester, made his first appearance on the scene in London, winning the high jump with 5 ft 8 in., the long jump with 19 ft 8 1/2 in., and the pole jump with 10 ft 6 1/2 in. Two years later Mitchell won all these three events again with the weight-putting into the bargain, and in 1871 he again was champion in these four competitions, his high jump on this, occasion being 5 ft 9 1/2 in., half an inch better than the old record. Mitchell's performances in 1871 certainly show him to have been a fine all-round athlete, his high jump being, as we have said, 5 ft 9 1/2 in., his long jump (in which he tied with E. J. Davies) 20 ft 4 in., his pole jump 10 ft, and his weight putting 38 ft. 8 1/2 in. In these later days the competition is so keen that would-be champions have to become specialists, and we thus hear less than we used to of 'all round champions'.

Mitchell's performance was never eclipsed until M. J. Brooks, a freshman from Rugby, came up to Oxford. Brooks in his first year jumped 5 ft 10 in. at the Inter-Varsity sports, and a few days later eclipsed this by a performance of 5 ft 11 in. at the championship meeting. He was a tall, cleanly built, and rather thin man, with a good deal of strength as well as spring, and his manner of jumping was very striking, although not very graceful when he got over great heights. He took very little run, and in fact almost walked up to the bar, springing straight over it with his legs tucked up high and well in front of him, and invariably looked, when his legs were once over, as if his body would fall crashing on to the bar; but he nearly always managed to jerk his body forward again and to alight upon his toes. When he did knock down the bar he did so with his elbows or body, being apparently able to get his feet over almost any height. The year after his first appearance Brooks was in no sort of form, and was beaten by M. G. Glazebrook, another Oxonian, who did 5 ft 9 1/4 in. at the Inter-Varsity gathering, and was credited with 5 ft 11 in. at the championship meeting. We can recollect, however, that Glazebrook's 5 ft 11 in. was rather a doubtful record, as he knocked the bar pretty heavily, but without bringing it to the ground. In 1876 Brooks disposed of his own and Glazebrook's joint record by jumping 6 ft at the University sports at Oxford. For so many years it had been considered an impossible feat to jump 6 ft that the excitement at the performance was very great, and the Honorary Treasurer of the O.U.C.A., then as now an enthusiastic admirer of 'records', threw his hat into the air, oblivious of the fact that the old Marston Ground was covered with puddles, in one of which the hat alighted. On this occasion the take-off was from cinders, but at the meeting at Lillie Bridge a fortnight later the competitors, who had a very fine warm day, took off from the grass, and Brooks cleared on this occasion 6 ft 2 1/2 in. We have heard from 'Bob Rogers', who was on the ground as official time-keeper and was standing close by, that Brooks' feet went two or three inches above the bar when he cleared this remarkable height. At the championship meeting three days later Brooks again cleared 6 feet, another magnificent performance, as he took off from very wet spongy grass. This was his last performance in public.

The next few years produced one or two good jumpers, but Brooks' record still seemed quite unapproachable. In 1878 a Northerner, G. Tomlinson, who in face and figure seemed a smaller edition of F. T. Elborough, won the championship with 5 ft 10 1/2 in., and we believe on other occasions cleared 6 feet. He was a very pretty jumper, but took his leap a bit sideways. Another fine performer was the Cantab, R. H. Macaulay, another all-round performer, who, when he became after some seasons of football a bit too heavy and stiff for jumping, developed into a fine quarter-mile runner. Macaulay when m his first year at Cambridge was able to clear nearly 6 feet, and in 1879 he won the championship with 5 ft 9 1/2, in. He was a very strong, loosely built man, and his style of jumping was to take off a long way from the bar and go over with a great bound and with his head and shoulders well up, so that at the moment of the clearing the bar the body was almost perpendicular, not leaning back as was the case with Brooks.

The only jumper, however, who up to the present has rivalled the reputation of Brooks is the Irish athlete P. Davin, a member of a very well-known athletic family, his elder brother, M. Davin, having made a great reputation as a weight-putter, and another brother, T. Davin, having won several Irish championships at high and long jumping. In 1880 P. Davin is reported to have beaten Brooks' record by clearing 6 ft 2 3/4 in. at his native place at Carrick-on-Suir, and in proof of the record we believe that the certificates of two local justices of the peace as to the correctness of the measurement were lodged with the Field. There is indeed not the least reason to doubt the bona fides of the performance, but it is perhaps natural that a good many Englishmen should have suspicions that Irish patriotism might manage to elongate a measurement by a quarter of an inch when the downfall of Saxon supremacy could be secured thereby. In 1881, Davin came over for the English championship and won with a leap of 6 ft 0 1/2 in. His appearance was watched with great interest, and he certainly showed magnificent power on that day, winning the long jump as well with a leap of 22 ft 11 in. Davin was a tall strong man of quite 6 feet in height, and might almost be described as a young giant, being, although very well-shaped, a strong, heavy man. His style of leaping was quite different from that of Brooks, as he trotted up towards the posts and with one prodigious bound in the air went clean over the bar. In one of his leaps, when he was clearing about 5 ft 9 in. height, we saw him take off six feet before the bar and alight six feet on the other side, and when over the bar his body was almost perpendicular. In fact he took a downright honest leap at the bar in much the same way as a man would leap over a hedge and ditch from a road.

Of late years Ireland has certainly produced many fine jumpers, and there can be little doubt that it is an amusement for which the Celtic race has a natural aptitude. For the half dozen years preceding 1886, both the high and long jump championships have fallen more often to Irish and Scotch competitors than to native Englishmen.

The Scotchman J. W. Parsons, who was English champion in 1880 and 1883, deserves a word of notice. Compared with Brooks and Davin, he may be ranked as a small man, and, if our recollection serves us aright, stands about 5 ft 9 in.; yet in 1883 he cleared 6 ft 1/4 in., which, when compared with his height, shows him to be a performer almost of the calibre of the other two. The champion of 1885 – Kelly, an Irishman – cleared 5 ft 11 in., and it may probably be said with truth that the average of high jumping at country sports is better in Ireland than in England. Except, however, in jumping and weight-putting, the average performer at English sports is better than the average Irishman.

The improvement made of late years in long jumping is even more marked than it has been with high jumping, and it seems almost absurd to us nowadays, when almost every fair sprinter can clear 20 ft, to know that up to 1870 every championship was won with a leap of less than 20 ft. The truth is that it was not till some years after sports had been instituted that the value of speed as a factor in long jumping was discovered. The old jumper took a short run and a big spring; the modern long jumper starts fifty yards from the take-off, sprints up as hard as he can, and is going his hardest when he takes his leap. The result is that the mere impetus takes him the extra foot or two over the ground by which the moderns excel their predecessors.

In practising, therefore, for the long jump the athlete must prepare himself in much the same way as the high-jumper and sprinter, taking care not to get stiff. There must also be a constant and assiduous practice in jumping, as the main element of success is to get a good take-off at full speed from the right spot, and this is much easier said than done. Indeed, it is the commonest thing, even in championship and other first-class competitions, to see the competitors 'muff' their take-off, or sometimes take off a foot before the line, and so be credited with having jumped a foot less than they have actually covered.

The theory upon which the rules of long jumping appears to be founded is that the jumper is clearing a river or a pit. Thus a board is placed flat with the ground, or a line marked, and the jump is measured from the starting line. The ground after the line should be hollowed out, so as to make it impossible for the jumper, if he over-run the line, to get a jump at all. If he fall back after alighting from his jump, the jump is lost; and the distance is, of course, measured from the taking-off line to the first part where the hindmost heel touches the ground upon alighting.

We have said before that it is no uncommon matter to find a sprinter clearing his 19 or 20 feet, not really because he is a born jumper, but simply from his pace, and from his having learnt to take-off when going at full speed; but out of the scores of men who can cover 20 feet, only very few can reach 21 feet, and the man who can jump that extra foot is a good performer. Nearly all these good jumpers seem to attain the extra foot or more by the kick or jerk which they get from the back either at the moment of taking-off or in mid-air. We have seen many jumpers in mid-air throw out their legs well in front of them with a jerk of the back, and alight a foot farther than the place where they seem bound to touch the ground. There is a good deal of art in knowing exactly how far the legs can be safely shot out, for if this be overdone the jumper will fall backwards and lose his jump. In fact, there is a great deal more skill in long jumping than is generally believed, and it is one of the competitions in which men show most uncertain form, for the slightest attack of the nerves may prevent a man getting anything like a decent take-off, or may make him forget his usual trick of throwing out his legs, causing him to skim along the ground, or jump too high in the air. Year after year sees men who have jumped 21 1/2 or 22 feet at Oxford or Cambridge, fail to reach much more than 20 feet at Lillie Bridge; and there is little time to recoup a bad beginning, as at most each jumper does not have more than six tries.

The long-jumper, like the sprinter, may be a man of almost any size or weight. He may be a giant like Baddeley or Davin, or a little light-weight like E. J. Davies, a short middle-weight like the Irishman Lane, or a tall middle-weight like Lockton. All these, together with J. W. Parsons, of whom we have spoken before as a high-jumper, have probably been capable of clearing 23 feet upon a good day, and yet it would be hard to say that as regards physique they presented any one quality in common.

We have said that it was not until 1871, when Davies and R. J. C. Mitchell tied for the championship with 20 ft 4 in., that 20 feet was cleared at a championship meeting, and before Davies appeared on the scene only one Inter-Varsity winner had cleared 21 feet, this being in 1868; and at that time A. C. Tosswill, the hero of the performance, was considered an absolute phenomenon. In 1882, however, Davies, who had by this time developed into his true form, threw all the preconceived notions of jumping ability into the shade by showing himself capable of clearing 22 feet almost any day he liked. He won the Inter-Varsity jump, in

1872, with 21 ft. 5 in., and the championship of the same year with 22 ft 7 in. In the championship of 1873 he did not compete; but in 1874 he again covered 22 ft 5 in., having in the Inter-Varsity jump of that year, a few days before, cleared 22 ft 10 1/2 in., then the record of the sport. Up to that time, indeed, Davies was as much the superior of the jumpers who had preceded him as was Brooks a few years later in the kindred sport of high jumping, and his case was like that of Brooks in another point, that the first man who rivalled his great reputation came from Ireland. In the Irish Civil Service sports of 1874 Davies was beaten by J. Lane, who cleared 23 ft 1 1/2 in. We never saw Lane jump, but gather from a sporting annual that he was 5 ft 8 in. in height, and weighed in 11 st 2 lb., a good weight for a man of that height. It is still somewhat a moot point whether Lane's jump ought to be received as a genuine performance, as it has been averred with vehemence, and denied with equal vehemence, that there was a fall in the ground. In truth, however, it is very difficult indeed, when it comes to an inch or two, to judge between one jump and another, as a little wind more or less behind the jumper, or a slight drop in the ground, may make a good deal of difference. It is seldom, also, that the run for the jump is on perfectly level ground, as it is impossible to place the jumping ground, with its prepared surface and hollowed pit, in the middle of the levelled running path. For several years, therefore, and we might almost say up to the present day, the question must remain undecided as to which of the pair was the best of all jumpers. Their performance was never even approached for several years.

In 1878 the Universities turned out simultaneously a pair of fine jumpers, C. W. M. Kemp of Oxford, one of a very wellknown athletic family, and E. Baddeley of Cambridge. At the Oxford and Cambridge meeting, Kemp, who was a light-weight, wiry, and of more than medium height, beat Baddeley by a few inches, winning with 22 ft 2 3/4 in. Kemp was, we think, not quite so good, but more certain than his opponent, and always jumped with great coolness and judgment, never failing when fit to get a good jerk in mid-air and fling his legs well out in front of him. At the championship meeting, in the same year, Baddeley turned the tables on his opponent, winning with the fine jump of 22 ft 8 in. on perfectly level ground. Baddeley was a very tall, heavy man, weighing over 13 stone, strongly and loosely built, and was also the hammer-throwing champion in 1878 and 1882. He occasionally made a poor show at long jumping, through failing to jump sufficiently high and skimming too near the ground. As he had a great natural spring in his muscles, it suited him better to leap a trifle higher than his lighter opponent Kemp.

Lockton, who made his mark also as a sprinter and hurdler, was another magnificent long-jumper, having time after time done over 22 feet in public. When a lad of seventeen at school he entered for the long-jump championship, and as Davies, who was also entered, did not put in an appearance, Lockton was indulged with a walk over. In 1875, 1879, and 1880 he also won this championship, on the two latter occasions clearing over 22 feet. Indeed, Lockton, from the time he was eighteen, was always good for 22 feet; and cleared within an inch or two of this distance at his school sports, when still at school.

Lockton did not figure prominently at sports after 1880, and since his time it is hardly too much to say that most of the best long-jumpers have been Irishmen or Scotchmen. Parsons, of Edinburgh University, who was, as we have described, a light-weight of medium height, not only cleared 6 ft 1/4 in. at the championship at Lillie Bridge in 1883, but on the same day won the long-jump championship with 23 ft 1/4 in. The weather was fine and warm, but as he was neither aided by wind nor drop in the ground, the double performance on the same day marks him as a marvellous jumper. Parsons, like Kemp, jumped always with great judgment, never taking off short of the line, and throwing his legs well out in front of him.

In 1881 P. Davin won the English championship at the Aston Grounds, Birmingham, with a jump of 22 ft 11 in., but was aided by a decided drop in the ground. Davin's long jumping was like his high jumping; he had a remarkable natural spring in his muscles and jumped well into the air with perfect grace and no twisting of the back or jerk of the body. Two years later he is credited with having, at Portarlington, in Ireland, covered 23 ft 2 in., just half an inch more than Lane's jump of 1874, and there does not seem to be any fair reason for disputing the record. In 1882 the championship again fell to an Irishman, T. M. Malone, who was a slighter man than Davin, but jumped in exactly the same style. Malone, who was also a fine sprinter, has since earned a great reputation as a professional runner in Australia. Since then an Irishman, J. Purcell, has won our championship, jumping in exactly the same style, being able to clear over 22 feet. In fact there is no doubt that there is an Irish style of long jumping which most of the English jumpers are physically unable to imitate. Experience may almost be said to show that in natural 'springiness' the Celtic muscle is superior to the English.

WEIGHT-PUTTING

At first sight it would seem that jumping and heavy-weight throwing were the very opposite poles of athletic sport, but experience shows this to be very far from the truth, and in many cases the champion at weight-putting or hammer-throwing will be found to be either an active or a retired jumper. The truth is that both strength and elasticity of muscle are required for weight-putting and hammer-throwing, and it is therefore not hard to understand why both these latter competitions are more natural to, and are more practised by, the Celts of Scotland and Ireland than by the English. Both competitions, however, form part of the regular programme of an English athletic fixture, and are included at the Championship and Inter-Varsity meetings.

The rough-and-ready experiences of the pioneers of the athletic movement decided that a 16-lb. weight and a 16-lb. hammer would give the best test of an athlete's ability to manipulate a heavy weight; at the present day, therefore, in England nearly all the weight-putting competitions are with a 16-lb. weight, which is put 'without follow' from a 7-foot square. In Ireland, Scotland, and America, however, the putting, hurling, or slinging of heavier weights is often practised. In the present work we think it better to confine ourselves to noticing the English practice of the sport alone.

The English rule for the sport of weight-putting as formulated by the Athletic Association runs as follows: 'The weight shall be put from the shoulder with one hand only, and without follow, from a 7-foot square. The weight shall be of iron, and spherical, and shall weigh 16 lb. All puts shall be measured perpendicularly from the first pitch of the weight to the front line of the square or to that line produced.' The definition requires perhaps a few words of explanation. The weight must first be 'put' from the shoulder, not 'bowled'. There have been cases where men with fine muscles of the arm and chest have been able to 'bowl' a 16-lb weight like a cricket ball farther than it can be put in the legitimate style. In a legitimate 'put' the elbow is directly below the hand and close to the side where the weight is delivered. Secondly, there must be no 'follow', that is, after the weight is delivered the 'putter' must draw back and not allow the impetus given to his body to carry either foot over the front line, or he will be 'no-balled', to borrow a phrase from cricket. Thirdly, the weight must be of iron. There really seems to be very little reason for this restriction, which, as a matter of fact, gives an advantage to men with large hands. A leaden weight is smaller and more handy, and a man with a small hand has better command over a leaden ball, and can certainly put further with it. The restriction of the nature of the metal has probably been instituted for the purpose of getting one fixed standard for estimating the relative value of performances at different places.

The main point to learn in weight-putting is to 'get one's weight on' – to use a rowing phrase – that is to say, to employ mere arm-work as little as possible, and to get the impetus for propulsion from a rapid spring and turn of the body. The method adopted for securing this by all good weight-putters is the following. The putter balances his body on the right leg (supposing him to be right-handed and putting with the right arm), with his right shoulder thrown back and the weight on his right hand close to the shoulder; he then raises the weight up to the full stretch of his arm two or three times to stretch the muscles, the left arm and leg usually being thrown forward to balance the body. A quick hop is then taken about three feet towards the mark; at the end of the hop the left leg touches the ground, but the right shoulder is kept back, and the weight of the body is still on the right leg. A sharp spring is then taken towards the scratch line and the body swung rapidly round a half turn, so that when the weight leaves the hand the right shoulder and leg are forward, and the left shoulder and leg behind. The weight is thus propelled more by the swing of the body than by the jerk of the arm. The best weight-putter, therefore, is not necessarily the tallest, heaviest, or strongest man, but he who can bring, roughly speaking, the greatest momentum by the turn of his body to the delivery of the iron ball. It thus gives a scope for agile strength; youth has its opportunity to compete with the matured power of riper age, and often a quite small light man is able to put really great distances; of course, however, height and weight have great advantages. An attempt was, indeed, we believe, once made to induce Chang, the Chinese giant, to enter for one of the championship meetings, it being thought that he must necessarily be able to put a great distance, as he would have been like an ordinary man throwing the weight out of a first-floor window. We fancy, however, that had the Celestial competed he would not have been in the hunt with the more skilful Britons.

For many years the weight-putting record was held by E. J. Bor, a gigantic member of the L.A.C., who put 42 ft 5 in at the championship of 1872. This was never surpassed until 1885, although there were plenty of fine weight-putters in the interval. R. J. C. Mitchell, the high and long jumper, twice won the championship with puts of over 38 feet, and the two brothers J. and T. Stone, of Newton-le-Willows, also figure in the list of champions, the elder brother having won in 1867 and 1868, and the younger in 1875, 1876, and 1877. The latter was a fine specimen of manhood, weighing 14 stone and being over six feet, but beautifully proportioned, and no mean performer at a sprint. He was, however, beaten in Ireland in

1876 by M. Davin, an elder brother of the two famous jumpers; although, in 1877, Stone in England beat the Irishman, putting over 41 feet with a leaden weight. In 1878, 1879 (summer championship), and 1880 the champion was W. Y. Winthrop, an ex-Cantab and popular member of the L.A.C., whose prodigious feats of strength in other matters would require a volume to record them adequately, the most famous being, if report be true, the upheaval of a flagstaff by his own unaided efforts at a well-known watering-place in the North. In 1882 the championship fell to a Northerner, G. Ross of Patricroft, who was, we believe, a policeman. Ross 'put' in a most unusual style, and was rather a puzzle to judges and referees. He commenced as if about to bowl the weight, but straightened his arm with a jerk, which brought the elbow into the side just before the weight left the hand. In the championship of 1882 he put 42 ft 4 in., only one inch less than Bor's record. Ross was not a very big man, nor yet very agile, but had enormous strength of arm, and his remarkable ability was, we think, due to his style of putting, of which he was, as far as we know, the first and last exponent. The next two years' championships fell to Owen Harte, a giant from the Irish constabulary. In 1885 Scotland had her turn, the champion being D. J. Mackinnon, of the London Scottish Football Club, the best weight-putter we ever saw. He was quite a young man, about 6 ft 6 in. in height, and broad in proportion, although not fleshy. He was always a conspicuous object in the football field, where his gigantic form towered over the scrimmages. He put in his championship win 43 ft 1/2 in., thus finally disposing of the old record. A few days afterwards, however, this performance was beaten at the Irish championship of 1885 by J. O'Brien, another member of the Irish constabulary, whose performance was 43 ft 9 in. This has since been surpassed by the 'put' of a Canadian, G. R. Gray, who accomplished 44 ft 9 in. at Dublin in July, 1888. Gray was only of medium height and size, which makes the performance still more wonderful.

It is hardly to be expected that the youthful undergraduates of Oxford and Cambridge should produce weight-putters of such excellence as their runners and jumpers. The best exponent of the art at the Universities, J. H. Ware, who won the event four years in succession from 1882 to 1885, was, however, a really first-class performer, having on occasions put over 39 feet, and it was unfortunate that he was unable to compete at the championship in 1886. Ware, like most of the other fine weight-putters, was a giant in height and build.

HAMMER-THROWING

Hammer-throwing is a sport which in its present form has come to us from over the Border, although the 'hurling of the bar or sledge' was, as we have already seen, one of the sports of merry England. Since the introduction of the sport into modern athletic meetings, the weight of the hammer has always been the same as that of the weight used in weight-putting, viz. 16 lb; but the rules as to length of handle, the length of run allowed, and measurement still vary. The original rules, followed both at the championship meeting and the Oxford and Cambridge sports, allowed the hammer-thrower to use a hammer of any length, to take as much run as he liked, and throw from any place he liked, the judge marking the place where the thrower had his front foot at the moment when the hammer left his hands. The measurement was then taken in a straight line from the thrower's foot to the pitch of the hammer. At the championship meeting after 1875 a 3 ft 6-in. hammer and a 7-foot run without follow alone were allowed, although at the Oxford and Cambridge sports the old rules went on until 1881, and even now the Oxford and Cambridge rule is different to that used at the championship meeting. In America, and at some Scottish meetings, the hammer is thrown standing, without a run at all. The rule of the Athletic Association, however, which was used at the championships until 1886, and followed at nearly all the places in England where the sport is practised at all, ran as follows: 'The hammer shall be thrown from within a circle of 7 feet in diameter. The head of the hammer shall be of iron, and spherical, and the handle shall be of wood. The head and handle shall weigh together 16 lb. The total length of the hammer shall not be more than 4 feet.' In 1887 the circle was enlarged from 7 feet to 9 feet. We must confess to thinking that the limited run, short hammer, and no follow make hammer-throwing a fairer, prettier, and more skilful sport than the original form of the competition.

The main point to learn in throwing the hammer is to get as much impetus as is possible upon the body by rapidly spinning round, the arms being held perfectly rigid with the hammer grasped in the hands. At the moment when the greatest impetus is obtained, the hammer is let go, an extra push being given at the last moment by a jerk of the whole body. 'No actual arm-work is used at all, the strain falling mainly upon the back and loins; indeed, one or two famous hammer-throwers, like W. Lawrence of the O.U.A.C., have only used one arm to hold the hammer. The hammer is swung round, when once the thrower has begun his spin, at right angles to the body in its vertical position, and the arm and handle thus act as one and the same lever. A very slight grasp of mechanical principles will show that the hammer-head is, as it were, attached to the circumference of a revolving circle, the motive power being supplied by the spinning human body at the centre. At the moment of leaving go, the centrifugal force causes the hammer to fly off in a straight line. It follows that the hammer will fly farthest when the greatest momentum, i.e. weight and speed combined, can be produced. It is therefore obvious that, where an unlimited run is allowed, the heaviest man, provided he can acquire enough skill to spin round fast without falling over, must inevitably be able to throw the hammer farthest. Height also will be a great advantage, as it will enable a larger handle to be used, and the weight starting from a higher point, will travel farther before touching the ground. Under the old system, when the art had been brought to the highest degree of perfection, the spectator could hardly help arriving at the conclusion that one athletic sport at least had passed the line which divides the sublime from the ridiculous. Three or four heavy men would come out, wielding what looked like a poker of 5 feet in length, and would spin round five or six times like teetotums with almost inconceivable rapidity, after which the missile would hurtle forth north, south, east, or west, no man knowing in which direction it would be likely to fly off. As a result, not only was the sport dangerous to spectators, but it came with many of them to be considered as the comical element of the meeting. Dangerous we say it was to spectators. On one occasion an Oxford athlete neatly picked off a college scout, who, however, escaped with a broken arm; but the unfortunate judges were almost in peril of their lives at each throw, being somewhat in the same enviable position as we have recently been told is the engineer who fires a big gun on one of her Majesty's ironclads. With unskilful performers also there was even more comedy and more chance of a tragedy, as they had absolutely no control over their weapon, and in their efforts to spin round rapidly found often that, instead of having thrown the hammer, the hammer had thrown them.

Hammer-throwing was introduced into the Oxford and Cambridge programme in 1866, and has always since been cultivated both at Oxford and Cambridge. It has, however, never taken root at any other athletic centre in England, and the championships have, with one exception (when a Londoner beat the Cambridge winner by 6 inches, with a very poor throw), been won either by University men or by Scotchmen or Irishmen. The sport is very popular in Scotland, and has also taken firm root in Ireland.

In 1873 an Oxford man, S. S. Brown (known as 'Hammer Brown', to distinguish him from numerous other Browns of the same college), eclipsed all previous performances by throwing over 120 feet; but in the succeeding year another and a greater hammer-thrower appeared at Cambridge in the person of G. H. Hales. Hales was an immensely tall man, 6 ft 4 in. or so, we should say, and practised hammer-throwing more assiduously probably than any one has ever done before or since. For some years he was continually making records and then eclipsing them with better ones, his final performance being 138 ft 3 in. in 1876. He used a handle of very great length with a leaden head, and certainly was a magnificent exponent of the science, spinning round many times with great rapidity, and being able on nearly every occasion to throw the hammer where he wished, which was not the case with some of the preceding champions, who threw very erratically.

Under the rule of the A.A.A. the thrower has only room for a couple of turns in his circle of 9 feet, and is bound to keep himself and his weapon under proper control, as if he 'follow' his hammer outside the circle he loses his throw. For the last ten years most of the championships have been won by Irishmen. One of these, Dr. W. J. M. Barry, is credited with the record under these rules, having thrown 134 feet 7 inches, a magnificent performance. The received record for a standing throw is 99 ft 7 in., which was thrown by C. A. J. Queckberner at New York, though I have been informed that a Scotchman, K. Whitton, has covered over 100 feet with a standing throw. It is difficult to settle records with so many varying rules.

Another pastime which is very popular in Scotland, but has never found favour in England, is that of 'tossing the caber'. It is an interesting sport which combines both strength and skill. The caber is a beam or small tree, or trunk of a tree, heavier at one end than the other. The athlete holds this perpendicularly, with the small end downwards, balancing it in his hand against his chest. He then 'tosses' it so as to make it fall on the big end. The usual performance at show meetings is to bring out a caber so big that none of the competitors can toss it clean over. A piece is then sawn off, and another round is tried. If more than one of the men toss it clean over, the farthest toss and the straightest fall mark the winner.

Another sport which is less frequent at athletic meetings than was the case a dozen years ago is that of throwing the cricket ball. The secret of a good throw is, as all cricketers are aware, to keep all the joints of the arm loose until the throw is taken, and then to stiffen at once with a simultaneous jerk the muscles of the shoulder, elbow, and wrist. The Oxford cricketer, W. H. Game, has we believe thrown the farthest distance on record, something over 127 yards with a good strong wind behind him; and the Etonian, W. F. Forbes, is credited with having done some magnificent throws while he was still a schoolboy. It is a pity that so fine a sport, which ought to attract the entries of many cricketers, is being allowed to fall out of the programme at open meetings.

Yet another sport, not often practised, but very popular with spectators, is pole jumping. A pole of from 10 to 12 feet in height, shod with one or in some cases three iron spikes, is used, and is grasped with palms facing each other, one hand above the other, that hand being uppermost which is on the opposite side to the foot from which the spring is taken. As a rule, the lower hand is placed upon the pole a little below the height of the bar which the jumper is about to clear. A short run is then taken, the pole planted firmly in the ground, and the holder makes his spring. When the pole reaches the perpendicular, the jumper, who holds his body perfectly rigid, by strength of back, arms, and wrist swings himself horizontally over the bar, throwing the pole back behind him so as not to knock down the bar with it. The skilful jumper often raises his body some way above his hands, and so clears a height which at first seems impossible. Of course the high-jumper has a great advantage at this sport, as his first spring is a great deal higher than that of any ordinary novice attempting the sport, and it is an almost invariable rule that the good pole-jumper is a fine performer at a high jump, as is the case with T. Ray, the champion, who has cleared 11 ft 6 in., and is good for 11 feet upon almost any occasion. At the present time Ray is probably able to jump a foot higher than any other man in England.

A friend has told us that he once saw a small acrobat at a circus clear far greater heights by the simple process of clambering up the pole like a monkey as soon as it was poised, and then dropping over the bar; but we have always felt inclined to believe that this story was on a par with that other, of an Indian juggler who threw a rope up in the air and then climbed up it and disappeared. Something, however, of the trick suggested is employed by Ray, who shifts his hands up the bar when his pole is poised in the air. The sport certainly gives scope to fine athletic qualities, as the pole-jumper must be a high-jumper, and also agile enough to raise his body by help of the pole over the bar. The pole-jumper is thus usually a light-weight, but this is not the case with Ray, who is a well-shaped man of decidedly heavy build. His success is no doubt partly due to the effect of an athletic tradition, as he comes from Ulverston, a place which has produced many fine pole-jumpers, one of whom was E. Woodburn, the champion of 1874, who probably ranks next in order of merit after Ray and Stones. We believe that the Ulverston lads are often to be seen after their day's work practising pole-jumping on the cinder heaps which are so conspicuous an ornament of that flourishing town.

Broad jumping with poles, which has been practised for centuries in the fen countries for reasons of utility, has never been adopted at athletic meetings, which is somewhat strange, as it would be a fine branch of legitimate sport. There are one or two other games or sports which occasionally find a place in an athletic programme. In country meetings especially the spectators often like the introduction of the comic element, and this taste is provided for in different ways. 'Three-legged races', or as they are sometimes called, 'Siamese Twin' races, are competitions between pairs of men running stride by stride with the left leg of one runner tied to the right leg of the other. If they fail to keep in stride the pair necessarily tumble over. Then there is the 'sack race', in which every competitor gets inside a sack, which is tied round his neck, and some shuffle while others bound towards the winning-post. Of late years, however, the place of these two old-fashioned sports has been taken by what is known as the 'tug of war', which is the dignified title given to a pulling match, in which teams of equal numbers pull against each other. This is really one of the oldest of English sports, and long before it was cultivated as a regular sport was played at schools under the title of 'French and English', and even, we believe, forms part of a nursery game known as 'Oranges and Lemons', a somewhat mysterious title, of which we have been unable to discover the origin. Quite decently the Athletic Association, at the urgent request of many club committees, have framed a special rule for the tug of war, as disputes were frequently arising as to the right of competitors to dig holes in the ground, or to sit down during the pull to prevent themselves being pulled over. The present rule, which is printed later on amongst the other competition rules of the A.A.A., obliges the competitors to keep on their feet and prevents them making holes in the ground before the start. There is no doubt that the sport is a highly popular one, and there is equally little doubt that combination is most important for success. The experienced team does not attempt to shift ground, but pulls in the rope by a series of tugs, taking the time from the leader. One of the strangest of the athletic competitions we have ever seen is the tug of war as practised in the United States. There the opposing teams sit down, facing each other, in two pits filled with soft earth, and pull sitting, getting into a dreadful mess during the process. The hindmost man of each team wears a broad belt with iron bars on it, and, directly an inch of rope is pulled away from the other side, this hind-man (called 'the anchor') whips the rope round the bars to prevent its being pulled away again. After five minutes or so the miry opponents are told to desist, and usually one side is found to have won by a few inches. We must confess to thinking the English tug of war a better test of skill and pluck than the American game.

5
Training

When the great athletic movement first became popular in England there was much strenuous opposition to it, not only from timid parents but also from the medical profession. Upon whatever ground this latter opposition was based, there is no doubt that the parental prejudice was not so much to the athletics as to the 'training'. To the athlete of early times as well as to his friends and relations the essential part and chief characteristic of training was not the taking of proper preparatory exercise, but the sudden and violent change of diet. 'Going into training' was taken to mean the commencement of a peculiar diet of half-cooked beefsteaks and dry bread and the reduction of the daily drink to a minimum, and not to imply the beginning of the proper training or cultivation of the muscles required for a race. Even to the present day the word 'training' is applied in its popular connotation to the choice of diet alone. It is scarcely to be wondered that, in an age which considered that eating and drinking would do more to make a runner than the practice of running, the system of training adopted would be a mistaken one, and that the mistake should be glaring. Men going into training adopted a course of diet which did not agree with them, and accordingly became ill in body and ill in mind.

Of the very oldest system of training, which is now thoroughly obsolete, little need be said, as no amateur of recent years has thought of following it. It was a method which may almost be called pre-athletic, as it was m fact nothing but that adopted for training for the prize ring. The weight was to be reduced to its minimum at all hazards; the liquid consumed was to be a maximum of two pints a day, the edibles were almost entirely meat and bread, and the natural physical result of such a diet was counteracted by daily purging medicines. Sweating, meat-eating, and purging constituted the old system of training, and those who wonder how such a custom could ever have been adopted must recollect that it was chiefly applied to men of the lower classes, used to coarse food, and with no highly organised nervous system. It needs no argument to show that such a method could not be beneficial, or even practicable, to an amateur, who takes up athletic sports as a recreation, and not as a business.

However, while from the first amateurs admitted that the old plan was wrong, a movement happened which is well known to historians. The old creed was overthrown, but some of its principal errors were admitted in a modified form into the new system. Although common sense and practical experience are beginning at last to convince the athletic public that the less alteration a man makes in his ordinary diet when he goes into training the better he will fare, yet there are many who still start training for races handicapped by the traditional belief in the efficacy of a meat diet, daily 'sweating' runs for the sole purpose of reducing the weight, and the rigid abstinence from every drop of liquid which can possibly be dispensed with. The present writer, who has practised the opposite method, although according to the old canons of training he is by build and habit of body the very man to whom the rigid rules should have been applied, steadfastly declines to believe in any system of diet whatsoever which leads to eruptions of the skin or of the temper.

There is certainly this apparent justification for the traditional course, that, as a rule, people in modern times do not adopt as frugal and temperate a habit of diet as they should, and a great many of them are either without the inclination or without the opportunity of taking sufficient exercise. There is no reason why an athlete who desires to get fit should lead other than a natural life, or alter an ordinary natural diet more than is rendered necessary by the increased amount of exercise which he has to take. The ideal diet for a man who is engaged in active training of his body for a race is, and should be, that which under ordinary circumstances would be best for a healthy man who is obliged to take a very large amount of active exercise. What that diet is, is a matter for scientists to decide (or to differ upon, as they usually do in such matters), and a practical athlete can only speak of it empirically; but, happily, scientists and practical athletes are of one opinion at the present day in thinking that no diet which obliges a daily course of physic can be a healthy one. Physic may be, and often is, necessary during training, to remedy any mistake which has been made in diet; but it should be used as a remedy, and not as a part of the diet.

A further difficulty which arises in laying down any regimen for training is the indubitable physical fact that no two men are alike in their internal economy any more than they are in their outward features; and when proverbial philosophy informs us that 'one man's food is another man's poison', it becomes impossible to speak merely from practical experience with any absolute confidence. When, however, it is understood that the problem 'What should an athlete eat and drink when in training?' resolves itself into nothing more than this, 'What is a healthy diet for a young Englishman who wants to get his muscles hard and keep his wind good?' it will be seen that it should not be difficult to give some short and simple rules for guidance.

Plain cooked meats, and a reasonable quantity of fresh fruit and vegetables, should form the staple articles of diet. Beef, mutton, and chicken are, no doubt, more digestible than veal and pork, and therefore should be more frequently eaten, as indeed is the usual custom in ordinary life; but to treat veal and pork as so much poison, as some trainers do, is simply silly. Taken occasionally by a man who is accustomed to them, they form a pleasing change, and, where a healthy man has an appetite for any food, one can pretty safely say that he is able to digest it. Fish is light and nutritious, and may judiciously be taken at any meal in the day. Soup is, doubtless, not so strengthening as meat, and not so good for the wind; but if a man is fond of soup, he is much better with it than he would be in vainly attempting to relish the mutton of which he is sick. In fact, as long as the food is plain and simple, and neither too much of it is taken nor too little, the athlete is not likely to go far wrong. Eggs, when not hard-boiled, are both light and wholesome, but to take them upon the top of a heavy meal of other things is usually a mistake, and leads to the usual result of over-feeding – biliousness.

The most rigid of the trainers of the present day give chops or steaks and eggs for breakfast; beef or mutton again, with watercress, &c, and vegetables for lunch; and beef or mutton again in the evening, together with stewed fruit or rhubarb, and blancmange or rice-pudding. This is a good sample of diet, we have no doubt; but variety is pleasing, and as soon as any food, however healthy, begins to pall, it should be changed for something which, although less digestible, will please, and therefore reinvigorate the trainee.

As regards eatables, ordinary common sense can tell a man that heavy pastry, or 'stodgy' sweet puddings, or highly spiced dishes, are not healthy food, and that the less that is taken of them the better for the athlete; but, at the same time, one requisite for a healthy diet is that a man should like it. Porridge makes an admirable dish for breakfast, but not to a man who doesn't like it. Pepper and mustard may possibly be deleterious (as we have heard) to the coats of the stomach, and tea without sugar may possibly be healthier than tea with sugar; but if a man dislikes his beef without mustard, or his tea without sugar, he had much better use these condiments than go without them, and he will do well to have kidneys and bacon (which after all are not poisonous) for breakfast, rather than to force down his throat the admirable porridge which he may not happen to like. Nothing which is unpalatable should be eaten as a duty.

Another point to which an athlete in training should attend is the quantity of his food. The youthful aspirant to athletic honours usually begins by gorging himself, thus falling a victim to the same old error that for feats of strength the one thing needful is to eat strengthening food. The old system, as we have before said, was applied chiefly to pugilists of the lower classes, who, when not in training, probably got less and worse food than they really required; accordingly it suited them to eat more when they went into training. At the present day the well-to-do classes, with their three meat meals a day, eat more than they need. Doubtless their natural powers of digestion increase when they begin to take the increased amount of exercise which training for a race involves; but if, as soon as fresh air and exercise increase their digestive powers, they immediately increase the amount of food they take, they will end their training as they began it – short-winded and overfed. In this, as in other matters of diet, it is difficult to give exact advice, but our strongly expressed opinion is that it is better to run the risk of eating too little in training than to run the risk of eating too much. A strong and healthy man may easily weaken himself by over-feeding, but he will not be at all likely to reduce his strength by taking less food than he absolutely requires.

Many men in training have their chief meal in the middle of the day, and a great many doctors recommend this as more healthy, saying that the digestion is stronger in the earlier part of the day, and that when the body is jaded after the day's work it is not fair to put a strain upon the digestion in its weakened state. Whether this view be right we do not pretend to say, and content ourselves with offering the practical advice that the athlete should dine at that hour when he feels most hungry. Men who are accustomed to dine in the evening may, we think, advantageously stick to their old practice when in training, and take their chief meal after their day's work. Of one thing only we feel convinced, that a man in training (unless his consumptive powers be as abnormal as those of Milo of Crotona) does not want a heavy lunch and a heavy dinner as well. If he dine in the middle of the day, his breakfast and supper should be lighter in proportion, and if he dine late he will want only a light lunch of a chop, or a plate of cold beef and vegetables, with little or nothing else. On the whole we prefer the system of a good breakfast, light lunch, and a moderate dinner after the day's work.

Of recent years trainers of crews or athletes have come round to a sensible view of what should be eaten. In our opinion, however, their views on the question of what should be drunk are not equally sound. For one thing it is obviously unreasonable to prescribe exactly the same amount of liquid for a small man and a big man, and to say that this quantity, and no more, must be taken whatever the amount of the day's work has been, and whether the day has been cold or warm. Yet this is a course which we have constantly seen adopted. The old theory was, as we have said, that a man, to get down his weight and make his body hard, should take the smallest quantity of liquid that he could possibly get on with. That theory is practically extinct, but it has left its legacy behind in the fixed notion of the trainer that there must be a definite amount of liquid fixed for each man and each meal. In speaking on this point we necessarily have to follow the same line of argument which we have adopted with regard to eating. It stands to reason that a man taking violent exercise and perspiring freely requires more liquid than he does during his ordinary life. But – and it is a very important 'but' – the majority of men drink a great deal more than they want, by which we do not mean that they take too much alcoholic stimulant, but that they take too much liquid, to the great harm of their digestions; and in this kind of over-drinking we believe teetotallers are the worst offenders. It is also a well-known fact that taking too much liquid does more to make the body fat and heavy than taking too much solid food. The conclusion we arrive at is, therefore, that a man who goes into training needs more drink than he does at other times, but should take less than he is in the habit of taking, unless he is more temperate than the majority of his fellow-creatures are. The athlete in training should never drink between meals unless he is absolutely thirsty, in which case he should drink to assuage his thirst and not for enjoyment; and at meal times he should drink as much as he reasonably feels a craving for. If the drink be unnaturally stinted, the man will soon break down, his skin will get unhealthy, and his sleep and digestion will be impaired. Doubtless it is quite true that a couple of good-sized cups of tea at breakfast, half a pint of liquid for lunch, and a pint at dinner is enough for most men in training; but to hold that a man who finds himself parched after his exercise at four o'clock is to wait until his dinner at seven before he can touch a drop of liquid is to turn a useful generalisation into a ridiculous rule. Rigid rules as to the quantity and quality of diet and exercise are not to be relied upon, and the effect of giving a man so much beer for dinner, and telling him he must under no circumstances have any more, leads to most absurd scenes and unsatisfactory results. Some great brawny fellow – perhaps the strong man of the crew – eyes his pint of beer with a wistful gaze, and does not take anything more than just a sip when he cannot possibly get his food down without it, in the vain hope that at the end of dinner he will have enough left to have a really good drink, and cease to feel thirsty for the first time during the day. It needs no doctor to say that the man who eats his dinner under such circumstances will fail to get the full benefit out of it, notwithstanding that he has fulfilled the requirement so dear to dyspeptics of eating his food dry.

It is often urged in reply to the argument that rigid rules of diet are a mistake, that if you give a man carte blanche to eat and drink whatever he thinks good for him, his wishes will be fathers to the thought that everything for which he has contracted an unhealthy fondness will be beneficial. To this we answer that a man knows perfectly well when he has eaten enough, and, in fact, cannot eat too much when in active exercise without finding it out; that the same rule applies to drink, and that if a man is unable to keep himself from taking solids and liquids which he does not require he will never be of any account as an athlete. The absurdity of the old system is shown from the fact that it was the frequent custom of the 'owners' of professional pugilists and pedestrians to put a watchman in attendance to see that their particular 'pet' in training did not sneak surreptitiously into public-houses or carry little bottles of liquid about with him in his pocket.

So much must be said as to the quantity of liquor. In the meantime there are other vexed questions as to the drink of the athlete. Until quite recently a man who trained upon teetotal principles was considered a *rara avis*, and the old English trainers believed in English beer as much as they believed in English beef and mutton. Of recent years, however, not only have temperance principles been widely preached, but the larger number of the oarsmen and athletes from America and Canada have adopted the system of training upon water alone, and taking no alcohol in any shape during training. From the views we have expressed above it will be seen that we are not likely to take one side or the other with great ardour, as we believe that there should be no violent change in the manner of living when a young and healthy man goes into training. We must confess, however, to have a strong leaning towards the Transatlantic or teetotal method of training. Whether alcohol be good or not we leave doctors to decide, but of all people in the world the athlete who is not over-trained least requires its stimulus. We believe doctors still differ upon the question as to whether it is nutritious to any degree, but all agree that it is very hard to digest, and this alone should be a strong argument against its use. Of one thing we feel confident, that if a man drinks water at his meals as a natural habit he will be very unwise to leave it off for beer or claret. If, however, he is accustomed to drink beer or wine, it is a hard thing to say that the athlete should give either up and take to water if he doesn't like it. We have seen men well trained upon beer, upon claret, and upon weak whisky-and-water, and are quite willing to admit that these beverages have done no harm. Any other wines, however, for a man in robust health are, we think, bad in training, as they excite the nerves and interfere with sound and quiet sleep. Of course, if a man is getting stale, good strengthening wine may do him a world of good; but as long as the athlete is not in this state, the glass or two of port, which he is often recommended to take, is exceedingly likely to do harm, and can hardly do any good. While, however, advocating training upon temperance principles, we wish to make it clear that circumstances and idiosyncrasies alter cases. A man with a naturally weak nervous organisation may find that old ale or a glass of port after dinner may prevent his training off through the work he has to undergo, and if such men take to the practice of athletic sports they must train on principles that suit their particular cases. With strong healthy men, however – the only men who in the present age of keen rivalry can indulge with perfect safety in athletic sports – we think that upon general principles the less alcohol they take the better.

So far it will be seen we have not suggested that a man in training should undergo any very serious trials and privations. There is one thing, however, which he must learn to do without, and that is smoking. While we are quite ready to admit that a moderate use of the comforting weed is not injurious to the health, there can be very little question that it tends to shorten the wind, and does so more especially when tobacco is indulged in between meals and not after them. Very probably many men, and especially sprinters training for short races, have smoked during training and done themselves no appreciable harm, as their smoking has been confined to a cigar or a pipe immediately after dinner; but even these cases, we should think are rare. The uses and functions of tobacco may almost be described as totally incompatible with the cultivation of athletic excellence. Tobacco is a narcotic; it is no doubt not only pleasant, but may be wholesome, to men whose nerves require soothing after hard brain-work and worry, but, except under abnormal conditions, an athlete in training can hardly want a narcotic; he wants to be brisk, vigorous, and robust, and anything which tends to make him lazy must do him harm for athletic purposes. In fact, to take a broad view of the uses of tobacco-smoking, it appears obvious that the men of the present day are almost universally adopting it, not because they are a degenerate and dissolute lot, but because the high pressure and forced mental activity of modern life have rendered a craving for it as a sedative only natural. But a man who requires a sedative to maintain his nervous balance is hardly likely to be a fit subject for the trainer's hands. By all means, then, let the man in training avoid smoking, and if from suddenly giving up the habit he finds he is unable to sleep, let him wean himself from smoking as quickly as possible.

Another mistake which a young lad just taking to training often falls into is to take too much sleep. With the old maxim that 'six hours' sleep is enough for a man, seven for a woman, and eight for a fool', we do not altogether agree, but experience shows that in ordinary cases seven hours of sleep are quite enough for a man who has not been taking any enormous amount of exercise during the previous day, and that eight hours is the maximum which can under any circumstances be beneficial to a man who is living a regular and temperate life. A young lad of eighteen or nineteen probably requires more sleep than an athlete who has passed out of his nonage and is fully developed, but at the outside more than eight hours' sleep should never be taken. Too much sleep engenders fat and makes the athlete slack, listless, and disinclined for his day's work. We have always wondered how the University freshmen, when they are just sent into training for the spring races, manage to survive the ordeal. They are gorged on meat, eggs, etc., three times a day. They have port wine and figs in the evening, and are sent to bed at ten to sleep until they rise in the morning again at eight o'clock to commence a fresh attack upon mountains of steaks and chops. Even quite apart from the food they take, the men would be slack and torpid from the amount of lazy sleep to which they are condemned.

Another point which is often disputed is the advantage of early morning work. All are, we think, agreed that a man should get into the open air and clear his lungs before breakfast. By these means he gives himself an appetite for his food, and the improvement in the wind which comes from thus getting out must soon be obvious. But it is a far more difficult matter to decide whether a man should do anything more before breakfast than get air into his lungs. Some men we have known actually to go hard spins before breakfast, others have taken walks of a mile or two, others merely stroll out and walk a quarter of a mile or so just for an 'airing'. Which of these courses should suit any particular individual depends both upon his constitution and his previous habits. Our own opinion is that as a general rule a man should never neglect to get out before breakfast, be it wet or fine, but should refrain from anything like work. We have seen so many men collapse in their training as soon as they tried work before breakfast that we are sceptical of its good results. But a walk of not more than a mile before breakfast is sure to do good to a healthy man. We need also scarcely say that, wet or fine, warm or cold, he should sleep with his window partly open. There can be no quiet sleep for a man in a confined atmosphere.

There is no reason why an athlete who makes his training consist of a sound and healthy system of living should break down in health, but without doing that he may nevertheless find himself *hors de combat* from some minor evils. Before a runner puts on his first pair of running-shoes he should pare his toenails close down to the flesh, or the pounding on the toes will result in the nail being pushed up at each stride. In a few days after this the nails will probably turn black, and in a week or two the runner may find himself minus one or two of them. All danger of this, however, is obviated by not allowing the nail to protrude in the slightest degree beyond the end of the toe. Occasionally the feet get tender from the exercise, and when this happens the athlete will do well to give up the cinder-track for the grass for a day or two. Soaking the feet in alum and water is also much recommended as a cure for tender feet. Prevention, however, is better than cure, and the best preventative is a soft washleather sock coming over the ball of the foot. This is also comfortable, and acts as a safeguard against blisters. With blisters the best thing is to prick them with a needle as soon as the water has collected in them; after this has been squeezed out, the old skin should be left on to protect the new skin growing underneath. If there are blisters on the foot half-formed, and the athlete is liable to them, the skin is best toughened and rendered least liable to them by taking a salt-and-water footbath in the evening. The tight shoes which are necessarily used by runners are also apt to create corns, which must be treated by the usual remedies which are known to housewives or to practitioners for the removal of these unwelcome visitors. The best means, however, to avoid blisters, corns, and such like ailments is to take a great deal of care in selecting a perfectly fitting pair of shoes; but of this we shall speak anon.

Strains of the muscles are more serious matters, and are sometimes very hard to cure; there is always, too, a danger that a slight strain of a muscle may get worse if rest be not taken. Experience shows that there is very little risk of the muscles giving way from anything but overwork in warm weather, but in cold weather muscles strain or snap without any warning; indeed, so many accidents of this kind happened at Oxford that notices were posted m the dressing-room at the old Marston ground warning runners not to go out into the cold without first rubbing their legs with a horsehair glove or with the hands, and not to undergo any violent exercise without taking a short trot to warm the muscles.

This precaution should certainly never be neglected at any time when the weather is at all chilly, and in the winter especially it is foolhardy to dispense with it. Slight strains of muscles are best treated by partial rest and the use of opodeldoc, or a mixture of arnica and opodeldoc as an embrocation. Of late years, too, the runners have frequently taken to using Elliman's embrocation, a mixture which was originally used by trainers of horses alone. A composition still frequently used by pedestrians is that which was recommended by Charles Westhall in his little book to which we have referred before in terms of praise. Westhall's recipe is as follows : 'Spirits of wine, 1/4 pint; spirits of turpentine, 1/4 pint; white vinegar, 1/4 pint. Mix these with a fresh egg beaten up, and give the bottle a good shake before using the mixture.'

If the strain of the muscle be very severe, something else besides an embrocation is required. Complete rest must be the rule, and if there is a swelling from injury to a joint this should be reduced by bathing in hot water. People frequently make the mistake of putting a sprained ankle immediately under a stream of cold water; cold water is invaluable to strengthen the muscle after the inflammation has gone down, but a hot fomentation is what is required to reduce the swelling. When the swelling has gone down, the 'cold tap' and embrocations are useful. Upon the same principle, too, that horses are 'fired', the outside of the ankle is often painted with iodine.

We have said before that one of the most satisfactory features about athletic sports, both to competitors and spectators, is that the winner wins on his own merits, and not from any superiority he may have obtained in equipment or apparatus. The oarsman may be helped to victory by a good boat, and the cyclist by a good machine, but the athlete can hardly win a race by having better shoes or knickerbockers than his opponent, though he often does win a race with worse legs than his rival, but with a better head. The apparatus of an athlete is simple and requires little description. His shoe should be of thin, good leather, which cannot possibly stretch, so that when once it fits the foot it may never wear loose. A shoe which slips on the foot in the slightest degree may not only impede the runner, but will assuredly blister the foot. The athlete, therefore, should get a pair of shoes to fit him like gloves, and then he will have all that mechanical skill can do for him. As we have said before, he will probably find it wise to wear a thin chamois-leather sock over the ball of the foot and toes. The ordinary running-shoe has only a single thickness of leather over the heel, and of course no spike there. The hurdler and jumper, however, who have to take every precaution against slipping, have two spikes in the heel of their shoes in addition to those in the toe, while the walker has a similar shoe with double thickness at heel and toe, and without any spikes. One other point only has to be attended to, and that is the length of the spikes. Obviously the harder the track is the shorter the spikes should be, so that upon a grass-track longer spikes are needed than upon cinders. For the tracks at Oxford, Cambridge, or Lillie Bridge, spikes of less than 1/2 inch in length will probably suffice if they be sharp; but the hurdler or a sprinter, who may be called upon to run over heavy grass, wants a shoe with at least 1/2-inch or 3/4-inch spikes. Most 'cracks', therefore, have several pairs of shoes with spikes of different length, and make their choice according to the state of the track over which they have to travel. In races over very long distances, shoes with very short spikes, and sometimes without spikes at all, are used, as the jar and concussion of travelling so far with a thin spiked sole may make the feet so blistered or tender as to drive the runner off the path or knock him to pieces before the end of the race.

Of the rest of the athlete's stock-in-trade there is little to be said. The knickerbockers or drawers, whether they be made of silk, merino, or thin flannel, are just knickerbockers and nothing more. They should be roomy enough not to interfere with the movement of the thighs, and should be short enough not to hamper the knee. A primrose to some people is a primrose and nothing more, and even to an athletic author a jersey is only a jersey. A word may perhaps be said, however, about the practice which some men have recently tried to introduce from

America of wearing sleeveless jerseys, which display the whole of the shoulder and the armpit. There is nothing to be urged in favour of the practice. A light sleeve over the shoulder cannot possibly impede a runner any more than a cobweb would, and the appearance of a runner with his shoulders and armpits uncovered is far from picturesque. Happily, when a runner appears so clad, his usual fate is to he marched off the track, and told that he will be allowed to come on again as soon as he is properly dressed, so we are little likely to be troubled with sleeveless jerseys in the future.

As regards the athlete's dress, it is very curious to notice the difference of custom in and out of the Universities. In London and the provinces the different competitors appear in different colours of knickerbocker and jersey, and, in addition, many clubs have a club-badge or emblem which each runner of that club sports upon his jersey. The result is that a big handicap shows a pretty variety of different hues. At Oxford or Cambridge every runner appears in virginal white, save the selected few who have represented their University at Lillie Bridge, and are therefore privileged to wear their white knickerbockers and jerseys trimmed with the blue ribbon of their club.

6
Athletic Meetings

If there be little to say of the individual athlete's requisites there is much that is interesting to note in the requisites for the meeting at which the athlete figures. The days are now gone when the champions of each neighbourhood met upon, the village-green, and took off their boots to run upon the nearest level piece of turf which was handy. A club which undertakes to hold a meeting has now to find a ground, prizes, officials, and a variety of implements and conveniences, which render the undertaking anything but a simple one. The first requisite of all is of course to get a ground, and it is of grounds therefore, that we first propose to speak.

In London, Birmingham, Oxford, Cambridge, and other great centres of amateur athletics there are regular running grounds, which can be engaged by a club which requires them. Nearly all the regular paths are 'cinder tracks', although of late years one or two have been made (chiefly for cycling purposes) not with cinders, but with burnt ballast or red brickdust. The making of a good path is a difficult and expensive undertaking, including as it does levelling, draining, and laying down of the cinders or brickdust. Excavation is made to the depth of from 12 to 18 inches, 12 inches being generally considered sufficient with a dry gravelly soil, while in a clay soil the full 18 inches is required. If the excavations be of 12 inches, about 5 or 6 inches of this is filled up with large brick rubbish, or what is known as ballast gravel – i.e. large stones which allow the water to drain through. Over the top of this, 3 or 4 inches of rough cinders are placed, so as to leave room for a layer of 3 inches of fine sifted cinders or brickdust upon the top. These 3 inches of fine stuff have to be put on in thin layers, to be watered from time to time and continually rolled. For the purpose of assisting the drainage, the centre of the path is usually raised slightly higher (not more than an inch) than the sides, and gullies are made at the side leading down to cesspools to carry off water which may collect after a sudden shower. When a good path is once made it wants little but rolling in wet weather and watering and rolling in dry weather to keep it in good condition. After many years, when the fine stuff off the top has been blown or carried away, and the coarser stuff below is working up, the top dressing may have to be renewed. Perhaps the better course is after each season to sprinkle a thin layer of cinders over the top of the path to keep it fresh.

Just at the present it would seem that fashion is changing round from black cinders to red brickdust as a top dressing for running tracks. The brickdust was, as we have said, originally used for cycling, but upon the inner path made at Lillie Bridge for wheels many foot-races were held with great success. No doubt the brickdust which has a slight mixture of loam is harder, and thus better suited for wheeling, and the fact that both Myers' 48 3/4 sec. for a quarter and George's 4 min. 12 4/5 sec. for a mile were accomplished upon the red track at Lillie Bridge seems to show that it is hardly less fitted for pedestrian contests. Probably, however, Myers and George both chose the inner track at Lillie Bridge, well knowing that the old cinder track upon the outside was getting worn out and in poor condition. The drawback of the red paths is that they get very hard and dead in wet weather, while a really well drained cinder path like that at Oxford or Stamford Bridge keeps its lightness, in spite of the ram, in a wonderful manner. We should not be surprised if the cinder track of the future for running purposes were to be a mixture of cinders and burnt brick ballast in equal proportions.

Until 1866 the Oxford and Cambridge sports were held upon grass courses either at the Christchurch cricket ground at Oxford or at Fenner's cricket ground at Cambridge. In 1867, however, the Universities moved up to London to the cinder track at the old Beaufort House at Walham Green, upon which the championship meeting of the previous year had taken place. The Beaufort House track was certainly not a good one, being loose and ill-drained, nor was its oval shape well suited for fair racing; however, it sufficed for championship and Inter-University meetings until 1869, when both meetings were shifted to the newly opened ground of the A.A.C. at Lillie Bridge. After it was got into working order the Lillie Bridge ground was certainly a very good one, perhaps as good and as fair a track as has ever been made. Like most other good paths, it was a third of a mile in circumference, but its chief merit in our opinion lay in the fact that the turns were well graduated. Although the corners were apparently sharp, by making the path slope downwards to the corner, the runners were prevented from running wide, and were given four straight stretches, one on each side of the ground. This, we think, is the right shape of path for every race under a mile, and especially for handicap races. The Cambridge ground at Fenner's is also constructed on this principle, there being no long gentle curves as there are at both ends of the ground at Oxford and at Stamford Bridge. Until 1876 the London Athletic Club used Lillie Bridge for their meetings, but the following year they took possession of their own private ground at Stamford Bridge. After that the Lillie Bridge track was undoubtedly left neglected, and in its latest years the old outer track was not good, the gravel underneath having worked up. In many places also the path was treacherous, the new cinders which had been placed at the top giving way under the feet of the runners. The Stamford Bridge track is, we think, about as badly shaped as a ground can be for any short races, but the track itself underfoot is almost as good as possible. The path is only a quarter of a mile in circumference, the lap consisting of two straight stretches of 120 yards each at the sides and two gradual curves of 100 yards each at the ends, and the quarter-mile races, as they were originally run upon the ground, were run over 200 yards out of 440 upon a curve. The ground was soon improved by a very long 'straight' of 250 yards extending up one side. The 250 yards and 220 yards races were run off on this long straight, and the first 250 yards of the quarter-mile races were also contested over this ground, which accounts, in a great measure, for the fast times done some years ago in short races at Stamford Bridge. In long races, where the pace is not so great, probably the long slight curves do not interfere with the times. Recently the long straight has been built over, and the ground is again left with the old defects. We are strongly of opinion that in every path there should be as much straight and as little corner as possible, or, in other words, that the path should be quadrangular with rounded corners, and not an oval with the two sides flattened. The fault of long curved stretches is also conspicuous at Oxford, though not to such a degree as at Stamford Bridge; but, on the other hand, there is no long straight at Oxford, and in a 300 yards' race on the Oxford ground half the distance has to be run round a curve. The long curves are most unfair in handicaps, and also in any race where there is a large field, as one runner passing another may have to come right out from the inside of the track and then have to come in again at once so as not to lose ground; besides this, the continual running in a curve must necessarily shorten the stride, and more ground is lost thereby than upon a short but sharper turn. The old Marston ground, although laid in a swamp and rightly deserted by the O.U.A.C. in 1877, was, we think, made in a better shape than the Iffley Road ground, although the cinder track at the latter place is certainly very fast and dry. The Cambridge track at Fenner's is both well laid and well-shaped, the only drawback to it being that the levels are not true. The starting-points of the quarter-mile, 300 or 220 yards races are higher than the finish, so that many of the fast times made over these distances at Fenner's are really untrustworthy. The Fenner's track, too, was built with the intention of making competitors run with their left hand to the inside of the track, the contrary being the practice at most other running grounds. Of recent years, we believe, the Cambridge runners have accommodated themselves to the general system, and run the other way round the ground, so that any times made by Cantabs running up-hill can scarcely be disregarded. Another well-known track, which has been remarkable for several fast times – that of the Aston Lower Grounds at Birmingham – was open to the same objection as Fenner's, on the ground of levels. In the Aston ground there was a drop of over 6 feet in the 300 yards course, and rather more, we think, in the quarter-mile course, the part between the finish and the beginning of the quarter being a stiff up-hill. As a result, the Records Committee of the A.A.A. has declined to take any notice of any performance done over less than a lap of a track which is not properly levelled; but it accepts performances where competitors have covered more than the full lap, and so run both up-hill and down-hill. Even this, however, can hardly be considered strictly fair, as experience shows that more time is gained running down a long and steady decline than is lost by coming up a short stiff incline. The Aston records can hardly, therefore, be considered satisfactory under any circumstances.

In considering the famous running grounds upon which so many cracks have toiled and 'spun', we have rather wandered from our main subject, that of athletic meetings. All the classical events of the year are held over regular running paths, but for an immense number of country and provincial gatherings there is no cinder track at hand. The committee arranging for the sports have therefore to procure the best field obtainable, which is usually the local cricket ground, and this has to be staked out with flags and ropes, so as to obtain as long a lap and as good turf as is possible. We are by no means so certain that where a well-shaped lap of really good dry level turf is obtained there is much difference in point of speed between cinders and turf; but it is very difficult indeed to get a piece of turf which will satisfy the requirements of a good running path in point of level and dryness. The majority of the fields used for local sports are cricket grounds of which the 'pitch' in the middle is perhaps beautifully level and in good condition, while the outside parts of the ground, upon which the races must necessarily be run, have probably been neglected. The majority of grass courses, therefore, are considerably inferior in every way to the regular running paths. Athletic 'cracks' of London and the Universities have got into the habit of thinking that no good thing can possibly come from grass courses, and are inclined to scout reports of any records having been made upon them. Still we would remind critics that there are grass courses and grass courses, and that a country cricket field mowed for the occasion round its edges is very different from the Private Banks cricket ground at Catford Bridge, Kennington Oval, or the Trent Bridge ground at Nottingham. The first and last of these are, we think, when the weather is favourable, little, if at all, inferior to the best cinder tracks that have ever been made, and we can quite understand how in longer races a grass course may suit some athletes better than cinders, there being less concussion at each stride. For a proof of our opinion we may point to the facts that H. R. Ball did his best and fastest quarter at Catford Bridge, Slade his fastest two miles at the Oval, Scott his fastest mile and Myers his fastest 1,000 yards at Trent Bridge. At the same time it is perfectly reasonable to feel doubtful about 'records' made over turf. The ground may not be level, the measurements may not have been accurately taken, and may be incapable of subsequent verification, the only boundaries being posts and ropes which are usually removed as soon as the day's sport is over.

When the ground is secured, the next thing for the secretary (to whom, as a rule, all preliminary arrangements are entrusted) is to get the entries. This for club meetings is often not so easy as it would appear. For the purpose of attracting a good 'gate', a Saturday afternoon or a public holiday is the favourite day for sports, and in the season the athlete has so many meetings to pick and choose from that something attractive is required to entice him. The usual enticement, we regret to say, is the best and most valuable prize which the finances of the club can stand and which the rules of the A.A.A. allow. Some years ago the A.A.A. stepped in to try and put a stop to pot-hunting, and limited the value of prizes which can be given in handicaps to 10*l* 10*s*, a sum which in our opinion is much more than is sufficient. At the present day, however, prize-getting is so much a business with the amateur athlete that the charge of 'pot-hunting', which a dozen years ago was considered discreditable, has now practically ceased to be a reproach at all with the sporting community, which reads with avidity notices in the paper that Mr A. or Mr B. has won 60*l* worth of prizes 'during the past week'. At the present day secretaries are glad enough to get the entries of men who really keep the prizes they win and do not, under the mask of amateurism, earn a living by selling their winnings. But our business at present is with the competitors as they are, and not with competitors as they should be, and we hasten to admit that there are still a few just men in Gomorrah.

Partly, however, to keep out the semi-amateur class, and partly to give the handicappers every opportunity of adjusting the starts fairly, every competitor is compelled to send in his entry for a meeting upon a regulation 'entry form'. By filling up and signing this he pledges himself to the assertion that he is an amateur within the meaning of the A.A.A. definition, which is printed on the paper, and he also gives an account of his last three performances in public, stating the amount of his start and the result in each race. If any wilful misstatement is found on these entry forms, the committee of the A.A.A. punishes the offender by suspension or disqualification.

Entries are usually made to close a week before the day of the meeting, to allow the handicappers (for at a club meeting the majority of events are handicaps) a few days' leisure to allot the starts. As a rule, however, when the meeting is on a Saturday, entries are frequently received on Monday morning, a very reasonable practice, as men who have run well on one Saturday are often inclined to enter for a meeting on the next Saturday, and might be unable to do this if their entries for the next meeting were bound to be in by the Saturday evening. The regulation entrance fee for a handicap is half-a-crown, and one of the most useful regulations of the A.A.A. enjoins that no entry shall be accepted unless accompanied by the fee. Secretaries of sports being anxious, however, to get as good fields and as many half-crowns as possible, to help to defray the cost of the prizes, are continually infringing this regulation, and in consequence unpleasantness frequently results. Secretaries of clubs enter their members, or friends enter their friends, and now and again the man whose name is entered fails to put in an appearance, being dissatisfied with his start, or is wrongly handicapped with too great a start, owing to the handicapper not having sufficient information with the entry to be able to identify the runner or gauge his abilities. In the first case, the absent runner now and then repudiates his liability for the fee; in the second case, if the runner turns up and wins the race the other competitors are loud in expressing their dissatisfaction. All this would be obviated if the secretaries would only do their duty and decline to take any notice of an entry not made upon a proper form and accompanied by the proper fee. In the long run we think this honest course would be the best policy, for if there is unpleasantness at a meeting one year the entries are sure to fall off at the next meeting promoted by the same club.

The secretary's duties before the meeting are by no means light; every competitor expects to see the starts published in the sporting papers a few days before the meeting, to have a programme and ticket of admission sent to him in due course, and the interests of the press have also to be studied. The press men expect interleaved programmes which will enable them to make their notes with more convenience, and a free right of admission to every part of the ground. With the old and capable representatives of the recognised papers this claim is no doubt a perfectly proper one, and clubs which want their meetings properly reported have no right to expect that this should be done unless they are willing themselves to afford facilities for the report. Sometimes, however, the representatives of papers which have very little concern with athletic meetings act in a way that is not above reproach. Knowing perhaps little or nothing of athletics, they freely criticise the decisions and proceedings of competent officials and stir up ill-feeling amongst athletes; and if by any chance they are not allowed in the centre of the ground, or are not treated with the amount of respect to which they deem themselves entitled, the readers of their paper are informed that the mismanagement of the meeting and the incompetence of the officials were outrageous. Happily, we think, of later years this nuisance has somewhat abated, and another practice which threatened to become a greater nuisance, the providing of reporters with liberal refreshments, has also been pretty well discontinued. The 'chicken and champagne' method of dealing with critics cannot fail to be pernicious, in however humble a manner it is employed.

Another and most important duty of the secretary before the meeting commences is to provide proper accommodation for the competitors. If the sports be on a running ground which has regular dressing-rooms upon it this is easy enough; but at country meetings tents have to be erected, and a liberal supply of towels, baths, water, chairs, &c., provided, as nothing is more disagreeable for competitors than insufficient accommodation. Care must also be taken to see that all the implements and apparatus required for the meeting are ready. Upon one occasion an important meeting had to be put off for half an hour because there was no pistol upon the ground to start the race with; and often have we seen a similar pause in the programme because there was no worsted or tape for the winning-post, starts were not marked out, and no measure was handy, no bar for the jumping-posts, no ground set apart for the weight-putting, and so forth. It need also scarcely be said that it is a grave offence for judges and officials to neglect their business, or to arrive late upon the ground. We have already given in a previous chapter a sketch of an athletic meeting and its officials, and, whether the meeting be a championship or a small local affair, the same requisites and the same method of conducting it apply. It is rare nowadays to see an ill-conducted meeting, and the rapidity and smoothness with which a big fixture is got through in a few hours is often highly creditable to the organising and administrative ability of voluntary sporting associations. It is no uncommon thing for heats of sprinting handicaps to be run off with only three minutes between each heat, the clerks of the course getting their men out upon the ground to the very minute. One thing we can say with confidence is, that the rule – always rigidly enforced – for putting back a competitor who oversteps his mark before the pistol is fired has not only reduced sprint racing from chaos to order, but has rendered the work of starters and officials easier, and has largely tended to improve the management of meetings. It would be, perhaps, unnecessary, after what we have written, to enlarge upon the right method of getting through a meeting, and we had better, perhaps, leave the rules for competitions recommended by the A.A.A., and now almost universally employed, to speak for themselves.

RULES FOR COMPETITIONS

OFFICIALS.

The officials shall consist of –
1. A Committee, in whose hands shall be placed all matters which do not relate to the actual conduct of the meeting itself, and who shall have a final decision in all cases not provided for in the rules of the meeting.
2. Two or more Judges, whose joint decision shall be final in every competitor, and with whom shall rest the power to disqualify any competitor.
3. A Referee, who shall decide in the event of a difference of opinion between the Judges. The decision of the Referee shall be final in all cases.
4. Two or more Stewards, or Clerks of the Course, whose business shall be to call out the competitors of each event, and to assign to each his distinctive badge.
5. One or more special Judge of Walking, a Timekeeper, a Starter, and one or more Marksmen.

ENTRIES.

1. The Committee shall reserve to itself the right of refusing any entry, without being bound to assign a reason.
2. Entries shall not be received unless accompanied by the entrance fees.
3. Competitors in handicap competitions shall be required to send with their entries full and definite particulars as to their last three performances, if any. The entry form shall be so drawn up as to make it easy for the competitors to give the information required.
4. All entries shall be made in the real names of the competitors.
5. Competitors in youths' races must state their age and previous performances; and, if required, must furnish certificates of birth.

PROTESTS.

1. All protests against a competitor, or against a competitor's qualification to compete, shall be made to the Secretary of the Club, in writing, before the prizes are distributed; and if the protest shall not be made good within one calendar month, the prize shall be awarded. Every protest must be accompanied with a deposit of five shillings, which shall be forfeited in case the same shall appear upon investigation to have been made on no reasonable ground.

STATIONS.

1. Competitors in level races shall draw lots for their respective places on the post before leaving the dressing-room. Each competitor shall be supplied with, and wear during each contest, a distinctive number corresponding to his number in the programme.
2. In handicaps, stations shall be awarded according to the numbers on the programme.

MEASUREMENTS.

1. All tracks shall be measured twelve inches from the inner side of the path.

STARTING.

1. All races (except time handicaps) shall be started by the report of a pistol. A start shall only be made to the actual report of the pistol.
2. The starter shall place the competitors on their allotted marks, and shall, if necessary, have the assistance of marksmen for this duty. If any competitor overstep his mark before the pistol has been fired, the starter shall put him back one yard from the distances up to and including 220 yards, two yards up to and including 440 yards, three yards up to and including

880 yards, and five yards up to and including one mile. These penalties to be doubled for a second offence, and disqualification to follow a repetition of the same offence.
3. All questions as to starts shall be in the absolute discretion of the starter.

GENERAL RULES.

1. Every competitor must wear complete clothing from the shoulders to the knees (e.g., sleeved jersey and loose drawers).
2. Any competitor may be excluded from taking part in the sports unless properly attired.
3. No attendant shall accompany any competitor on a scratch (except in bicycle races) nor in the race, nor shall a competitor be allowed, without the permission of the judges, to receive assistance or refreshment from anyone during the progress of a race.
4. Wilfully jostling or running across or obstructing another, so as to impede his progress, shall disqualify the offender.

STRAIGHT SPRINT RACES.

1. Straight sprint races shall be run on a part of the cinder path or grass so staked and stringed that each competitor may have a separate course. The width between the strings shall not be less than four feet, and the stakes shall not be less than forty feet apart.

WALKING RACES.

1. In walking races, cautions and qualifications shall be left to the decision of the judges of walking.

HURDLE RACE.

1. The hurdle race shall be over ten flights of hurdles, on a level grass course of 120 yards straight. The hurdles shall

stand 3 ft 6 in. from the ground and shall have level top rails and shall be placed ten yards apart. Each competitor shall have his own line of hurdles, and shall keep to that line throughout the race.

STEEPLECHASING.

1. The hurdles shall not be higher than three feet. Every competitor must go over or through the water; and anyone who jumps to one side or the other of the water jump shall be disqualified.

HIGH JUMP AND POLE JUMP.

1. Each competitor shall be allowed three jumps at each height. Crossing the scratch without displacing the bar shall not count as one jump. All measurements shall be made from the ground to the centre of the bar.

THE BROAD JUMP.

1. Each competitor shall be allowed three jumps, and the best three competitors of the first trial shall be allowed three more tries each for the final. The farthest jump of the six attempts shall win. If any competitor falls back or steps back after jumping, or crosses the taking-off line with either foot, or so swerves aside that he pass beyond the taking-off line, such jump shall not be measured, but it shall be counted against the competitor as one jump. All jumps shall be measured to the taking-off line, from the edge of the heel-mark nearest that line, along a line perpendicular to that line.

THROWING THE HAMMER.

1. The hammer shall be thrown from within a circle of nine feet in diameter. The head of the hammer shall be of iron, and spherical, and the handle shall be of wood.

The head and handle shall weigh together 16 lbs. The total length of the hammer shall not be more than four feet. Each competitor shall be allowed three throws, and the best three competitors of the first trial shall be allowed three more throws each. The farthest throw of the six shall win. All distances shall be measured from the circumference of the circle to the first pitch of the hammer, along a line drawn from that pitch to the centre of the circle.

PUTTING THE WEIGHT.

1. The weight shall be put from the shoulder with one hand only, and without follow, from a 7 ft square. The weight shall be of iron, and spherical, and shall weigh 16 lbs. All puts shall be measured perpendicularly from the first pitch of the weight to the front line of the square, or that line produced.
2. In throwing the hammer and putting the weight, crossing the scratch shall count as a try.

THROWING THE CRICKET BALL.

In throwing the cricket ball the distance thrown shall be calculated from the centre of a scratch line; and the thrower, in delivering the ball, shall not cross such scratch line. Three tries only shall be allowed, and crossing the scratch shall count as one try.

TUG OF WAR.

The teams shall consist of equal numbers of competitors. The rope shall be of sufficient length to allow for a 'pull' of twelve feet, and for twelve feet slack at each end, together with four feet for each competitor; it shall not be less than four inches in circumference, and shall be without knots or other holdings for the hands. A centre tape shall be affixed to the centre of the rope, and six feet on each side of the centre line two side lines

Putting the shot – the first position. Putting the shot – the second position.

parallel thereto. At the start the rope shall be taut, and the centre tape shall be over the centre line, and the competitors shall be outside the side lines.

The start shall be word of mouth. During no part of the pull shall the foot of any competitor go beyond the centre line. The pull shall be won when one team shall have pulled the side tape of the opposing side over their own side line. No competitor shall wear boots or shoes with any projecting nails, sprigs, or points of any kind. No competitor shall make any hole in the ground with his feet, or in any other way before the start. The final heat shall be won by two pulls out of three.

The rules are, we think, so plain and straightforward that they require but little comment as to their practical working. One or two remarks, however, naturally suggest themselves. As regards officials, it is a truism to observe that the best laws in the world are no good unless they can find capable administrators; and the first and most important thing to make an athletic gathering successful is to get officials who are up to their work. In London and large athletic centres this is now by no means difficult, as every year there is an increasing number of old athletes who retain sufficient love for the sport to give their aid. At country meetings, however, the difficulty is much greater, not only from there probably being no men with great experience in the neighbourhood, but sometimes also because there are local interests to be conciliated, and some of the subscribers to the meeting have to be asked to officiate in order that no offence may be given. The presence of these willing but incapable officials sometimes leads to most remarkable results. We have seen a country J. P. (and a staunch old sportsman too) officiating as starter with a blunderbuss. His method of starting was as follows. He told the competitors that when he turned his back upon them they were to get ready, and were to start when they heard the gun. He no doubt thought, with great artfulness, that he must turn his back lest the competitors should see his finger tighten on the trigger. But as soon as this sapient starter's back was turned, off went all the competitors, and usually when they had gone about twenty yards the gun blazed. Another starter whom we saw (the local rector) rolled up his handkerchief in his hand, and prepared to start his men with the following successive formulas: 'Get ready. Are you ready? One, two, three – off', dropping his handkerchief at the 'off'. Early in the day his men found that he never called them back for starting before the word, so they first started about the word 'One', then at 'Are you ready?' and finally at 'Get ready'. The starter did not like to confess himself beaten, and, like a conductor who when he finds his orchestra will not follow him decides to follow his orchestra, as soon as his men started he gabbled out the remainder of his sentences and dropped the handkerchief as speedily as possible; by the time he had well settled down to something like 'Ge-ready – aready – wun-to-throff', the competitors were never more than five yards in front of him. The judges, too, have to be no less competent than the starter, for many sprint races are won by a few inches. The judge of sprinting contests should stand some yards away from the winning post, and directly opposite the tape or worsted.

When he has watched whose chest breaks the line first, he should let his eye follow that man, and immediately discover his name. At all well-managed sports every competitor is now obliged to carry a large number pinned upon his breast, so that the judges may identify him at once, and the clerks of the course take care that no man shall be without his number. Real dead-heats are very rare, many races being won by an inch, and even an inch is unmistakable to the experienced eye of a tried judge; but a man who has had little practice is often inclined to give a 'dead-heat' when there has been nearly a foot between the two runners. An untried judge, too, is often misled by a man who has been gaining on his opponent shooting past him after the post has been passed, and this is a mistake into which spectators very often fall. We have seen very bad decisions given by untried judges; at one meeting there was no tape, the only line being a chalk line marked on the ground between the winning posts, and the judging, which would in any case have been thus rendered difficult, became almost a farce, for whenever there was a close finish each man rushed up to the judges and claimed the race, and a general muddle and wrangle ensued. There is no more odious practice for a competitor than to claim the race from the judges by flinging up his arm or going up to speak to them, and it is with great regret that we have seen athletes who are good enough sportsmen to know better indulging in it. This, however, is by no means the worst offence we have seen perpetrated at a meeting, where the officials have been weak. In such a case the motley team of competitors of all classes is very liable to get out of hand, although a little display of timely firmness might have kept everything in order. If, as soon as a man misbehaves himself by jostling a competitor on purpose, or by declining to obey the judges' decision, he is promptly sent to the rightabout and disqualified for the rest of the meeting, the probability is that there will be no further trouble of any sort. An instance in point – rather a ridiculous instance certainly – was furnished at a Northern meeting, where a number of professional pedestrians entered themselves as amateurs, not desiring to take prizes, but merely to win money by betting about the heats for which they had been handicapped with a moderate start as 'unknowns'. Shortly before the racing came on the committee discovered the fraud, but were in a difficulty, as the 'pros' were attended by a number of backers, and stated that they would come out on the ground and run at all hazards. When the first offender appeared, as he had threatened, nothing was said until the men got upon their marks, when two stout officials quietly went up to the man, and without more ado seized him by the head and legs and sat upon him until the race was over. The man was then released and retired threatening vengeance, a threat which he never executed, and none of his companions appeared for the subsequent heats. The local committees of the A.A.A. give a very short shrift to a man who has declined to obey the judges, and the nuisance of disorderly meetings is being rapidly abated.

It will be noticed that the A.A.A. give a very free hand to the officials in the conduct of a meeting. The judges' decision is final, when they agree as to the result of any race, or as to the necessity of disqualifying a competitor on the ground. If the judges differ, the referee's decision is final. It has been found in practice that if there is a right of appeal even to the committee from the officials' decision there is much time wasted, and a great deal of friction; as in a loose body like the general committee of management, opinions may differ, and there may be conflicting interests, rival committee-men having rival *protégés* towards whom they may be apt to lean, although perfectly honest in their opinions. The committee, however, have left in their hands everything which does not relate to the racing itself and the declaration of the winners. Just as the judges' decision is final as to who are the winners of the races, the starter has an absolute discretion to call back the men even after he has fired the pistol, and either to declare a start or 'no start'. On one point only – a point which was only settled after much anxious discussion, and some considerable opposition – has the starter no discretion at all. If a competitor oversteps his mark before the pistol is fired, the starter is bound to put him back a yard in a sprint race, 2 yards in a quarter, and so on. It is contended by many that such a rule should not apply to a championship meeting; by others, that it is wanted more at a championship than at any other, as the temptation to get a flying start is stronger. A compromise between the conflicting views, that in a championship meeting the starter should be allowed a discretion to put back men or not as he thought fit, was finally rejected by the committee which framed the rules, it being thought, and in our opinion wisely, that a rigid and inflexible rule was better, as the starter could only judge of acts, and not of intentions, and would be unable to decide whether the overstepping of the mark was accidental or intentional. As it is, experience has justified the framing of the rule in its present shape, and under the present rigid laws there has been no attempt at a repetition of the fiascos of some old championship meetings, where men running in the hundred yards race were kept five minutes at the post making false starts, while there was every opportunity for the worst man to win by wearing out the patience of the starter.

The judges of walking have a similar discretion in deciding as to the fairness or unfairness of the walkers' gait, and this, too, is a decided improvement upon an old rule often employed, which obliged a certain number of 'cautions' before disqualification, although there was a special exception that there should be no 'cautions' in the last lap. The maxim upon which the A.A.A. rules were founded, was to give the officials a free exercise of their discretion; but it is obvious that for the rules to work well the officials must be men whose discretion is guided by experience and knowledge of the sport. A dispensing and discretionary power in the hands of a novice is apt to lead to blunders, but, as we have said before, there is seldom any difficulty, now that athletics have been in full swing for a generation, in finding judges who are both willing and able to act when asked, and the occasions therefore upon which the rules of the A.A.A. do not work well are very rare.

One of the officials, upon whom in a great measure success depends, although he is often not present at the meeting itself, is the handicapper. At most gatherings nowadays, there are more handicaps than level races; often indeed, especially in London, there are no level races at all. In fact, the ordinary programme for a club meeting near London is something of this kind: a hundred and twenty yards handicap (open), a quarter mile handicap (open), a mile handicap (open), a three-quarter of a mile steeplechase (open), a two miles walking race (open), a hundred and fifty yards, half a mile, and two miles handicaps (confined to members of the club giving the race). Perhaps also there is a level race at some special distance arranged on purpose to bring two or three 'cracks' together, or perhaps a handicap with a short limit (say a quarter of a mile, with a limit of 25 yards from the best runner of the day), this last race being designed to produce a field where there are no 'platers', but only good class runners. As meetings of this description take place by scores in every part of the country, it is obvious that none but trained handicappers, who regularly study the art, can be trusted to bring the men together. Before competitors became so numerous, handicappers could be found to do the work without reward, but first one and then another of the well-known handicappers began to demand payment for their services, and at the present day at least a score of men in one or another part of the kingdom are making a comfortable addition to their income by the exercise of their talents in this direction. The system in shorter races is to handicap by giving so many yards start, but in the longer races, whether of walking or running, the competitors often have so many seconds start of the scratch man allotted to them. A novelty in the way of handicapping was introduced in a cross-country race by the Thames Hare and Hounds Club some years ago, the runners all starting together, but being handicapped, in horse-racing style, by the apportionment of different amounts of weight, each runner being allowed to carry his weight in any way he chose. The novelty, however, was hardly a success, the runners who were heavily weighted (the top weight carried, we believe, 28 lbs) making most ungainly efforts, and the result would seem to show that man, as a running animal, is not able to carry anything more than his own weight with ease and elegance. We do not anticipate any change, therefore, in the old and received system of handicapping for man-racing.

The advantages of giving up a club meeting to the handicap-runners have been much questioned, and there can be little doubt that the rapid increase of handicaps was a necessary step towards the popularisation of athletic sports with the runners themselves. To make all open races level no doubt not only encouraged 'pot-hunting', but prevented those who were not really first class from taking part in races at all, as they would naturally object to form part of a procession at every meeting. Undoubtedly, also, there are many 'cracks' who were first encouraged to come upon the path by handicap prizes, and who have gone gradually down in the handicap scale until they have found themselves good enough to compete in level races or championships. The club treasurer, too, often feels that he cannot do without the handicaps, for while a level sprint might only produce four entries, i.e. four half-crowns, a sprint handicap might well produce eighty entries, i.e. eighty half-crowns, and there is a vast deal of difference between ten shillings and ten pounds of entrance fees. In the days, too, when there was something of a novelty and a pleasing surprise for any man to find himself a runner at all, the friends, sisters, cousins, and aunts of the handicap runners come to see their heroes run, and athletic clubs flourished and waxed rich; while many a cricket, rowing, or football club netted a nice little sum out of its annual sports, which came in as a handy addition to the club's revenues. At the present day there is rather a plethora of athletic meetings, and while the handicaps still draw large entries from competitors, who expect there will be at least three valuable prizes, we have something more than a suspicion that the public has been driven away from attending sports by being bored with a succession of these dreary competitions. In sprint races one lieat is very much like another, and, as a rule, the really good runners are unplaced, or give up against the unequal odds; while in a mile race, where there is a cloud of runners, none but the experienced eye can see who is making his way to the front, or really running above his form, and so doing well. The effect of this is that the public is beginning to get tired of the monotony of athletics, and of late years the attendance, of ladies especially, has become less and less frequent. In London the waning of the popularity of athletic sports with the paying public has been very marked of recent years, much more so than in the provinces, but generally it is admitted with perfect frankness by the promoters of athletic meetings in all large towns that there is 'very little money in athletics now'. At Birmingham there have been very few athletic meetings recently, and in London, Liverpool, Manchester, etc., the clubs are not so flourishing as they were formerly, owing to the falling off of 'gate money'. As we have hinted before, we behove one cause of this decadence is the mistake made by the managing committees of meetings in giving so few level open races. Certainly the big provincial meetings of the North, where there are plenty of level races, and where, even in the handicaps, the 'cracks' are leniently treated and encouraged to enter, command bigger 'gates' and better fields; and even Londoners are at last beginning to learn that one 'crack' will do more to make a success of a meeting than fifty 'crocks'.

At every meeting, however, there must be a certain number of handicaps, and for this it is indispensable that the handicappers chosen should be men up to their work. For the 'short limit' handicaps (which are such a success at the Civil Service meeting, and which we should like to see at every fixture, as they bring 'cracks' together, and yet prevent the same men from always winning) the handicapping has to be equally a matter of care and study, as a yard more or less may make or mar a good race; and there is little danger, when there are none but well-known men competing, of all calculations being upset by the appearance of a 'dark horse'. So far, indeed, has specialism proceeded in the athletic art that at many meetings there are different handicappers for the long and short races. The professed handicappers keep a book in which every man's performances are recorded, and their duties are certainly arduous, as to be exact in their calculations they have to get the best accounts of every event that has taken place in the country. It is not at all unusual for the athletes of one district to take journeys to other districts, while some of the semi-professional amateurs flit about all over the kingdom picking up prizes. As soon as any athlete wins or is placed in a race his scale of start has to be reconsidered.

About a decade ago the amateurs thought they could borrow with advantage a system employed by handicappers of professional pedestrians of framing all the starts with reference to a fixed standard, and not with reference to the pace of the man who is the best of the entrants. Under this, which is known as the 'Sheffield system', the standard fixed by the handicapper for 100 yards would be, say 10 sec., or for the quarter 50 sec., and each competitor would be handicapped according to the number of yards he would be outside 10 sec. or 50 sec., as the case might be. The result necessarily was that in nearly every case the best man in the handicap was not at 'scratch', but at some yards start. The system, no doubt, had its advantages, for it saved the handicapper a good deal of trouble in readjusting all the starts for each race according to the varying ability of the man at 'scratch'. There was also this further advantage, that the handicappers throughout the country all adopted the same standards of merit for the imaginary scratch men, and it thus became very easy to handicap a stranger from another district, by simply finding out upon what mark his own local handicapper considered this stranger should be placed. The Sheffield system, however, was swept away by the growing desire, both of the public and of the men themselves, to see 'bests on record' accomplished at meetings. Several instances occurred of the real scratch man in a handicap starting, under the 'Sheffield system', with some yards from 'scratch' and winning the race with a performance which would have been a record had the whole distance been covered. The 'crack' who had done a record performance was thus deprived of the credit of it, as it was obviously impossible to establish a 'record' for 148 1/2 yards, 436 yards, or 596 yards, in cases where the scratch man had had a few yards start from the imaginary ' Sheffielder'. The Sheffield system was soon given up at Oxford – we believe it was never tried at Cambridge – and it was abandoned by the L.A.C. in 1877. At the present day it is entirely unknown in the South, though sometimes employed elsewhere.

No meeting now is without an official time-keeper, and at some important gatherings, as we have seen, there are three such functionaries, all of whom time each race. There are, of course, many advantages in having each contest timed. The athletes themselves and the spectators like to know whether the races have been fast or slow; and for purposes of future handicapping, or of comparing the worthies of one period with those of another, timing is indispensable. Indispensable, however, though it may be for certain ends, timing is merely a means, and not in any way an end in itself: a fact the present generation of athletes – which has simply gone mad upon 'times' and 'records' – appears to have forgotten. By saying that the athlete of to-day considers timing an 'end' and not a means, we mean that he thinks it is a fine display of skill on his part to cover so much ground in so little time, without taking any ether fact into consideration – an opinion upon which we venture to differ with him.

There can be no question about the public fondness for a 'record'. A club which owns a ground of its own is rather inclined to give races at distances where there is a particularly good chance of lowering the existing record; and committees of clubs giving sports frequently advertise in the sporting papers that such and such runners will compete, and that it is confidently expected that 'the record will be lowered', &c. To such an appeal spectators never fail to respond by attending in large numbers. For the manufacturers of bicycles or the owners of running-grounds which are let to the public, we can quite see the advantages of promoting records with a view to bold advertisement; but amongst athletes and others, the present writer is heretical enough to believe that the worshipping of records is idolatrous, and inconsistent with the creed of the true sportsman.

But before we go into this question at any length there is something more to be said as to the practice and difficulties of timing.

'Timing' in foot-races requires even more care than 'timing' in other sporting contests, for a mistake of a fifth of a second may make all the difference between a good or an ordinary performance. To ensure accuracy of timing there must not only be a good watch, but a person who knows how to hold it. In most stop-watches the watch is started by a simple pressure of the thumb or forefinger upon a knob or pin which removes the catch and puts the works in motion again. To drop for the moment the fact that some watches start quicker than others, the apparently simple process by which the man who holds the watch sets it going is not so simple as it seems, and there are plenty of opportunities for differences to arise between one timekeeper and another. If, say in a hundred yards race, the timekeeper waits for the sound of the pistol to start his watch, he himself standing at the winning-post, about 1/10 of a second elapses before the sound reaches him. If he takes the start from the motions of the body, it is a most difficult question, when the men are upon tip-toe at the mark, to know which motion of any one of them is a motion made after the pistol is fired. In either case when the sound of the pistol is heard or the first motion noticed, the timekeeper has to arrive at a determination to start the watch from the sensations of his eye or ear; he has then by will to convey that determination to the muscles of his finger, and the watch is then started by him. Recent experiments in physiology have shown not only that the process of thinking and volition takes an appreciable time, but that there is also an appreciable difference between the rapidity of thought and volition in different individuals. Practice and experience, as in everything else, tend to quicken the rapidity of the action of the will or thought, which travels quicker over beaten tracks. We of course wish to steer clear of physiological discussion as far as possible, and to confine ourselves to practical experience of timekeeping; but it is necessary to point out that the individual qualities of timekeepers may make the results they arrive at untrustworthy. As a general proof of the truth of what we say, we may call attention to the fact that novices who try to time races invariably make the times 'fast', i.e. they are very slow in starting the watch, although they are not so slow in stopping it at the moment the tape is reached, as by watching the runner up to the tape they know almost the exact moment when the pressure of the finger to stop the watch will be required. Before quitting the subject of the liability of the timekeeper to error, we would suggest that there should be a definite rule laid down by the A.A.A. for the guidance of starters as to what point should be taken for the start – the flash of the pistol, the report, or the first motion of the runner. Most timekeepers profess to start from the motion of the runner's body, but we are inclined to think with some of them this is a mere profession. Obviously they must only look at one runner, and if he were left upon the mark they would be 'out' altogether, a fact which we never yet heard an official timekeeper admit. In any case the starting from the motion of the body is fallacious, as one runner usually begins to move perceptibly before the others.

Besides these complications, there is the further set of difficulties created by the watch itself, though with the splendid pieces of mechanism which are now made expressly for this purpose the uncertainty is minimised. The dial of the stopwatch is usually marked into fifths, and with some of the older watches there was this fact to be considered: the hand 'jumped' from fifth to fifth round the dial, there being of course a fifth of a second between each jump. Obviously, therefore, there might be almost a whole fifth of difference between two occasions when the same time was registered on the dial. For instance, upon one occasion when 10 1/5 was registered on the dial, the hand might, just at the instant before the watch stopped, have made its jump to the fifth, while upon the other occasion the hand might have stopped at an infinitesimal period before it took its jump to the two fifths mark upon the dial. It is clear, therefore, that, as a good sprinter travels a shade over two yards in a fifth of a second at the end of a hundred yards race, two men might each have been fairly timed at 10 1/5 seconds in a race, although the one was two yards in front of the other. As for a very long time there were nothing but watches which jumped fifths even at first-class meetings, it is obvious that as regards the times made at these meetings, they are quite untrustworthy as to one-fifth of a second's variation. At the present day there are some watches (although there are not many belonging to private individuals, their cost being large) which, at any rate as far as the human eye can distinguish, travel evenly over the dial. As a matter of fact, the wheel which regulates the motion has such small cogs that the jumps are divided into twenty or thirty per second. The hand, therefore, can really be stopped at any place on the dial between the fifths, and the dial then has to be surveyed through a magnifying-glass, and a conclusion arrived at how far it has travelled between one fifth and another.

All this process, however, though exceedingly wonderful and the result of admirable workmanship, is also liable to error. The slightest warp of the straightness of the hand between the fifths may lead to doubt, and even supposing the mechanism perfect the human eye can and does make mistakes in deciphering the result which the machine has registered. The watches of which we speak are of course so made that the 'seconds' hand travels round the whole of the dial; but the watch is made to be carried in the pocket, so that there is very little space between the fifths of seconds on the dial, as each fifth occupies 1/300 of the circumference of the dial. It is thus obvious that the human eye can easily be deceived in reading the dial, and it must be recollected that as soon as the next race comes on the watch has to be got ready again for this, so that it becomes impossible to verify afterwards the result registered on the dial. On account of the difficulty of reading the results on the watch many timekeepers carry a magnifying glass with them, and although this makes the reading easier and perhaps more accurate, the whole process becomes still more complex. On the whole, therefore, it appears that there is every possibility of a mistake being made to the extent of a fifth of a second, or even rather more, in the timing of races; and some years ago when timekeepers had less experience and timing instruments were inferior, there was even a greater possibility of error than there is now. We cannot help thinking how strange it is that in these days of science no more satisfactory method of timing races has been invented than that of a watch started by a man who observes the start from some distance off. In these days of electric science it seems to the unscientific mind of the present writer that it ought not to be difficult to time by an apparatus, which could be fixed on every recognised running-ground, set in motion by the firing of the pistol, and stopped by the breaking of the thread at the winning-post. In such an apparatus the difficulty of deciphering the result marked on a small dial need not occur, as the hand or hammer registering the result might work upon a dial of any size. There need be no difficulty in the size of a dial in a fixed apparatus, and the consideration of expense hardly ought to arise when it is considered that sixty, eighty, or a hundred guineas are often given for the best timing watches.

Closely connected with the subject of 'timing' is that of 'records'. We have already given our opinion that in short races it is somewhat unsatisfactory at present to place reliance upon a 'fifth' of a second, and it is well known that in any race up to 220 yards the difference of a fifth of a second may make a 'record'. But quite apart from questions of timing, the state of the path, or of the weather, and especially the direction and force of the wind, may make a difference of two or three-fifths of a second in a sprint, or of the same number of seconds in longer races. The inference would seem to be obvious that the fact of a man having covered a certain space of ground in a shorter time than any other runner, does not by any means necessarily prove that the man who has performed the feat is the best man who has ever run that distance. If this result is borne in mind, we can see no reason for placing the acquisition of a 'record' as the summit of an athlete's ambition. Yet this is exactly what is done by both athletes and the public at the present day, who consider the possessor of a 'record' a man far more to be envied or admired than his companion who has met one by one his best opponents and beaten them. The popular opinion, too, having once laid down a record as the highest possible distinction, has encouraged athletes to the most absurd limits in honouring the record. Records are gravely chronicled at distances which are never run as races, and we hear that Myers has made a record at 130, 360, or 1,100 yards, or that George has shifted the record for three miles and three-quarters, these record times having been taken by a man stationed at a particular post to note the time as the runner went by. Another practice which in our opinion is illegitimate is that followed by the cyclists who allow a record to be secured at any time whether in a race or not provided they are satisfied of the 'timing'; and an aspiring amateur accordingly may go down accompanied by a time-keeping friend, and may try day after day to lower the record for six or seven miles, which he at last does when he is favoured by exceptional conditions. After this he retires happy in the possession of a record, and his satisfaction remains undiminished until his bosom friend comes down the next week and after another set of futile efforts at last 'cuts' the record by a second. However, our concern at present is not with cycling records, and we only state our grievance against their system because we think that the 'record nuisance' has in a great measure been promoted by enterprising manufacturers of bicycles, and first forced upon the cyclists by the 'makers' amateurs', while from the cyclists the infection has spread again in its most virulent form back amongst the athletes. Recently the Amateur Athletic Association has been engaged in revising and settling the athletic records, and in arriving at the results (which are printed elsewhere) they were guided by the following principles, which, as it will be seen, carefully exclude all 'times' not made in legitimate competitions:

> It is decided that the running records to be dealt with shall be the '100, 120, 150, 200, 220, and 300 yards, quarter-mile, 600 yards, half-mile, 1,000 yards, three-quarters of a mile, one mile, one mile and a half, and then each mile up to ten, after which the only distances to be examined and authenticated shall be the fifteen, twenty, twenty-five, thirty, forty, fifty, seventy-five, and 100 miles.
>
> The walking records to be dealt with shall be only the mile records as above mentioned, but the one, three, and twelve hours walking record shall also be examined and settled.
>
> The other competitions to be investigated shall be the 120 yards hurdles, long, high, and pole jumps, putting the (16 lb) weight, and throwing the (16 lb) hammer.
>
> The only records to be accepted shall be those made in public competitions, and held under A.A.A. Rules and by a recognised club.

> Questions of gradients, wind or other favourable conditions, shall be taken into consideration when deciding any individual record.
>
> A record shall include any performance in the United Kingdom.
>
> The record of a foreigner or colonial done anywhere in the United Kingdom shall be considered an English record.

It will thus be seen that in future the A.A.A. propose to restrict the making of records within reasonable limits by only recognising those which are authenticated and made upon fair grounds under fair conditions, in legitimate competitions and at recognised distances. These regulations will prevent any second-rate runner from securing a record, and will make it more likely than of yore that the 'record-holder' will be the best man over the distance. In spite, however, of these reforms in the system – reforms which it is as yet doubtful whether the public or the press will be content to accept – we are still inclined to object to record-worship upon wider and deeper grounds than that the system is inconclusive and carried to absurd limits.

Our general indictment against the system of paying reverence to a record because it is a 'record', is that the system is unsportsmanlike, and has demoralised the whole of the present generation of runners. The essential merit of every athletic contest, as of every other contest of skill or endurance, is for one man to be pitted against another man. The rivalry and the desire to win and not to lose bring out the pluck, the skill, and the endurance of all the competitors. It is in a contest with his equals or his betters that a man becomes, as the Greeks would have said, 'better than himself', and our own poets have expressed in many different ways the joyous exultation of the brave warrior when he knows he will meet a foeman worthy of his steel. From the days of chivalry up to modern times one of the things which has made the English nation brave has been the praise bestowed upon the knight, swordsman, boxer, or runner who was ready to encounter anyone who challenged him. At the present day that part of the nation which patronises the athletic ground awards more praise to the man who has scampered past a field of inferior runners quickly than to the man who has pluckily met and beaten other 'cracks' in a level race. Had this view prevailed in the Middle Ages the champion knight would not have been he who kept the ring against all comers, but he who knocked down with his lance twenty 'dummies' in the quickest time.

Our complaint against the athletes and the public is that they do not see that it is the competition of equally matched antagonists which brings out all the manly qualities of the Englishman, and that this alone is the true raison d'etre of athletic sports. They did not come into vogue to show the capacities of the human body as a running or jumping machine, but to teach young Englishmen to train themselves in coolness, courage, endurance, and good temper, by pitting themselves against their equals in fair contest. When a man makes a record (as in bicycling) with several pace-makers and no opponent, or when (as often occurs on the running path) a crack starts at scratch in a handicap especially made (as freely stated in advertisements) to give him an opportunity of beating the record, he has everything to win and nothing to lose; he wants no pluck nor skill to defeat his antagonists, as there are none who start level with him. All he has to do is to lay his feet to the ground as fast as nature will permit him, and if he accomplish the task set him, one feels inclined to parody the familiar sentence and say, 'it is magnificent – but it is not sport'.

It would, however, make little difference to the welfare of the sport whether the public liked level races or record-handicaps best, if the taint had not spread to the athletes themselves. A suspicion of bias always attaches to the *laudator temporis acti*, but at the risk of incurring that suspicion we feel compelled to express an opinion that the great 'cracks' of the present day are not over-fond of meeting each other. The desire of winning the title of champion is still strong enough to bring most of them together once a year, but upon any other occasion it is the greatest difficulty in the world to induce two 'cracks' at the same distance to meet in a race. One day one is seeking a record in the South, and on the same day another is running at a country handicap in the West, while a third who is great at the same distance is at a big Birmingham meeting, also trying for records on the Aston track. On a Bank Holiday the same phenomenon is also to be observed, although the motive on this occasion is not to make records but to win 'pots'. If there are three good quarter-milers in London in the spring, it may be predicted with great confidence that one of them will be at Woodbridge, another at Colchester, and the third at Newmarket. All this cowardice (to use a plain word) is discreditable to the sport, and it is fostered and encouraged by the system which takes as the test of a man's merit, not the quality of the opponents whom he has beaten, but the 'time' in which he has performed. The sooner, therefore, that athletes learn that time is a test of speed but of nothing else, the better for the sport. The race is not always to the speediest, and to possess speed without pluck or judgment is to have very little title to genuine merit. To conclude with an old athletic aphorism, 'Fast times do not make the runner', and with this remark we will close our case against timing and records.

There is one other practice which, in our opinion, has been carried to absurd limits at athletic meetings. At a great many meetings boys' races are included in the programmes. That a good, strong, lusty schoolboy, who is continually playing cricket or football, should come out and race in public is sensible enough. Athletic sports have now been in full swing for a generation, and many of the runners of the past are bringing up possible young champions of their own. At first sight, therefore, it seems a genial and sportsmanlike notion for races to be given at meetings for the sons or young brothers or nephews of the members of clubs. But this idea, like some other good ideas, has led to cruel absurdities. At the Civil Service and Private Banks and other meetings, little boys of six years old, and even less, are to be seen racing in boys' handicaps, having, of course, prodigious starts from the scratch markers, who are much bigger lads. For our own part, we think it is neither good for the minds or bodies of little boys to run hard races at public meetings at all, and we should like to see boys' races restricted to those over twelve. But even of races for elder boys there are far too many. There are so many, in fact, that a regular class of boy-champions is springing up, and certain boys run at twenty or thirty meetings during a summer, and bring home as many prizes. This early 'forcing' of juvenile talent can hardly be considered a healthy system, and yet the practice is yearly extending rather than decreasing. Every school, great or small, has its athletic meeting now, and we think that schoolboys had much better confine themselves to their own school races, and their own games and paper-chases, until they are good enough to compete at men's meetings in men's races. Another drawback about these boys' races is the immense amount of squabbling to which they give rise at country meetings. The only way for the handicapper to get his boys together at the finish is to find out the age of each, and a very large number of frauds are perpetrated by boys who either themselves understate their ages or whose friends do the cheating for them. So many of these 'mistakes' have there been that the Athletic Association has been obliged to pass a very stringent rule which confines boys' races in most parts of the country to purely local events. Only a short time ago a case came before the Southern Committee of the A.A.A. of a boy who had been entered at different sports under four different names, his ages being variously given from 11 1/2 years to 14 years, and his height from 4 ft 2 in. to 4 ft 8 in. His real age was 16, and his real height 5 feet. This is no doubt an exceptional case, but the number of instances in which a boy's age has been understated a year, 'quite by accident', is large enough. A system is not bad in itself because bad people abuse it, but apart from these abuses we think the practice of encouraging boys' races at open meetings a pernicious one. If there are to be boys' races at all, let them be confined to those introduced by members of the club holding the meeting, and to competitors who are over twelve years of age.

Having dealt with the boys, we will end our criticism of athletic meetings with the veterans. Some clubs give races to 'veterans' – a 'veteran' in the athletic sense being usually a man over thirty-five years old. We do not see that there is anything wrong in giving those who are *rude donati* an opportunity of coming out again to exhibit themselves to the rising generation of runners, but in practice the veterans' race is usually rather an absurd sight than otherwise. At one of these competitions, which is an annual affair, an old gentleman, who must by this time have passed his allotted span of three score years and ten, comes out regularly to exhibit himself, many others who are well over fifty appear in the race, while a good many younger men compete whose bodies from disuse have so far thickened about the middle as to render their movements anything but graceful. On the whole, we think that the veteran who is too slow to take part in the ordinary races 'lags superfluous on the stage' of athletic sports.

7
Athletic Government

One of the most remarkable features about modern English athletic life is the capacity of the athlete for self-government. As soon as any game or sport becomes popular in any district, or throughout the country, clubs are formed; the clubs conglomerate into district associations; and the latter finally become gathered together into a national governing body. All these bodies, from the smallest club to the largest association, are the outcome of voluntary effort; they are worked, as a rule, in a sensible and businesslike manner, and the officers, in almost every case, are unpaid. Football, cricket, cycling, athletics, paper-chasing, have all their governing bodies; and at a week's notice the best team at any sport can be picked from the whole country, or the popular opinion as to any change or innovation in the sport ascertained. All this discipline and organisation is so well known nowadays as to excite little notice; but when fairly considered, it is really marvellous, and most creditable to the capacity and sound sense of the English sportsman.

The 'Jockey Club' of athletics, the Amateur Athletic Association, did not take its rise until comparatively late in athletic history. For a great many years the Amateur Athletic Club, which was formed in London from the chief University and London athletes of the day, and which instituted the championship meeting in 1866, assumed a position in athletics like that of the M.C.C. in cricket, and no other governing body was needed. From various causes, however, the chief of which was the rising strength and popularity of the other great metropolitan club, the L.A.C., the A.A.C. gradually began to decay. The original members of the A.A.C. ceased to take any active part in its welfare, and the few new members who joined became members simply for the purpose of training upon the club-ground at Lillie Bridge, the club holding no other sports except the championship meeting. To such a stage of apathy had the club sunk in 1876 that an unfriendly critic declared it had only three active members – the secretary, the pony, and the roller. Up to this time the L.A.C. meetings – the most important in London – were held on the A.A.C. ground at Lillie Bridge; but in 1876 a final rupture occurred between the A.A.C. and L.A.C. over 'gate-money' arrangements, and in 1877 the L.A.C. departed to its own ground at Stamford Bridge. In 1877 and 1878 the championship meeting still was held without objection under the management of the A.A.C. at Lillie Bridge, upon the Monday following the Oxford and Cambridge sports, although a strong feeling was growing up in London and the provinces that the date of the fixture gave an unfair advantage to University men. The real truth of the matter was that in the twelve years that had passed since the foundation of the championship meeting, the state of athletic society had undergone a vital change, and the A.A.C. had failed to 'move with the times'. In 1866 and the next few years the University runners were by far the most important section of the athletic community, both in number and merit, and provided about two-thirds of the entries to the sports, while the few Londoners and provincials who were athletes were in a social position which enabled them to find leisure enough to train in the spring to meet the University runners. Before 1878 a new class of runners had sprung up both in London and the provinces. The provincial runners were (as they still are) for the most part drawn from the 'mechanic, artizan, and labourer' class of the community. In the North they were accepted as amateurs; at Lillie Bridge, where the Henley definition of an amateur held good, they were, according to the rule, excluded; although, as a matter of fact, either from accident or from design, their entries were often accepted. The bulk of the London runners, although of quite a different class from the provincials, were clerks or business men who were tied to their desks during the day, and were unable to train except in the evening. The only chance, therefore, that many of them had of getting fit for a spring championship in March or the beginning of April necessitated their practising in the dark. From different reasons, therefore, in London and the provinces athletics had become a summer pastime, while at Oxford and Cambridge they were pursued mainly in the winter months. The three University terms are short, and the various sports have all to be accommodated; so the arrangement both at Oxford and Cambridge is, that athletics and football are cultivated in the two winter terms, the summer term being reserved for cricket and boating (and examinations). It became obvious, therefore, that a summer championship would place the University men at a disadvantage, while a spring fixture would give them a decided 'pull'. Soon after the opening of the Stamford Bridge grounds, the L.A.C., then under the management of Messrs. James and William Waddell, placed itself at the head of the agitation for the summer championship; and, after much fruitless negotiation and discussion, the L.A.C. runners in a body 'boycotted' the spring championship at Lillie Bridge in the spring of 1879, and it was accordingly confined to the University men and a few provincial athletes, including Webster, the walker, and Warburton, the long distance runner. In the summer of 1879 an opposition championship was held on the Stamford Bridge ground, under the management of a committee consisting almost entirely of London runners, together with some few secretaries of clubs from the Midlands; but the Northerners, who had by that time formed themselves into a Northern Counties Athletic Association, held aloof, as they were standing out for the contention that a championship meeting should be open to any amateur, of whatever social position, provided he had never run for money. The summer championship was a decided failure, in spite of the presence of W. G. George, who won both the mile and five-mile races, two-thirds of the winners being from the L.A.C alone. Early in the spring of 1880 the Lillie Bridge championship was again advertised for the usual date, and again notices were given by the London runners that they should decline to compete.

The dispute also with regard to the amateur definition was still unsettled, the provincials maintaining in a body that the 'mechanic, artizan, or labourer' class should be admitted as amateurs, provided they had never run for money. The wide definition had already been accepted by the Northern Counties Association – a body then consisting of some sixteen strong clubs – while in the Midlands a similar body, consisting of some eight or nine clubs, was already in process of formation. Under the circumstances, it occurred to some of the leading athletes at Oxford, early in the spring of 1880, that the best way to settle both burning questions was by a general conference of representatives of leading clubs; and it was further thought that the invitations to such a conference should be issued in the joint names of the Oxford and Cambridge clubs. A notice was accordingly issued in March by the presidents of the two University Clubs, inviting secretaries of all recognised athletic clubs to meet at Oxford on April 24. As soon as the notice was circulated the advertisements of the usual Lillie Bridge championship were withdrawn, and it was tacitly agreed between the disputants to settle the question of spring or summer championships at the Oxford meeting.

It is probably no breach of confidence after so long an interval to say that the 'Oxford Conference' had several narrow escapes of falling to the ground. Each different party was anxious to keep away from the meeting unless some guarantee for the preservation of its interests was given, and this was of course impossible. Even at Cambridge some opposition was got up in the University club against the holding of the meeting, and early in April the guiding spirits of the movement at Oxford were at their wits' end for an expedient to realise their cherished project of founding a general governing body for amateur athletics. Finally the well-known tastes of Englishmen were recollected, and it was decided to invite every delegate to attend a meeting in the afternoon and a dinner in the evening. How far the latter part of the suggestion availed to overcome scruples it is, of course, impossible to conjecture; but in the result the meeting came off on April 24, 1880. A set of resolutions to submit to the assembly was drafted by Messrs. Wise, Jackson, and Shearman of the O.U.A.C., and on the evening before the meeting they were further discussed in conjunction with Mr Walter Rye, who had come down from London for the purpose. The gathering was attended by twenty-seven delegates representing fifteen clubs, the Northern Association (sixteen clubs), and the Midland Association (nine clubs), and at that meeting was founded the Amateur Athletic Association, which, at the end of six years, consisted of 154 clubs representing about 20,000 athletes.

As the foundation of the A.A.A. represents a new and important era in the history of athletic sport in this country, it may perhaps not be amiss to give a few further particulars of the men present at this first meeting at Oxford and of the resolutions there come to. The representatives present were J. G. Chambers and A. G. Payne (of the A.A.C.); E. Storey, L. Knowles, and R. H. Macaulay (of the C.U.A.C.); C. Herbert and H. Tomlinson (of the C.S.A.A.); J. W. Macqueen (of the German Gymnastic Society); J. Waddell (of the L.A.C.); J. Anderton and Frank Smith (of the Midland Counties Association); R. Mullock (of the Newport, Monmouth, A.C.); C. E. Barlow, T. G. Sharpe, H. C. Faram, and T. M. Abraham (of the Northern Counties Association); J. Ingman (of the Northampton A.C.); C. F. Turner and J. E. Dixon (of the North of the Thames Cross Country Union); C. N. Jackson, W. N. Bruce, and M. Shearman (of the O.U.A.C.); J. Suddaby (of the Reading A.C.); J. Gibb (of the South London Harriers); W. Rye (of the Thames Hare and Hounds); W. Waddell (representing the United Hospitals A.C.); E. R. Wood (of the Woodbridge A.C.); and B. R. Wise, who, as President of the O.U.A.C., took the chair. At this meeting it was decided that the Championship Meeting should take place in the summer, and be held in rotation in London, the Midlands, and the North, and that it should be open to all persons who had never competed for money; that the clubs present should associate themselves into a body, to be known as the Amateur Athletic Association; and that the objects of the body should be: (1) to improve the management of athletic meetings, and to promote uniformity of rules for the guidance of local committees; (2) to deal repressively with any abuses of athletic sports; (3) to hold an annual championship meeting. It was also decided that 'all races held under the sanction of the Association be confined to amateurs, and that the following be the definition of an amateur: "Any person who has never competed for money, with or against a professional for any prize, and who has never taught, pursued, or assisted in the practice of athletic exercises as a means of obtaining a livelihood."' In order, however, to guarantee the independence of individual clubs it was understood that this rule should not interfere with the right of any club to refuse the entry of any person to its own sports whenever it thought fit. As regards prizes it was arranged that in no handicap should a prize of greater value than 10*l* 10*s* be allowed, and that every prize of a greater value than 5*l* should be engraved with the name and date of the meeting. The execution of these provisions was to be entrusted to a committee, consisting of certain *ex-officio* members, the representatives of a few leading clubs, and of elected members. A large number of names were proposed for election, but the following ten were chosen for the first year: The Earl of Jersey, and Messrs. Anderton, Barlow, Herbert, Jackson, Lockton, Macaulay, Rye, Shearman, and Waddell. Probably it was in recognition of the services of the Oxford men in setting the Association on foot that in the choice of the officers for the first year Lord Jersey was elected President, and Messrs. Wise, Jackson, and Shearman, Vice-President, Treasurer, and Secretary of the new body.

Since its institution the Amateur Athletic Association has had a career of even success. Although it proceeded cautiously at first, as there was a good deal of opposition to be met, it has of recent years assumed a wholesome arbitrary power over all athletic meetings held in England; and it insists that the main provisions which are necessary for the maintenance of fair play and genuine amateurism shall be respected. The body occupies in fact the same position as the Jockey Club in the sport of flat racing on the turf, insisting that all meetings shall be held under its laws, proclaiming meetings at which such laws are not followed, and punishing athletes for any unfair practice in connection with athletics. Rule XVIII of its present code provides for the suspension of any athlete who wilfully competes at a meeting held by any club or managing

Throwing the hammer.

body which is not either, (1) affiliated to the Association, or (2) registered as an 'approved' club after application to the local officer of the Association, and both the affiliated and the registered clubs are bound to advertise their sports as being held 'under A.A.A. laws'. Such advertisement does not necessitate the adoption of the 'competition rules' given before, which are merely recommended, although as a matter of fact they are now almost universally adopted; nor, as we have seen above, is the club giving sports 'under A.A.A. laws' obliged to accept any entry of which it may for its own reasons disapprove. The only compulsory laws of the A.A.A. which must be observed at every meeting are the following, and it will be admitted that they are not such as to interfere unduly with the freedom of any club which is desirous of giving sports:

1. All competitions must be limited to amateurs. 'An amateur is one who has never competed for a money prize or staked bet, or with or against a professional for any prize, or who has never taught, pursued, or assisted in

the practice of athletic exercises as a means of obtaining a livelihood.'

2. No person must be allowed to compete while under a sentence of suspension passed by either the A.A.A., National Cyclists' Union, Swimming Association of Great Britain, Scottish A.A.A., or Irish A.A.A.
3. No 'value' prize (i.e. a cheque on a tradesman) must be offered.
4. No prize must be offered in a handicap of greater value than 10*l* 10*s*.
5. Every prize of the value of 5*l* or upwards must be engraved with the name and date of the meeting.
6. In no case must a prize and money be offered as alternatives.
7. All prizes shall be publicly presented on the grounds on the day of the sports.
8. All open betting must be put down.
9. All clubs holding and advertising their sports 'under the laws of the Amateur Athletic Association' must have printed on their entry forms 'the definition of an Amateur' as adopted by the Amateur Athletic Association.

It will be seen that it has throughout been the main principle of policy of the A.A.A. to insist upon the orderly management of meetings and the suppression of unfair practice, but yet not to interfere with the free right of any club, whether affiliated or 'approved', to appoint its own officers and manage its own meetings, provided they respected the essential laws of amateurism. Unfortunately, during the whole of the year 1885 the amateur world was thrown into disorganisation by a vehement dispute between the A.A.A. and the National Cyclists' Union, a body which occupies a similar position as the recognised governing body of amateur cyclists. Like many other party conflicts, this arose out of a very small matter and grew into serious proportions, rather through misunderstandings than through ill will, on both sides. The point in dispute was the management of cycling races given by athletic clubs, and generally of all meetings where there were both foot-races and cycling races, the cyclists claiming to have absolute control over every cycling race, wherever held, and the A.A.A. resisting the claim of the Cyclists' Union to interfere with the management of meetings of the affiliated clubs of the A.A.A. Happily, at the end of the year 1885, terms of arrangement were concluded between the belligerent associations, which we think were, to use a well worn phrase, 'honourable to both parties concerned', and have certainly made the interests of both bodies so far identical as to strengthen the position of each with the amateur public. All mixed meetings since the arrangement are advertised under both rules, the foot-races and other athletic sports being under the A.A.A. rules, and the cycle races under the N.C.U. rules, the N.C.U. undertaking, in the case of meetings held by the clubs affiliated to the A.A.A., not to make any order (except at the invitation of the A.A.A. club) upon the committee of that A.A.A. club to alter its decision.

We have probably said enough of the A.A.A. and its objects and principles to convey some idea of the work it performs. Soon after its foundation it was found necessary to put the greatest possible administrative power into the hands of the local associations in the North and Midlands, and the A.A.A. may now practically be said to consist of three bodies in the North, South, and Midlands, the general committee only sitting as a court of appeal from the decisions of the local committees, and the general body of clubs rarely meeting more than once a year, to effect alterations in the rules, and to supervise the management and expenditure. It has naturally been a matter of time and trouble to get the Association known and its power felt throughout the kingdom, and for its present strong position the A.A.A. owes a great debt of gratitude to its present honorary secretary, Mr Herbert, of the Civil Service Athletic Association, in whose hands the management of the body has been since 1883. In the early days of the Association also, it owed much of its success to the support of the Press, most of the sporting papers of influence giving assistance and encouragement to the movement for the organisation and purification of amateur athletics.

So far, however, we have presented the bright side of the picture in sketching the history of a body which has undoubtedly by its influence brought all classes of athletes and all districts into communion, and has also done much to remedy some of the grosser abuses of the sport. On the other hand, those who are familiar with the working of athletic meetings and athletic clubs know that outside the Universities, and a few other similar places, the state of amateurism has never been so bad as it is at the present day. When open races were first thought of, nearly all the competitors were 'gentleman amateurs'. It was soon found that, hard as it was to define an amateur, it was still harder to define a 'gentleman' for athletic purposes. The 'gentleman amateur' was replaced by the 'amateur', who was what his name represented, a man who competed for love of the sport, and respected the rules of honour and fair play. Then came the time when athletics were at the height of their popularity, when the 'gate-money' taken at the meetings was enough to support a club without paying much attention to subscriptions of members, and when meetings began to spring up throughout the country. This prosperity has led perhaps almost inevitably to decay. Thousands of men of every class of the community, but, for obvious reasons, chiefly those of the lower class, found that by taking up amateur athletics there were prizes to be won, which were readily exchangeable for cash, and opportunities also could be provided for making money by betting in those mysterious ways which had long been so familiar upon the turf and with the professional pedestrians. The result is that the last state of amateurism is worse than the first, and that the ranks of so-called amateurs are crowded with athletes who have absolutely no further thought in entering for races than the amount of money they can, by fair means or foul, extract from them. Probably not one tithe of the malpractices that are committed are so obvious in their nature as to render it possible that they can be brought before the notice of the Athletic Association; but we imagine that an evening spent with any of the committees of that body would astonish an uninitiated patron of athletic sports, for he would discover the existence of an amount of petty swindling, deceit, and unfair play, which would give him but a poor opinion of the modern amateur. Men who have belonged to clubs and have run under their club-names refuse to pay subscriptions; they enter for races, and when unsuccessful decline to pay their entrance fees; they attempt by every conceivable kind of trick, such as making omissions or ambiguous statements in their entry forms, to induce the handicapper to give them longer starts than they would obtain if they made a full and fair disclosure of their last three performances; and lastly, there is over and over again grave suspicion of 'roping', men who ought to win suddenly losing in a way which is unaccountable, except upon the hypothesis that they are paid to lose. All this has tended in a great many districts to drive gentlemen out of the field, as they do not care to associate with the semi-professional amateur, or take part in a sport where such practices are rife. The existence of these abuses, too, has even led to the corruption of the genuine amateur. Knowing well that many of those with whom he may find himself competing are dishonest, and being too honourable himself ever to indulge in malpractices, he fancies he has discharged his duty to the community by always running to win, and respecting the laws of the meeting, and that when this is done nothing further is to be expected from him. Thus, of late years, many amateurs, against whom no suspicion of dishonesty can possibly arise, are ready to go off to any meeting where they can pick up a 'pot', and when they lose to raise protests against the winner. It is sad to find that the 'win, tie, or wrangle' policy has increased a good deal upon the running-path within the last few years.

Upon the whole, therefore, the state of amateur athletics throughout the country can hardly be considered satisfactory. A great many athletes who pass as amateurs are not only professionals in truth and fact, who make a living out of the sport, but, what is worse, many of them are making a living out of it by dishonest means. It is difficult, however, to see how, in the turn which the movement has taken, things could have happened otherwise. The athletic movement which commenced with the 'classes', and first drew its strength from the Universities and public schools, has finally, like most other movements and fashions, good or bad, spread downwards to the 'masses'. The encouragement and interest given to the amateur contests by the non-athletic public caused the popularisation of the sport to be very rapid, and when the taste caught the 'masses' it became easier for them to take part in amateur sports than in professional pedestrianism. Without casting any reflection upon the conduct of the masses as a whole, it is obviously impossible to expect that with many of them the money to be gained by betting or 'squaring' races will not offer irresistible temptations. Nor, again, is it to be expected that the 'mechanic, artisan, and labourer' ranks will always have, when a valuable prize is at stake, as much sportsmanlike feeling and nice sense of fair play as one could rely upon finding in the much-ridiculed 'gentleman amateur' of past days. As soon as any sport has become so popular that money is to be made out of it, and men engage in it upon whom the loss of reputation has little effect, it may be prophesied with certainty that abuses will arise. Such abuses have arisen in athletics; but it is of more importance to find a remedy for them than to discuss their origin.

The foregoing will, however, serve to explain in some manner the true position of the Athletic Association. The objection has often been brought against this body, as well as against other similar bodies, that it has been productive of no good because it has failed to purify the sport which it governs. All that a governing body of sport can be expected to do is to keep order and punish open offences against its laws, and it can no more render its subjects good sportsmen and amateurs than an Act of Parliament can render citizens virtuous. What the A.A.A. does for the true amateur is this: it assures him that wherever he goes to run under A.A.A. laws he will find competent management and fair play – a fair field and no favour – but it cannot prevent the genuine amateur from rubbing his shoulders against many a false amateur whose motives in running as an amateur are obvious, though no complaint can be made of his public behaviour.

Before discussing the possible remedies for the present state of amateur athletics, a few words may be said as to some of the leading athletic clubs. We have already pointed out that in some respects the runner has an advantage over the oarsman or the cricketer in being independent of his fellows, able to choose any time for training which may suit him, and that in competitions he wins or loses upon his own individual merit. This independence of the athlete, however (employing the term to include the walker, runner, hurdler, and so forth), is rather a serious drawback to the success of athletic clubs. Rowing, cricket, football, cycling, tennis, and gymnastics, are pastimes as well as competitions, and the members of clubs devoted to pastimes have plenty of reason to bring them together at other times than the days of competition. A club devoted to athletics alone had, until paper-chasing came into vogue, little social attraction, as compared with other clubs. The popularity of paper-chasing during the last few years has caused a large number of clubs to spring up throughout the country, which exist to promote paper-chasing and cross-country racing during the winter, although they hold athletic meetings during the summer season. However, with paper-chasing clubs it is not our business to deal in the present chapter, although it is worth mentioning that quite a fourth part of the clubs affiliated to the A.A.A. are Harriers or Hare and Hounds clubs. But if the paper-chasing clubs are put out of the question, it may almost be said that there are no clubs in the true sense of the word which exist purely and solely for the cultivation of running, jumping, and throwing of weights, with the exception of those which are fortunate in possessing running grounds with a cinder-track of their own. Of these the number is very limited, but their work in collecting, promoting, and forming athletic talent is wide and far-reaching. Ever since the time when athletics became part of the regular University life, the Oxford and Cambridge University Athletic Clubs have brought out and brought together all the men with athletic capabilities in their different colleges. The management of the two clubs, and the system pursued for the cultivation of athletic skill at the two Universities, is so identical, that it can hardly be of any advantage to give separate sketches of both;

the writer will, therefore, in the main give an account of his Oxford reminiscences.

The Cambridge athletes formed themselves into a club in 1863, and their home has always been the cricket-ground at Fenner's, which they share in common with the University Cricket Club, the latter using the ground and pavilion in the summer term, and the athletes in the autumn and spring terms, the cinder-path of course running round the cricket pitch. Until the end of 1876 the Oxonian cinder-track was out in the fields at Marston, quite a mile from the centre of Oxford, and in some very low-lying meadows, which made the track and grass decidedly swampy. In the next year, however, the Oxonians removed to their present ground in the Iffley Road. The University athletic clubs are open to every member of the University without any formalities of proposing and seconding, but everyone who wishes to train upon the club grounds, or run in the Freshmen's or University Sports, must pay his subscription to the University club and become a member. There is, however, at Oxford, and we believe also at Cambridge, an exception. For a limited time before any college gives its sports a member of that college, who is not a member of the University club but wishes to have a few days' practice upon the ground, can obtain permission through an arrangement between his college and the University club. As a general rule, however, those members of the colleges w-ho run at their college sports are members of the club. At Oxford, in the writer's time, the only formality necessary for membership was to go to Rowell's, the silversmith's, in 'The High', and pay the subscription over the counter.

The athletic season begins immediately after the commencement of the October term, and at Oxford after luncheon the athletes in twos and threes may be observed wending their way over Magdalen Bridge to the ground. Before long they may be seen scampering also in twos and threes over the path or over the hurdles, or essaying the hurling of weight and hammer. At Oxford athletics are an eminently sociable sport. You run 'spins' with your friends, or take the long-distance runner a lap upon his way; then, perhaps, a try at the long jump or the weight, or you hold the watch for the practising half-miler; then the final breather, and the return to the pavilion; then a warm at the fire, and the walk back in the dusk of the short winter day with the friend, when the form of the 'coming' Balliol man is discussed, or the chance of the London stranger winning the 'Exeter Half'. Oh, glorious days of youth and training, before the race of life has begun, and some companions have shot to the front and others have fallen to the rear, while some have dropped out of the running, and will never more meet an antagonist in any field!

A man whose soul delights in running can get as much as he wants at Oxford. The season begins in the autumn with the 'Freshers' alias the Freshmen's Sports, open to all who are in their first year at the university, and from these it is soon seen what new men will have a chance of their 'blue' in the spring. Then come the series of college meetings, some score in number, about half of which are in the autumn term and half in the spring. Every college meeting has its strangers' race, open not only to strangers from Cambridge, London, and elsewhere, but to all those of colleges other than the one holding the meeting. To enter for the race all that is needed is to write one's name in the book at Rowell's, entrance fees to college strangers' races being things unknown, and you will be handicapped by two members of the O.U.A.C. committee, to whom the particular distance is allotted. A college meeting itself is always a festive scene. It is not promoted for the benefit of the few cracks in each college. Men turn out for the handicaps who have never put on a shoe before, and in the level races the winners of previous years are penalised. Everyone has a chance of a prize, the value of the prize is happily small, and no one is aggrieved at losing. As a rule, too, a man who is a 'blue' – that is, has run for his university at any particular event – stands out of the races at his own distance in his college sports to give the other men a chance. All is good sport, even though the winners' times are sometimes so slow as to promote the mirth of the London 'crack'.

When the 'college grinds' are over the Varsity sports come to finish up the season. They always take place about a week before the end of the Lent term, and it is from the result of the different races at the Varsity sports that the representatives for the Inter-Varsity gathering are selected by the committee of the Club. From the very earliest time the Oxford men took a sensible course with regard to the prizes at the University meeting, and for the last fifteen years the winner and second man in each race get exactly the same prize – a silver medal. To have earned the 'O.U.A.C. medal' is honour enough for the Oxford athlete, and it is better far to give the winner a trophy which shows upon the face of it in what sports it was earned than to give valuable prizes to a class of amateurs who ought to be above coveting them. There is something, however, which the University athlete covets more than his medal, and that is the 'blue'. The system of Varsity 'colours' certainly has its amusing side, and a stranger may well be bewildered at the number of coats and caps of gaudy hue which are in the possession of an Oxford or Cambridge athlete. Every college has its colours; then there is something distinctive for each club of every college from which the initiated observer can gather whether the wearer of the coat and cap he sees is a cricketer, or an oarsman, or something else. Then with the cricket coats there must be a fresh difference, to mark the man in the college eleven and the man who is not in it; and similarly with the votaries of the river, a man gets a different cap when he reaches his college 'torpid', and yet another when he is promoted to the 'eight'. The outward and visible sign, then, of the Varsity man's upward progress in an athletic career is the donning of a fresh coat or cap, or a piece of ribbon which he wears proudly as a badge of merit. Mere college colours, however, are considered to count for but little as compared with the dark or light blue colours which show that the wearer has represented his University in a contest against the rival University. The Oxford eight each year is clad in dark blue flannel coats and caps; and the Oxford eleven who meet Cambridge at Lord's, and the nine athletes who are sent up to London as the 'first strings' to compete against Cambridge, have a like honour, although there is of course a slight difference which distinguishes the rowing, cricket, and athletic coats and caps, the oarsman wearing a white badge of crossed oars, the cricketer a white crest, and the athlete a white laurel wreath upon the cap and the breast pocket of his coat.

This hierarchy of coat-wearers doubtless causes wonderment to the astonished stranger, but those who, from experience in other parts of the kingdom, know how soon a genuine sport can be corrupted by greed and money-making considerations, cannot see anything but good in a system which makes the chief distinction something which cannot possibly foster any undesirable quality except perhaps a little harmless vanity.

To return to our athletes then, the Oxford or Cambridge runner looks forward, as the supreme goal of his ambition, to the right to wear a blue coat or cap. Only the winners of the nine events which are included in the programme of the Inter-University meeting are awarded this honour, and those who run as 'second' or 'third' strings in London only hold the 'half-blue' – that is, they can wear blue trimming upon their jerseys and knickerbockers when running, but may not sport the blue coat or cap. With the conclusion of the University sports the athletic season closes at the Universities, and the ground is handed over to cricket until the following October.

It remains to speak of the organisation and management of the University athletic clubs. Generations of undergraduates come and go, and the President of one year is not in residence the next year. Neither at Oxford nor Cambridge then could the clubs be placed upon a sound and lasting basis without the assistance of some permanent official. Luckily for both Cambridge and Oxford, they have been fortunate in this respect in obtaining permanent treasurers. At Oxford, the old athlete, C. N. Jackson, tutor of Hertford College, has long and ably managed the business concerns of the O.U.A.C., while at Cambridge the popular Dean of Jesus, the Rev. E. H. Morgan, has long held a similar position with his club. With the exception, however, of the permanent treasurerships, the remaining offices of the University clubs are entirely managed by the undergraduates themselves. At the beginning of every October term at Oxford (and we believe at Cambridge a term earlier) a general meeting of the representatives of the college athletic clubs is called. One man attends from each college to give the vote of those he represents. At this general meeting a president, secretary, and four other committee-men are chosen from amongst the athletes who will not have passed their fourth year of residence before the next Inter-Varsity sports, and will therefore still be eligible to compete against Cambridge. The president, secretary, treasurer, and committee manage the club affairs, fix the dates of sports, and choose the representatives for the Inter-Varsity contests. The Oxford and Cambridge meeting in London is managed jointly by the committees of both clubs, each of them deriving a substantial addition to its income from the 'gate money' taken from the large crowd of old University men and others who never fail to attend the 'Inter-Varsity Sports'.

To pass from the Universities to London. Here we find one club based almost upon the same lines as the University clubs, and, like them, doing excellent work in promoting the growth of a healthy amateurism in the metropolis, although of late years it has had far greater difficulties to contend with than are ever likely to befall the University clubs. The London Athletic Club was founded in 1863 under another title, but in 1866 took its present name. Like the Oxford and Cambridge clubs it first held its sports at the old Beaufort House Ground, and then moved in 1869 to the new ground of the A.A.C. at Lillie Bridge, where its meetings were held until 1876, and it has now been for ten years upon its own ground at Stamford Bridge. The Amateur Athletic Club, which started with great prospects and seemed even more permanent than the L.A.C. in 1869, when it opened its ground at Lillie Bridge as the head-quarters of English amateur athletics, gradually died a natural death, and now does not even exist in name. Up to 1880 the L.A.C. had an unbroken career of success, and, in fact, really became rather overgrown. The business of a club carried on by unpaid officials naturally must fall into the hands of one or two energetic men who carry it on with little interference from the rest of the committee. It can hardly be disputed that the method in which the membership of the L.A.C. was for several years thrown open to many who neither had any connection with nor took an interest in athletic pursuits, tended to dissipate the *esprit de corps* which is so vital to the well-being and success of a club. The rising generation of athletes began to betake themselves to the less important paper-chasing clubs, and even when they belonged to the L.A.C.

as well as to other bodies most frequently ran under the names and colours of the smaller institutions to which they belonged. Such a sign might have warned the committee of the L.A.C. that the club was ceasing to cohere as it should. However, all went prosperously until about the year 1880, when that rapid popularisation of sport began which, as we have seen before, has tended in some measure to withdraw the support of the paying classes from athletics to other pastimes. The business of attending to a large ground and pavilions and keeping them in order is expensive, and little assistance can now be obtained from gate-money. The result was that when the L.A.C, in the autumn of 1883, suddenly lost its managing directors there was a debt of 1,000*l* to be cleared off, as well as a ground, which was acquired under very onerous conditions, to be carried on. It speaks much for the vitality of the old club that it has stood the shock and still keeps its place at the head of the London athletic organisations. Last year, when the members subscribed a sufficient sum to clear off the greater part of the debt, the club was reorganised and registered (with leave to omit the word 'Limited') as a company under the Companies Acts, with a liability limited to a small guarantee by each member. It is not too much to say of the L.A.C. that in times gone past it collected, formed, and brought out all the athletic capabilities of the metropolis; and it would have been a bad day for genuine amateurism had the club failed to weather the storm of 1883.

Besides the L.A.C. there are many paper-chasing clubs around London which cultivate flat-racing in addition, and may be considered as athletic clubs quite apart from their functions as promoters of cross-country racing. Two of these, the South London Harriers and the Blackheath Harriers, are old-established clubs, and the former owns a cinder-path of its own at Balham. All the paper-chasing clubs round London have a strong esprit de corps, which occasionally, we regret to observe, manifests itself in the expression of ill-will towards rivals. The L.A.C., however, occupies a different position from them all, having amongst its roll nearly all the leading London athletes of the last twenty years, and affording a centre and a ground for the meetings of most of the others.

There is little that need be said of the other clubs throughout the country which hold athletic meetings. Few of them are athletic clubs in the same sense of the word as the University clubs or the L.A.C. In a country district it is obviously out of the question for a club to exist upon athletics apart from other kinds of manly pastime. Neither Manchester, Liverpool, nor Birmingham has a club which owns a running ground and encourages athletic practice all the year round as does the leading London institution. In purely country districts the athletic meetings are promoted and managed by the local cricket, football, or paper-chasing club, or by a committee which is got together annually for the purpose of holding a meeting, and except for the purposes of that particular meeting has no corporate existence. Many of the large provincial towns, such as Huddersfield, have clubs with a permanent existence jointly devoted to cricket and athletics, as well as other sports, separate committees managing the different branches of sport. One of these clubs – the Huddersfield C. and A.C. – was, long before the London A.C. took a similar course, registered as a limited company with leave to omit the word 'Limited' from its name. These provincial clubs for combined athletic purposes are amongst the most flourishing and best-managed organisations in the kingdom, and perform excellent work in the cultivation and development of athletic energy.

The difficulties, then, which beset the path of a genuine amateur do not arise from want of material, but from the irruption into the amateur circle of men whose money-making propensities have gotten the better of their honesty. Thousands of men come annually from the Universities and public schools as well as from elsewhere, who could do nothing but good to themselves by competing in honest contests in running and jumping matches; but all present efforts have failed to separate from the genuine amateurs the class of those who take up athletics nominally as amateurs, but really as a means of livelihood. There are plenty of sheep and plenty of goats, and the questions which naturally arise are whether it is possible to separate them, and if so by what means; also, whether, if it be impossible to separate them, there are any means of preventing the decadence of athletic sports.

The genuine amateurs are all of one kind; they run because the exercising of their bodies gives them delight, and because, being Englishmen, they find it pleasant to have beaten an honest adversary in an honest competition. The summit of their ambition is to have met all comers and won a championship, or to have met all opponents from their club or district or from their University, or from the two Universities, and to have borne away the palm. The prizes they win are to be kept as trophies, and not to be parted with; and whether they care for handsome prizes much or little, their chief pleasure derived from the sport is the honour they have gained in their chosen pursuit. Let no one imagine we are drawing an ideal picture of the English athlete. There is a good deal of human nature in man, and there are very few runners, jumpers, or what not, who are above the temptations of winning a handsome prize. There have been plenty of genuine amateurs who have carried their love of 'pots' to an illegitimate extent, and have gone touring round the country to meetings at which they could not increase their reputation by winning, and which they have simply attended for pot-hunting purposes. These men, however, have won the prizes with the desire to ornament their homes with them, and not with the object of increasing their weekly stipends with the gains of athletics. Such are the sheep; but the goats are of various kinds. Some of them are men who run honestly enough on the whole, but as soon as they get a prize dispose of it promptly for what it will fetch; and we fancy that silversmiths and dealers in fancy articles could, if examined before a Royal Commission upon athletics, make some strange disclosures as to the number and importance of this class. Such men soon degenerate into the other class, who find there is more to be made out of betting or 'squaring' a race than out of the prizes, and who therefore never run honestly if it pays them better to do otherwise. As for a championship with these gentry, it is not worth running for unless the 'market' can be worked, or unless the competitor meditates taking a public-house and trading upon the reputation of being an ex-champion. The number of these sham-amateurs is large, and it is a serious question whether it is possible to exclude them from the amateur fold.

At the time when amateurism first came into existence upon the running path, the amateurs, looking at the state of professional pedestrianism, were rather inclined to consider running for money as being a bad thing in itself. Whether there is anything degrading in the notion of a man gently bred running, or playing cricket or football, for money, is a wide subject which we do not care to discuss at present, and upon which public opinion would probably adopt more liberal views now than it did a quarter of a century ago. The line taken up by the earliest 'gentleman-amateurs' was, however, that it was degrading to run for money, and that amateur athletics should be confined to gentlemen. Possibly the eventual solution of the present problem will be a return to the old practice, and the gentlemen who run and jump in matches will be able to confine the amateur competitions in which they take part to their own class. Such social distinctions, however, are very hard to preserve anywhere, and particularly hard in sport, and the difficulties of defining an amateur are nothing compared to the difficulties of defining a gentleman. One thing is certain: the attempt to confine open competitions to gentleman-amateurs broke down. In the country especially, where the sports were promoted by the help of subscriptions from the neighbourhood, people naturally declined to see the money they subscribed devoted to prizes to be competed for solely by gentlemen, and the gradual stream of public opinion from 1870 to 1880 flowed steadily in the direction of allowing any one to compete for a prize, whatever his social position might be, provided he cared to run for prizes in preference to running for money like a professional 'ped'. The result has been as we have seen, that with the rapid extension of the athletic movement throughout the kingdom, a large number of those who in former times would have become professionals have turned amateurs because amateurism is more lucrative. Of this class it may be safely said that they will never abandon the amateur ranks until they find there is more money to be made as professionals. The recognition and encouragement of an honest and open professional athleticism throughout all districts of the country would be the best possible means of purging the amateur ranks of those who have no business to remain in them. As soon as the large number of the mechanic classes, who cannot afford to despise the money which they can make out of their athletic powers, find that it is just as lucrative and just as honourable to compete as professionals, they will cease to call themselves amateurs, and amateurism will be the better for their departure.

As regards the lowest class of runners, be they professionals or amateurs, who run to the orders of their bookmakers, and win or lose races just as the monetary arrangements make it advisable, nothing can be done to drive these off the path but a vigilant exercise of power of disqualification, and a rigid suppression of all open betting upon the ground. Every sport which comes to the state of merely being a resource for betting will arrive eventually at a condition of rottenness which will make it the despair of a reformer; and if amateur athletics eventually get into the hands of the bookmakers, the sooner the sport 'goes under' the better.

If, therefore, amateur athletics are to be purged of their abuses, one can safely point to the direction which the reform must take. The suppression of betting upon the ground must be rigidly enforced at every meeting great or small, for if the runners are to become simply animals with so much 'money on them', it cannot matter a straw whether the stake for which they run is money or a cup; and, indeed, the running is much more likely to be honest with a money prize than with a cup which is not readily converted into money. Unless the runners are all genuine amateurs, running for honour and not for money, it is impossible when betting is rife to keep the sport pure, and the Amateur Athletic Association had better dissolve and cease its labours than try to stem a tide which will be too strong for it.

Granting, however, that betting can be suppressed or kept within reasonable limits, the movement to purify athletics from the sham amateurs must be in two directions. The real amateurs must try to encourage professionalism open and undisguised, for the establishment of recognised professional sports throughout the country would draw off from the quasi-amateur ranks those who take it up from interested motives. The other remedy is easier, and rests with the genuine amateurs themselves without requiring any assistance from the public patronage. The bona fide gentleman-amateur must give up the idea of earning valuable prizes, and must take to the system of running for medals of little value, or to earn his 'colours', as at the Universities, without any further reward.

In other sports, gentlemen are willing enough to toil and practise to gain honour alone. The cricketer plays assiduously for seasons, and is sufficiently rewarded by gaining a place in his county eleven, and athletics could be placed upon a sounder footing if there were more representative competitions which it would be recognised as an honour to win, or even to take part in, without any special stimulant. The body athletic has become corrupted by too much prosperity, and the proper method for its recovery is a severe course of ascetic training. When amateur athletics are again confined to men who show by their acts that they run for sport and not for gain, then the tide of public favour will flow back to them with full force, and athletes will have full honour in their own country.

We have purposely refrained during the writing of these chapters from rhapsodising upon the advantages of the cultivation of athletic excellence to the individual and the nation. In these days of endless writing, when many articles are indited which, like bad sermons, consist of a few texts largely diluted, it is usual to found all the possible praises of athletics upon two texts: the one from a classical source alluding to the necessary connection between mental and bodily soundness, and the other from a native source alluding to the connection between military excellence and playing fields. As no book upon athletics is considered complete without some allusion to these time-honoured friends, we have thus cursorily alluded to them at the end of our task, but have before preached no sermon upon these passages, for a very simple reason. We take it that at the present day it is but a waste of labour to demonstrate to Englishmen the advantages of manly sports, of hard exercise, and friendly competition. For the last five-and-twenty years the young men of England have flung themselves into the pursuit of hard bodily exercise and sporting competitions upon foot. The youth of the present day fresh from school, instead of spending his leisure time in seeing cocks fight or terriers kill rats, goes off to the football or cricket field, to the river or the running path, and finds his recreation in the exercise of his own body. The result of a generation of athletic sport has made the nation stronger, manlier, cleaner, and more sober than it was before the pursuit of athletics became a national characteristic. When the athletic movement first came into full force it found vigorous opponents. Mr Wilkie Collins in particular wrote a novel in which the wicked brother was an athlete – a heartless villain, without manners or brains, and the sworn companion of swindlers and sharpers; while the virtuous brother, who detested hard exercise and played the fiddle, had every conceivable virtue of morals and intellect. The public was thrilled by the novel but not convinced by it, and with reason. If anyone will take the trouble to study a school, a college, or any large body of men, he will find that the dozen best cricketers, footballers, or oarsmen will provide more clever scholars, and – what is quite as important – more capable and better mannered men than any average dozen of the others; and, indeed, it may safely be added that a dozen athletes will produce as many violin players as a dozen non-athletes. There may be, and doubtless are, plenty of strong hulking fellows in whom athletic propensities are joined with rough behaviour; but the manners of these are none the more rough because they have taken to athletics. Were there no field upon which their strength and spirits could be curbed and disciplined, it may safely be said that they would have been worse. No; the athletic movement has benefited the people at large. The lad or man who is a keen athlete is rarely mean, vicious, or a coward; the black sheep of the community are the loafers, and from a host of these a love of athletics has delivered England.

Other and graver objections are sometimes raised to the pursuit of athletics in individual cases. There are, no doubt, many instances of men who have undermined their health by too much training and competition, and there are doctors who shake their heads when they hear that their patient has been an athlete. Most athletes also know of a case here and there of a man breaking down or even dying in his prime under circumstances which at any rate point with some probability to a sport in which he indulged as the cause. We have already expressed our strong opinion that for many years a vicious habit of training was in force, and that even in the present day men are inclined to overwork themselves in their practice. Every system has its victims until it is understood, and the men who have suffered loss of health from an overdose of athletics are men who have abused a blessing, and, in the name of health and exercise, have placed themselves under an absurd and unhealthy diet and have worn out their vigour by persistent overwork. The present writer is hardly one who by his practice and his preaching can be taken for an alarmist, but he feels constrained to end what he has to say upon athletics with an appeal to the votaries of the sport not to abuse a good system. The number of those who have gained health, strength, courage and character from the practice of one form or another of athletic exercise is legion, and to a statistician dealing with averages a victim more or less is of small concern; but there is really no reason whatever why athletic sport properly conducted should have a single victim. When fervid athletes keep little boys from running in boys' races at public meetings, when school committees will put a stop to 'junior miles' and 'junior steeplechases', and when 'twenty-four hour' races and go-as you-please competitions are no more heard of, athletics will be purged of some current evils. When going into training means nothing more than living a regular and healthy life, and the daily exercise is taken to increase the strength and skill, and not to see how much the human body can do without failing, then no one except by his own fault can suffer any harm from athletic sports.

Some Sports Stand the Test of Time

Classic Guides

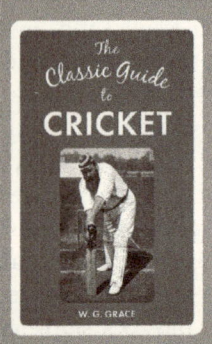

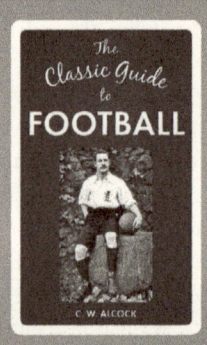

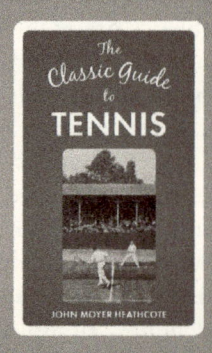

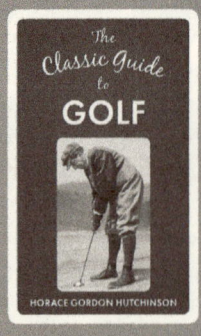

from Amberley Publishing

The Classic Guide to CRICKET
W. G. GRACE

The Classic Guide to FOOTBALL
C. W. ALCOCK

The Classic Guide to TENNIS
JOHN MOYER HEATHCOTE

The Classic Guide to GOLF
HORACE GORDON HUTCHINSON

The Classic Guide to SAILING
E. F. KNIGHT

Find us on Facebook
facebook.com/amberleybooks

Follow us on Twitter
@amberleybooks

w. www.amberley-books.com **T.** +44 1453 847800 **E.** sales@amberley-books.com